Defining America
in the Radical 1760s

ALSO BY JUDE M. PFISTER
AND FROM MCFARLAND

*The Creation of American Law: John Jay,
Oliver Ellsworth and the 1790s Supreme Court* (2019)

*Charting an American Republic: The Origins
and Writing of the Federalist Papers* (2016)

*America Writes Its History, 1650–1850:
The Formation of a National Narrative* (2014)

Defining America in the Radical 1760s

John Dickinson, George III and the Fate of Empire

Jude M. Pfister

McFarland & Company, Inc., Publishers
Jefferson, North Carolina

LIBRARY OF CONGRESS CATALOGUING-IN-PUBLICATION DATA

Names: Pfister, Jude M., author.
Title: Defining America in the radical 1760s : John Dickinson, George III and the fate of empire / Jude M. Pfister.
Other titles: John Dickinson, George III and the fate of empire
Description: Jefferson, North Carolina : McFarland & Company, Inc., Publishers, 2021 | Includes bibliographical references and index.
Identifiers: LCCN 2021037359 | ISBN 9781476679747 (paperback : acid free paper) ∞
ISBN 9781476643779 (ebook)
Subjects: LCSH: United States—History—Revolution, 1775-1783—Causes. | United States—History—Colonial period, ca. 1600-1775. | United States—Politics and government—To 1775. | Great Britain—Politics and government—1760-1789. | Revolutionaries—United States—History—18th century. | Dickinson, John, 1732-1808—Influence. | George III, King of Great Britain, 1738-1820. | Great Britain—Colonies—America—Administration. | Pamphleteers—Delaware—Biography.
Classification: LCC E210 .P45 2021 | DDC 973.2/7—dc23
LC record available at https://lccn.loc.gov/2021037359

BRITISH LIBRARY CATALOGUING DATA ARE AVAILABLE

ISBN (print) 978-1-4766-7974-7
ISBN (ebook) 978-1-4766-4377-9

© 2021 Jude M. Pfister. All rights reserved

No part of this book may be reproduced or transmitted in any form or by any means, electronic or mechanical, including photocopying or recording, or by any information storage and retrieval system, without permission in writing from the publisher.

Front cover image: Burning of Stamp Act, Boston, created 1903 (Library of Congress)

Printed in the United States of America

*McFarland & Company, Inc., Publishers
Box 611, Jefferson, North Carolina 28640
www.mcfarlandpub.com*

To my wife, Miriam

Acknowledgments

The list of those who provided insight and inspiration for this book is manifold. I am, as in previous works, greatly indebted to my colleagues at Morristown National Historical Park. Joni Rowe and Sarah Minegar oversee one of the finest research collections in the National Park Service. Particularly, the Lloyd W. Smith rare book and archival collection is seemingly never-ending in its ability to bring forth a wealth of primary material. The park's superintendent, Tom Ross, is due recognition for his support.

Further afield, Jane Calvert, professor at the University of Kentucky and editor of the *Complete Writings and Selected Correspondence of John Dickinson*, is due an especial thank you for her willingness to share her insight and vast knowledge of John Dickinson through innumerable emails. She also graciously provided access to the still in-draft versions of the Dickinson papers so that I could keep on schedule and for that I am thankful. The team at the Drew University library is to be thanked for their excellent assistance in all matters of reference and circulation of books. Johanna Edge and Andrew Bonamici are especially thanked. I also thank Bruce Spadaccinni for his insightful discussions with me on Benjamin Franklin and I thank Steve Newfield for his photographic assistance.

The King's Friends initiative, which oversees the publication of the Georgian Papers Programme, are to be thanked for all their efforts to make the papers of the Hanoverian kings electronically accessible, especially George III. Although a study trip to the Royal Archives at Windsor castle is appealing, it is certainly a convenience to be able to access the writings of the young George III from my computer in my office.

I finally want to thank Charles Perdue and the team at McFarland for being so accommodating and professional. They have taken words on pieces of paper and created a book; and for that I am grateful. Lastly, it goes without saying, but any errors that remain after assistance from so many wonderful people who offered their time are entirely mine and mine alone.

Table of Contents

Acknowledgments   vi

Preface   1

CHAPTER 1. Setting the Stage   5

CHAPTER 2. America: 1760   11

CHAPTER 3. The Era of the French and Indian War   31

CHAPTER 4. Escalation and Victory   49

CHAPTER 5. King George III and the Rise of American Resistance   69

CHAPTER 6. The Stamp Act and a Congress   88

CHAPTER 7. The Ink War on the Stamp Act   103

CHAPTER 8. A Farmer Pushes Back   124

CHAPTER 9. The Dimensions of Taxation   153

CHAPTER 10. Ancient Liberties   173

CHAPTER 11. James Wilson, Thomas Jefferson, and the Final Arguments for America   187

Appendix 1. Crevecoeur—What Is an American?   215

Appendix 2. The Language of the Stamp Act   219

Appendix 3. Language from the Repeal of the Stamp Act   221

Appendix 4. The Language of the Declaratory Act   222

Appendix 5. Massachusetts Circular Letter to the Colonial Legislatures: February 11, 1768   224

Appendix 6. James Wilson: From Considerations on the Nature and Extent of the Legislative Authority of the British Parliament	227
Appendix 7. Albany Plan of Union 1754	230
Appendix 8. William Blackstone: Excerpt from the Introduction to Commentaries on the Laws of England	233
Chapter Notes	237
Bibliography	249
Index	255

Preface

This book is the result of anecdotal observations over two decades which have consistently yielded similar results. Those observations dealt with the prevailing perception among the public concerning the crucible of the American Revolution. What were the events that precipitated the armed conflict in the 1770s? Many observers feel the Revolution sprang fully formed and articulated from the minds of the Founders. As though, almost as one, the seventy-five or so primary Founders suddenly woke up with their opposition to Britain completely formed and ready for action. Nothing could be further from the truth. The Revolution was the accretion of over a decade and more of thinking about the place of colonists and colonies in the British Empire. This decade of deep thinking was exceptionally radical in terms of the propositions put forth. Nearly every essay or article produced concluded with an unwritten prognosis—American independence. Naturally, this was never explicitly stated prior to actual warfare, but there was little room to maneuver toward any other outcome, especially to the more strident arguments posed by the Americans.

The overwhelming aspect impacting the uprising propelled by ink in the 1760s was the near simultaneous appearance of the greatest compilation of English law to appear up to that point. When William Blackstone set out to start his *Commentaries on the Laws of England,* he most certainly never anticipated that the Americans would be initiating a challenge against some of the very laws he was writing down for posterity. He never would have dreamed in 1765 that the America challenge would end in war. This ink war produced a veritable mountain of essays and pamphlets promoting every side of the debate from every perspective.

It has been estimated that "Altogether, between 1670 and 1764 as many as a thousand to twelve hundred explicitly political writings issued from colonial and British presses on matters of moment to the colonial British American world."[1] Those who would be the arch revolutionists of the 1770s were only getting started in the 1760s however. They had not yet become a galvanizing force and certainly were not yet openly agitating for independence.

Attempting to tell the story of the decade (1760s) which brought about revolution in the 1770s is the purpose of this book. Furthermore, the antecedents of the American Revolution, as incongruous as it may seem, carry back to the turn of the eighteenth century with the dynamic power struggles taking place in Europe. Without the centuries-long conflict between England and France spilling over to their North American colonies by 1755, the breach between Britain and the colonies might never have occurred.

Therefore, to set the stage for the 1760s, an understanding of the events plaguing Europe is necessary. To provide this background overview, a review of the Wars of Spanish Succession and Austrian Succession will be a part of the first few chapters. As the names imply, these two wars, and their ancillary side-wars, revolved around dynastic succession of continental Europe which threatened the balance between England and France, the two major powers of the time. Inevitably, the North American colonies became an associated battleground in which Britain would prove spectacularly successful; yet in that success would lie the seeds of the dissolution of its North American Empire.

The overarching guiding focus to the 1760s will be provided by two men—John Dickinson and King George III—who, each in their own way, brought about, however unwittingly, the revolutionary fever which gave us the Declaration of Independence in 1776. The words and actions of these two men will guide the primary emphasis in this narrative much as they did in the 1760s. From this study, a greater understanding and perspective will emerge for the nascent beginnings of the United States. Between the two men, John Dickinson was the radical, while King George III, nowhere near as conservative as his predecessors, was attempting to make sense of the charges against him and the British constitution. Historian David Jacobson, writing about Dickinson, noted:

> [H]is arguments in 1764 showed not essential conservatism, as historians have so frequently charged, but a belief in the more radical idea that fundamental rights could not be altered without the consent of the governed, an idea that clearly foreshadowed the American position in the Revolutionary crisis of succeeding years.[2]

Several perspectives will be explored. Why did Britain seemingly change decades of revenue policy against the American colonies? And, exactly why did the colonies feel the revenue policy of the 1760s would suddenly threaten their ancient rights and liberties? Beyond that, what were their ancient rights and liberties? The ancient English heritage involved more than legal rights, and that understanding was what first brought the colonial leaders together. Given that many of the early leaders were trained in the law, this was not surprising.

As already pointed out, when William Blackstone started to compose his monumental *Commentaries on the Laws of England*, why was John Dickinson in America starting to question the premise of some of those basic legal foundations in terms of their application to the colonies? How did the British so mis-read the attitude of the colonies and vice-versa? The 1760s, from the American perspective, was a decade of intense transition and exploration seeking to plumb the depths of British colonial administration without originally seeking to challenge the ultimate authority of the British system.

John Dickinson. The Miriam and Ira D. Wallach Division of Art, Prints and Photographs: Art & Architecture Collection, New York Public Library Digital Collections.

King James II (reigned 1685–1688) became the first English monarch who attempted to exert greater control over the colonies after being relatively unbothered for nearly eighty years. As Winston Churchill was to observe, "For the next fifty years successive English administrations tried to enforce the supremacy of the Crown in the American colonies and to strengthen royal power and patronage in the overseas possessions."[3] Charles II (reigned 1660–1685) had originally acquired the territory from the Dutch in North America which James II sought to exploit. James should not be seen as a colonial innovator though. He saw the wealth of the colonies as a means to bypass Parliament in his quest to rule as a Catholic authoritarian without the influence of the House of Commons. This move failed and left James's policy against the colonies unimplemented. Consequently, the Americans were given by chance greater control over their territory and James was removed as king. As will be seen, this attempt by James served to enhance the feeling of the colonists decades later towards perceived British encroachment of their rights.

Colonial governance was slow going however given Britain's other commitments. Seventeenth-century England was in no condition politically to exert much influence or dominance over North America. A civil war in England spanning nearly a century depleted the resolve for extensive colonial involvement.

The new king, William III, in his own efforts at colonial organization, oversaw the dissolution of royal governments in New England especially and refashioned many colonies to pre–James II operations. England sought in the later seventeenth century to structure the American colonies through various methods for the complete benefit of England, although it allowed the colonists some measure of self-government. This isolation would not last long.

As a powerful and confident England, soon Great Britain, maneuvered across the eighteenth century, it strove ever more consciously to draw the colonies into its orbit. This increasingly challenged the Americans in ways they had yet to experience.

Every political movement or agitation begins with an idea. An idea born of necessities that perhaps were unforeseen. This idea is written down, perhaps printed on a press, and distributed. From this, the idea is sent into the world to begin its life. Some are easily dismissed and never heard of again. Others linger but rarely take hold. Finally, a few become incendiary to the point of altering history. Such was the idea that began with the Sugar Act of 1764.

Spellings, grammar, and style of eighteenth-century writing have mostly been updated to reflect modern usage. For this book, it is more important to know what was said than how they said it. For those so inclined, referring to the original source as identified in the footnotes will lead the inquisitive to the original eighteenth-century style of writing. However, uppercase and italics seen in quotations throughout this book are taken from the original printings without alteration to ensure the emphasis of the author.

Chapter 1

Setting the Stage

This book is part biography of a time long past and part narrative interpretation of events during the decade (1760s) covered which have echoed down to us over the centuries. This is not to mean that those distant times will be compared to the present. Rather, those distant times will be surveyed through the lens of 250 years to determine if the story normally told and repeated about those times can be more accurately or meaningfully understood. There have been many fine, prize-winning studies of this time period, but few look at the intersection of the various tangle of events in both the colonies and England and Europe which produced the first serious organized resistance to Britain on a colony-wide basis in 1764 after passage of the Sugar Act.

Especially concerning are the approaches of King George III and John Dickinson. Both men have come to occupy positions in the American imagination that have changed little over two hundred years. They are dismissed as sideshows to the more "heroic" characters of the American Founding. Rather, George III and John Dickinson are the two most seminal figures during the 1760s and in multiple ways more heroic than those we normally exalt.

Many studies spend an inordinate amount of time attempting to compare and contrast the 1760s to current events. They tend to highlight the well-trod contours making sure not to deviate from the accepted course of events and primary characters involved in that time period. The closest equivalent for a compare and contrast to the 1760s would be the 1860s or even the 1960s. The radical (some would say) forces that drive change seem to manifest themselves, as if having been dormant, by springing to life when a decade ending in '60 starts.

Competing studies attempt to retell the time-approved sequence of events that Americans feel they must know to gain an understanding of the American past. We like our history, if not pre-digested, to be eminently digestible. No mental or patriotic heartburn should disturb our relationship with the past. Our comportment with the past must satisfy our contemporary worldview. This misguided approach to historical study is not worthy of serious debate. History must not be a tool to promote one linear conception of the past. What seems missing overall from the general, larger, discourse of colonial America is a more complete picture of certain British figures who are sacrificed to American interpretations at the expense of history. This book will seek to remedy that in some way. In fact, even certain American figures are seemingly forever bound to their respective roles as determined and assigned in previous decades and centuries. There seems at times to be a canon of historical narrative that cannot be challenged. Intriguing as this historiography may be, it is not the purpose of this book.

During the 1760s, as though a giant becoming aware of its power, colonial America came together for the first time to face the challenges of a revenue-starved Great Britain. This idea was radical; the colonies never saw themselves as a homogenous group. Instead, they worked, acted, and thought about themselves as separate from the other colonies. Each colony was singular, there was no plural in colonial America prior to the French and Indian War—from either the American or British (although much less so) perspective.

With that as the starting point this study of the 1760s starts to take shape. The defined parameters of colonial interaction were as one sovereign state to another. This insular perspective was not shared by Britain, whose actions would unwittingly force the colonies to begin to see themselves as one entity—which was how Britain essentially saw them but did not always treat them. The colonies were too early for a country, but nonetheless territories with mutual interests. These mutual interests took many forms: economic, cultural, social, and political. But among the greatest shared heritage the colonists found was their shared interest in their ancient legal heritage as Englishmen. That realization highlighted the radical temper of the language employed by the first essayists.

Understanding the rise of opposition to Britain during the 1760s starts with understanding the mind-set of colonists in a position to do something about the implementations in British policies toward America. Nearly to a man, leaders in colonial America saw themselves as Englishmen. In most cases, proud Englishmen. This perspective was re-enforced by the formal learning which comprised the school years. The most fortunate attended school in England; close behind this were those who studied with those who had studied in England or Europe. This continuity further strengthened the ties between America and England. Bonds of academic collegiality helped to ensure a structured approach to government and society.

By the 1760s, mass education was not something accepted by the larger population. Education was purely an upper-class domain, and for formal education, male. Women certainly did learn to read and write, but not in a formal classroom sense. In larger urban areas, lower-class boys did occasionally receive some basic education. Home schooling was of necessity a common element in eighteenth-century life and well into the nineteenth. Some colonies did make modest efforts at public education prior to the Revolution, but it was not until the new American government began operating in 1789 that a more full-scale effort to provide public education at the state level became more widespread. Major pieces of legislation such as the Northwest Ordinance of 1787 called for public education administered by states. There were also efforts undertaken to establish colleges and universities in America. These met with varying levels of success and did have some impact on making a formal education more possible for a greater number of young men as the century progressed. Religious schools (founded by denominations but not necessarily solely teaching religion) dominated in those areas more heavily influenced by individual sects. George, Prince of Wales, future George III, was a keen advocate for education. He was convinced that education was a key component in developing a virtuous and productive citizen. He wrote:

> Ardent love of one's country is most essential to the preservation of all republican governments, the inspiring therefore the minds of youth in the first dawn of reason with this passion ought to be the principle view of education; nothing will more effectively do this than example, and above all that of the parents, for youth is seldom [?] till those of riper years have made vice fashionable.[1]

It was into this environment that Americans first began to seriously question British colonial policy. One of the first to speak against that policy was also one of the best educated, John Dickinson. Dickinson had a thoroughly aristocratic education for an American. Born into wealth, Dickinson had all the advantages that accompany a privileged birth. His emphasis while a student at the Inns of Court in London focused on law and history; a winning combination for approaching British imperial policy in the 1760s. It was also Dickinson's great good fortune that he possessed an ability to distill complex details into pre-digested morsels that were accessible to all, not just those with an education.

As will be seen later, John Dickinson provided the responses to British attempts to raise revenue in the colonies which many colonists instinctively recoiled against. Dickinson would go on to become one of the longest serving Founders in the cause of American liberty. He arrived on the scene in 1764 and left active politics in 1789—twenty-five years of continuous service to the American cause, longer than many of the original Founders. Yet, he is defined by one act during those twenty-five years: his refusal to sign the Declaration of Independence. This one act, entirely reasonable on his part, has trailed him through history to the point it is the only thing most people know about him. From that standpoint alone, this book will provide what for most will be a new assessment of Dickinson; a view of Dickinson contained in the decade of the 1760s before the rejection of the Declaration of Independence. Similarly, George III will be studied in the years immediately before becoming king and shortly afterward for his writings. These writings, outlining his studies as a future monarch, show a young man intent on learning his destined role. He was not a reactionary, although he was not a deep thinker either. Still, he was nothing like the common portrayals we as Americans are forced to learn in school.

The intellectual landscape had seemingly been fashioned for someone like Dickinson to take advantage of as he started America's decade-long slide to revolt. Finally, Dickinson and the other early Founders benefited from the increase in printed material produced in the colonies from an ever-expanding number of printers. While printed works from England and Europe had been available for over a century by 1760, colonial printers had only begun to proliferate and produce titles in agriculture, law, commerce, government, and housekeeping. America's most famous printer, Benjamin Franklin, was instrumental in not only being a printer as such, but also in expanding the "power of the printing press" to multiple areas within the colonies. He was also active in the development of the tools of his trade—ink and paper.

The colonies have been seen to have developed in a positive way throughout the eighteenth century. This has been partly attributed to the relative isolation with which the British authorities observed their colonies throughout much of the seventeenth century. Yet, "by 1753 [Parliament] had passed over eighty acts relative to colonial trade and a number of others touching on such aspects of colonial life as indentured servitude for minors, the sale of land to aliens, and the naturalization of foreigners."[2] Depending on when the starting date would be, it could average out that Britain passed less than one act per year. Still, even with this possible oversight, the colonies expanded due to abundant natural resources, including land, and a growing population. "[I]n America, freed from the immediate pressure of a titled aristocracy and clerical hierarchy, they advanced rapidly ahead of their English contemporaries in the degree of their sovereignty over matters of law, religion, intellect, and aesthetic interest."[3]

During the first half of the eighteenth century as interest in the colonies increased, the British Parliament did take on several large issues impacting colonial trade. The Sugar Act of 1733, the Iron Act of 1750, and the Currency Act of 1751 were examples of major pieces of legislation that affected the colonies and in fact saw the colonies lobby for some of the legislation which a few saw as advantageous. There were also numerous iterations of the Navigation Acts which dated to the seventeenth century.

Navigation Acts (of which there were multiple versions during the colonial period) sought to:

> (1) maximize customs revenue collected in England; (2) increase the flow of commerce enriching English merchants; (3) stimulate English shipbuilding; (4) augment the number of English sailors, swelling the reserve for the Navy.[4]

Some acts failed to produce their intended consequences. The Iron Act failed and "showed that Great Britain could not guide the complex economic forces of the empire nor could it balance colonial and British interests...."[5] Governing the colonies exposed the fault lines inherent in managing a colonial empire. At some point, purely economic interests must be acknowledged and combined with the practical interests of government. By ignoring governing and focusing solely on the financials, the mother country would run the risk of neglecting the vital role of ensuring a level ground existed for the population of a colony. Political theorists had been publishing on this topic for decades by 1760. "For nearly a century, in formal political writing, they had effectively been testing, defining, and expanding the bounds of liberty in Britain's overseas possessions."[6]

Another example was the outlawing of private banks by extending the Bubble Act of 1720—which was designed to prevent the economic type of speculative bubble which creates fiscal mischief when it inevitably pops. Many of these moves by Parliament were not received well by businessmen in the colonies; "a tight money policy such as Parliament had imposed on New England struck the merchants hardest, and it put them in a sour mood toward Parliamentary interference in American affairs."[7] At this early stage, 1720, the colonies were still enjoying a relatively free approach to business in which only they had to concern themselves. Britain, on the other hand, had to concern itself with the financial well-being of its colonies worldwide. These early attempts to manage American affairs, especially business related, generated the first true opposition to British policy in the American colonies. Yet, even with all this Parliamentary activity, colonists still viewed the Crown as their special protector. This would lead to confusion, as we will see, during the 1770s (was Parliament, the king, or both, the American enemy?) when American leaders sought to pit one faction of the British government against the other. Manufacturing an enemy is always risky, but America would need one sustained "bad guy" on which to place its disapprobation when actual warfare began in 1775.

The first American to argue against Britain actively and systematically was John Dickinson of Delaware. It should be noted that Dickinson was also associated with Pennsylvania, but Delaware claims him (although he was born in Maryland). Dickinson had the educational attainments to enable him to approach these topics with much confidence. Dickinson also possessed the rare gift of being able to distill arcane concepts and topics into a narrative understandable by all readers alike. This was a crucial alchemy in a proto-nation with little wide-spread formal education. To have acknowledgment of the consequences of the situation the "betters" in society needed to have the support of those not so well off. It must be remembered that the American Revolution was very much a top-down undertaking. Indeed, that is one of the reasons the Revolution is often questioned as to whether it really was a revolution in the formal understanding of the term. Given that the wellspring of emotion originated with the highest levels of colonial society, was the American Founding Era a revolution? While the main figures studied in this book certainly represent the highest levels of American society, the debate over whether the American War of Independence was revolutionary will not be considered.

Chapter 2

America: 1760

This chapter will chart in broad strokes the society which the colonists, through much trial and error, had created by 1760. It was a society, modeled on English precedent, which valued its unique concept of being colonial. This can be found in the outlines of most spheres of public discourse—entertainment, government, law, manners and style, and language. By necessity these developed over 150 years in some isolation due to the great and perilous distance from Britain. However, these traits did not develop in a vacuum either.

In 1760, the American colonies were as content as any outpost of Great Britain could have been. Indeed, "[d]uring the first six decades of the eighteenth century, England had generally allowed her American colonies to grow, almost without direction."[1] By this point, the colonists had made a living along the eastern seaboard for one-hundred and fifty years. It was by no means easy, but the colonists had built something they could take pride in. More native-born Americans (European ancestry) lived in the colonies than immigrants by 1760. The second-, third-, even fourth- or fifth-generation colonists could by and large look back to their ancestors and feel a sense of accomplishment. Certainly, this is not to say there were no problems—there were plenty. However, in the eighteenth-century perspective, on balance, the long struggles of basic settlement seemed to not have been made in vain.

The larger continent beyond the coastal colonies was still unknown the deeper one went past the settled areas. In total, three world powers, Great Britain, France, and Spain, all claimed some territory in North America as their own. The lucrative trade prospects were too much to simply walk away and disengage from colonial settlement. The economic possibilities of colonial North America ensured it would forever draw the attention of a colonial power—if the colonies did not become independent. Even the term "the colonies" had taken on a unique meaning. There were thirteen in 1760 and each one saw itself as *the* colony; or at least the larger ones did—Virginia, New York, Pennsylvania. There was no real sense of cohesion among the separate colonies as each one saw themselves as independent of their neighbors up and down the coast.

The English took the examples of colonial administration from the Dutch and Spanish, both of which had more experience in the Americas. During the reign of Charles II (1660-1685) the English sought to consolidate the disparate tangle of colonial administration to administer taxation, trade, and defense more effectively.

Administratively, some of the colonies were originally outsourced; the "Crown had entrusted colonization to private interests licensed by royal charters."[2] This meant that some colonies were started as private investment ventures. In all, four colonies were founded by trading companies: the London Company chartered Virginia in 1606; Massachusetts Bay Company incorporated in 1629 to prop up the Plymouth Colony; the Dutch West India Company, in 1621, founded New Netherlands, later to become New York in 1664; the King of Sweden formed his own West India Company and founded a colony which became Delaware. Georgia, too, in 1732, could have been seen as having started as a mercantile venture under George II. The altruistic ideals of James Oglethorpe persuaded George II to create the colony which bears his name in part as a buffer to the Spanish in Florida. In 1752, less than twenty years after it began, Georgia became a royal or Crown colony.

A proprietary colony was an exercise in money making. The monarch provided a charter to a sole proprietor, or group, to establish a colony for their benefit and ultimately the benefit of England. The legal difference between a Crown and a private colony was more than just in the denomination.

A private non–Crown colony, also known as a charter colony, was structured between the monarch and the colonists of the specific colony. As an example, Connecticut constituted a charter colony in that the king and the colonists signed a contract specifying the terms and agreements under which the colony (in this case Connecticut by 1776) would be governed. As such, charter colonies were not specifically under the influence of the monarch as was the case with Crown colonies. A Crown colony (such as New Jersey by 1776) was directly governed by a representative of the monarch, a royal governor. A Crown colony was directly structured through the English monarch although most had an assembly elected by the colonists directly.

Crown colonies had a constitution or charter, from the Crown, and were semi-autonomous in government. A Crown colony "exercised many functions of a sovereign government: it could make assessments, coin money, regulate trade, dispose of corporate property, collect taxes, manage a treasury, and provide for defense."[3] They also usually included some language about an established religion. "By a gradual process, beginning with the dissolution of the Virginia Company in 1624 and ending with the extinction of the Georgia corporation in 1752, eight of the thirteen colonies became royal provinces, that is, their executive departments were in the hands of governors appointed by the King of England."[4] "Rhode Island and Connecticut, retained the right to elect their own executives through all changes of the colonial period, and they were the objects of suspicion to the British imperialists who feared the 'democratical pretensions of America.'"[5] The Crown regularly provided security and foreign policy (war) oversight for the colonies overall until the 1770s. The individual charter or proprietary colonies provided funds or in-kind services, a type of taxation. The policies that Britain began to enact during the 1760s were some of the first to deal with most of the colonies as Crown colonies. This was a new approach from both sides, and especially acute in New England, where charters allowed property owners great say over local affairs, in particular, taxation policy.

Colonial Virginia in the first decade of settlement was a rough, brutal, place. Without a steady cash crop, the early Jamestown settlers had great difficulty in ensuring a sustainable colony. During the life span of the London Company, 1606–1624, over 5,600 settlers were sent to Virginia. Of those, not even 1,100 survived the less than twenty years the Company was in existence.[6] It was very traditional in its approach to governing and maintaining order—it was a harsh life. There was nothing romantic about it. Conflict with local Indian tribes, internal conflict, and individual conflict made survival perilous. "Not a generation passed without a baptism of fire—without giving the colonists experience in the use of that unanswerable argument of sovereignty, military force."[7]

The Virginia colony was saved by tobacco. Virginia, from the beginning, nearly failed due to constant warfare with Indians, but profits from the cash crop of tobacco virtually restarted the entire enterprise. After a decade of disease and starvation and Indian wars, the colonists finally (c. 1618) found a crop which would provide them a steady, increasing, source of revenue and hence livelihood. The early colonists faced seemingly intractable problems over work requirements and governance before the rise of tobacco. Many of the colonists became despondent over their situation during the first decade and a few even joined local Indian tribes, abandoning their English colleagues. This naturally created further tension in an already tense environment. The London Company initially dreamed of emulating the Spanish in South America in exploitation of precious metals. This meant the London Company imagined gold and silver, and lots of it, for the taking. However, the English were destined not to repeat the experience with gold that the Spanish had. In anticipation though of great wealth, the London Company at first sent far more gentlemen than laborers, effectively handicapping the colony from the very start. It would take a decade, the character of John Smith, and near annihilation to save the colony.

Tobacco helped fuel the population increase in Virginia from around 350 people in 1616 to over 13,000 by 1650.[8] While tobacco did save Virginia, it was not enough to save the Virginia Company, which was foreclosed on by the English government, thus making Virginia the first Crown colony in 1624 after it was acquired by the British government representing the Crown. Maryland became the second Crown colony in 1632. As a Crown colony, Virginia developed quickly, aided by tobacco and the plantation economy resting on slavery. As such, Virginia became a wealthy and powerful economy much overshadowing its neighbors. Virginia also developed a taste for something far more dangerous in British eyes: a taste for self-government. "Colonial Virginians developed the American interdependence of elite rule, popular politics, and white racial supremacy. That distinctive combination increasingly distinguished English America from the mother country and from the colonies of other empires."[9]

The Pilgrims of Plymouth fame originally contracted with the London Company to settle in Virginia. Navigation errors and storms landed them instead at Plymouth in Massachusetts and they purchased out their contract with the London Company in 1624. This incident, with a loss of settlers, was one more reason the London Company failed in Virginia. Plymouth, an accidental settlement, survived but did not prosper. In 1691, after seventy years, Plymouth had only seven thousand residents when it was absorbed into Massachusetts Bay colony under the 1691 charter.

Massachusetts Bay colony was established in 1629 as a mercantile corporation—just ten years after the Plymouth settlement which was separate at that point. "Unlike the Plymouth band, the Massachusetts Company had a formal charter of incorporation from the king."[10] The Bay colony had learned from the problems of the Virginia colony. Instead of investors in London making decisions, the investors lived in the Bay colony. They also had more explicit guidelines on governmental affairs.

Delaware originally became part of Pennsylvania because William Penn convinced the Duke of York—holding Delaware after taking it from the Dutch, who took it from the Swedes—that he needed a coastal component to his new colony, thus Delaware became the three lower counties with ocean access. The Dutch of New Amsterdam surrendered to the claims of the Duke of York in 1664 without a fight. King Charles II simply decreed that his brother the Duke of York would have the land the Dutch occupied and the Dutch, unable to resist, acquiesced. The Duke granted George Carteret and John Berkeley the land which became New Jersey. Three colonies, "Pennsylvania, Delaware, and Maryland, the old proprietary system remained in force until 1776, keeping the governors equally independent of popular assemblies."[11]

Several colonies failed as private ventures and had to be directly taken over by the Crown, thus becoming Crown colonies. The investment needed for colonization was staggering in both money and personnel. Rarely did private concerns have the necessary funds to make a serious attempt at a successful colony. The competing aspects of trying to turn a profit ran head-long into the demands of human nature. The Spanish, with their example of literally shiploads of gold and silver, painted a too-rosy picture for some businessmen. Added to that, countless external variables such as weather, disease, violence, or crop failure could cause a colonial venture to fail.

Who Were the Colonists?

The colonists largely saw themselves as English, although Spanish and French influence was not far away. This was not just from the cultural influences of the colonists themselves. There was also the long influence of participation in the affairs of government that helped to frame how the colonists saw themselves. A tradition, albeit not everyone, participated in. Whether a royal colony or a proprietary colony, colonists for the most part were acquainted with a limited form of self-government, "For practical purposes the colonial assemblies, in their domestic concerns, were their own masters and their strength was increasing."[12] Especially in the realm of finances, "Propertied Englishmen cherished legislative control over taxation as their most fundamental liberty."[13] Of the three regions, north, middle, and south, New England had the most self-government overall. Virginia, by contrast, was a Crown colony with limited self-government. Several decades of gradually increasing stability and power during the eighteenth century had placed the American colonies in a position of being covetous of their political maturity within the British Empire. This was a powerful force which was constantly within the range of thought of Englishmen who jealously guarded their sacred rights and liberties. This perspective would come into full view during the 1760s, as "England had never discarded the institution of representative government which had sprung up in the middle ages" as a legacy of their Saxon past.[14]

Geographically, France was closing in from the west and north while Spain was from the west and south. Spain showed almost exclusive interest in colonizing South America and only as far north as Florida (and the west coast which the colonists knew little or nothing about). This left most of eastern coastal North America to the midwest available for the English and French to try and colonize. In 1760, neither influence was overly welcomed by either the colonists or the British, which by this time was the dominant cultural and political influence in the colonies. The cultural makeup of the colonists was majority English, and this certainly impacted their worldview. In fact, as will be shown later, the American above all Americans, George Washington, was during the 1750s quite English. During the French and Indian War, he actively sought a commission in the British army. Many of the most familiar names of the Founding generation were in 1760 the gentry and aristocracy of the colonies; they hailed from the leading families. The gentry in America were the wealthy merchants and lawyers of the North; the aristocracy were the great planters of the South. One aspect of English social life that flourished in America was the class system. "In all the colonies the ruling orders, in English fashion, demanded from the masses the obedience to which they considered themselves entitled by wealth, talents, and general preeminence."[15]

Demographics

The lifestyle in the American colonies during the 1760s was overwhelmingly agrarian. Land ownership for cultivation or other pursuits drove emigration to America for decades. There was so much land it was being given away in many cases. From the tip of present-day Maine to present day Georgia (and from Nova Scotia to Barbados—encompassing all British North America), the colonies spread out along the coast over some 1,500 miles. There were few if any settlements of consequence more than 250 to 300 miles from the coast. By the Revolution, some 25,000 had already moved beyond the mountains to permanently settle in areas which became Kentucky, Tennessee, and Ohio.[16] (It can be said that during the first half of the eighteenth century, virtually all settled communities were within 250 miles of the coast and near a river or tributary of some sort. Although outposts abounded further west, it took time to advance beyond the village stage.) Historian Francis Parkman wrote: "Along the skirts of the southern and middle colonies ran for six or seven hundred miles a loose, thin, disheveled fringe of population, the half-barbarous pioneers of advancing civilizations."[17]

Most of the population clustered along the coast in the Mid–Atlantic region into New England. This was not only due to Native American populations being more prominent beyond the 250-mile area. For most, the issue was the dense forest and difficult terrain. Also, to the east lay the ocean, the only source of communication with the wider world. Although there seemingly was unlimited land, the colonists could feel a sense of being constrained to the coastal areas as the main arteries of travel and communication. Settlement patterns that reached west did so invariably along water routes. Without water, the American interior would have been nearly impenetrable.

Impenetrable or not, colonists did make their way into the American interior. It was not easy to hack a road or settlement out of forests or swamps, but gradually over time they did. Without direct encouragement from the British government—in fact, the British were against it—settlers pressed deeper and deeper into the American continent in ever larger numbers. By 1760 proto settlements existed along not just river routes but along crude roads or paths that in many cases followed Native American routes.

For land transportation colonists relied on foot power, horsepower, or in rare instances carriages. Small conveyances drawn by one horse were utilized by single travelers or larger coaches for longer trips. By far those who traveled were on business of one sort or another. Historian Charles Andrews wrote a century ago, "Nothing but sheer necessity could have compelled men to drive these roads through the dense forests and tangled undergrowth, across marshes, and over rocky hills...."[18] Pleasure travel was not undertaken. The concept was not widely envisioned by most colonists. Those who did travel of necessity for business traveled as far as possible by water before resorting to overland transport. Water vessels came in a seemingly unlimited number of types depending on the need at hand. Certainly, they were wind powered before the advent of canals with flat-bottom boats pulled by horses later in the century and into the nineteenth century. And, the world changed again with the advent of steam power; however, in 1760 that was still science fiction.

The travails of travel could be exacerbated by regional geographic topography. The southern colonies experienced more problems in overland routes as has been noted; "in the colonies south of Pennsylvania ... the wide rivers, bays, and swamps rendered the land routes difficult and dangerous."[19] Climate too was a worrisome variable. The southern heat in summer was just as dangerous as the winter cold in the north.

Water travel led to a ubiquitous symbol of coastal life much romanticized today—the lighthouse. In the mid-eighteenth century, "the most important ... lights were in Boston harbor, off Newport, on Sandy Hook, on Cape Henry in Middle Bay Island, Charleston, and on Tybee Island."[20] Rivers boasted buoys to aid in navigation and pilots were frequently needed to assist maneuvering in tight channels.[21]

The more one traveled though the more one likely made calls for better public road systems. It may seem strange today, but the idea of a publicly funded road system was the exception rather than the rule in eighteenth-century colonial America. This became an issue after the Revolution when the newly independent states needed better, more reliable, transportation systems. Before independence, the colonies often were their own worst enemies in that standards of transportation systems could vary considerably from colony to colony. Still, by 1760, there was already one road that ran from New Hampshire to Georgia.[22] The road transportation system was also enhanced in 1738 with the passage of postal regulations throughout the colonies which by default required a maintained, standardized road system. While keeping close to the coastal areas, it was nonetheless a significant beginning in standardize road systems.

It is hard to overestimate the role the humble tavern played in these decades before, during, and after the Revolutionary War. They offered company, shelter, food, drink, news, discussion, and public venue space … the list could go on. Naturally, it goes without saying that quality varied dramatically between establishments. They were nonetheless a reliable staple of eighteenth-century American life. One common form of entertainment in taverns, besides gambling, was music. Rarely were there concerts or recitals such as might occur today. Rather, these performances were more informal gatherings where musicians could earn a little extra money while providing some pleasant interlude for guests. The cringe-worthy stories of travelers sharing bedding was all too true. Hygiene was nowhere near as regimented as today and overall cleanliness of inns was often a matter of debate with the mistress of the establishment. Still, without family or friends nearby, the best that travelers could hope for was finding a local tavern-keeper with similar approaches to one's expectations.

Outside of tavern life, nearly any occasion sufficed to counter the tedium of life. Religious festivals were always popular and seemed to carry a stamp of approval about them. These celebrations varied throughout the colonies depending on what religious variant one section followed. Naturally, Christmas and Easter were nearly uniformly followed. Thanksgiving Day (or some variation on a harvest festival) too found acceptance throughout much of the colonies.

Politically, the seaboard sought to keep power confined to the coastal areas. "Care was taken in all the colonies to keep the representation of the backcountry at such a point that control of the legislature remained in the hands of the seaboard counties."[23] (This would lead to many homegrown issues of near civil war. A prime example was Shays' Rebellion in 1786.) This also ensured fewer serious settlements in the interior and thus fewer conflicts with Native Americans and the French or Spanish. During much of the eighteenth century, the British controlled most of the territory from the coast west to the Appalachians. The French controlled to the west beyond the mountains while Spain controlled the southern areas beyond Georgia, which in fact itself was created as a buffer between British and Spanish lands. For a host of reasons, life was better along the coast.

Throughout the eighteenth-century standards of living rose throughout the colonies. While this impacted a small percentage of the population, its residual effects often helped those less favorably situated in life. This would be crucial during the years of war when those less favored by circumstances would be called upon to do the fighting. Some buy-in was necessary to induce these men to risk their lives and sacred honor; not their fortunes, which the signers of the Declaration of Independence pledged and which the average fighting man did not possess to pledge.

In 1760 the male and female white population in the colonies totaled approximately 1.2 million. By 1760, the original European settlement centers from the seventeenth century, Massachusetts, and Virginia, had expanded to include the entire eastern seaboard. The traditional immigrant had come to include, in addition to the English, the Scots and Scots-Irish, as well as the Dutch, Swedish, and German immigrants who were well established. (By far the largest number of immigrants where from Africa—admittedly against their will. "During the eighteenth century, the British colonies imported 1,500,000 slaves—more than three times the number of free immigrants."[24]) The outlines of British population dominance were securely in place by the mid-eighteenth century. The enslaved African population by 1760 numbered approximately 300,000 although it is more difficult to track due to poor record keeping. Amidst all this were some free Africans living in the colonies. Boston and Philadelphia vied for the most populous city. Again, record keeping makes declaring a clear winner difficult, however, "during the eighteenth century most colonial arrivals were African conscripts forcibly carried to a land of slavery, rather than European volunteers seeking a domain of freedom."[25] Therefore, during the eighteenth century more people came from Africa than any other country or continent.

Early demographics of colonial America show areas of immigrant destinations to more likely be Philadelphia, the most diverse city in America, or Charleston as opposed to Boston or New York. "The great migration of the eighteenth-century shunned New York as fully as it did New England."[26] This was a pattern which held throughout much of the eighteenth century even past American independence. Popular stereotypes created during this time have lasted well into the modern period. Just one example would be the term "Yankee," originally used to describe residents of New England and which gradually came to mean any American when viewed from skeptical foreign eyes.

One of the largest issues facing the colonists, regardless of where in the colonies, was land ownership. During the first decades of colonization in the seventeenth century, colonial leaders followed patterns of land usage developed in Europe. This became problematic when the absolute amount of land available in the colonies was truly grasped. Each region then had to try and adapt policies that acknowledged European practices but still dealt with the realities of seemingly endless land. These policies pointed toward a future of expansive land ownership and against massive estates passed from generation to generation. The American colonies never became an exact version of Europe or England although certain traits and characteristics clearly maintained a hold throughout the colonial period. It was impossible not to emulate England to some degree. Not only were the colonies English by government, they organized and functioned much like the mother country. This is not surprising. Those who came to America were by and large eager representatives of the results-oriented approach which pervaded England at the time. "England in the seventeenth and eighteenth centuries was a nation engrossed in applying ever-increasing energies to business enterprise—of which colonization in the New World was one branch for the employment of capital and administrative genius."[27]

Traditional European group prejudices were less observed in America but still contributed to the oftentimes chaotic colonial response to British policies. Even during the Revolution and immediately afterwards, regional, and sectional rivalries, held over from ancient European differences, nearly kept America from becoming America. Regional concerns, fueled in part by long-simmering Old-World antagonisms, created far too many issues than necessary as America emerged from two decades of transformation by 1789. Writers of greater and lesser recognition observed this transition and commented on it in numerous published works throughout the closing decades of the eighteenth century.

The roughly fifty years between 1714 (end of the War of Spanish Succession) and 1760 (the fall of Montreal) were generally good decades for the colonies overall within themselves and within the larger British colonial system. England enjoyed the benefits of their colonial policy:

> In the eyes of contemporaries most of King George IIIs subjects enjoyed an enviable standard of living: they were, by and large, better fed, better clothed, better sheltered, better rewarded for their efforts, than any other people with the possible exception of the Dutch.[28]

This expansion was not confined to one area; rather, all aspects of colonial life developed a more positive and forward-looking attitude. Social, economic, and political considerations all matured to greater or lesser extents than what had existed in America coming out of the seventeenth century. The relative peace in Europe allowed for the greater increase in emigration to America from Europe which started to include smaller ethnic groups which would become so vital to energizing the American cultural outlook in the late nineteenth century. Many of these groups had their first taste of freedom, just by traveling to what seemed like was literally a new world. They laid the foundations upon which further immigration occurred once America became more settled. And those who came undertook the arduous journey out of the same reasons we associate with most of the earliest settlers to American shores: religious or economic reasons. Indeed, those are still two primary reasons for immigrants to this day. Of the nearly 2,000,000 (enslaved and free) people living in America in the early 1760s, a full one-third were born abroad. While England sought to severely limit emigration to America, the colonies themselves generally ignored these rules and admitted anyone who arrived. In fact, the concept of citizenship developed into a legal issue during the eighteenth century in tandem with the rise in immigration. Citizenship conferred unique rights, and expectations, on those receiving it. Citizenship has always, since Greek and Roman days, been a badge of honor and pride, and contention.

Citizenship was a concept with huge implications. It determined rights and responsibilities and conferred status and a sense of dignity. Citizenship will factor into the larger discussions of the 1760s through the writings and arguments undertaken by authors on both sides of the debate about "Englishness" during that tumultuous decade. Citizenship is crucial to understanding the American founding. It was important as it formed the basis for admission to a community that could protect and nourish a person. The collective approach has always been attractive yet entrance into the collective has always been limited.

Throughout the colonies there were noticeable differences in how people lived. In large part this reflected the attitudes of those who originally settled the land. New England conformed readily to the stoic Puritan ideals of the founding families of Pilgrim lore. (Although the Pilgrims of Plymouth were not connected to the Massachusetts Bay outside of being geographical neighbors until the 1690s.) With a heavy emphasis on the church and community as the anchors of communal life, New England radiated the pious, God-centered evocation of the pulpit out into its towns. Each man had a separate worth apart from the theocratic government and maintained his own land as an owner, not a tenant. "The colonists substituted an English way of living within nature for the ways that had long sustained the natives in New England."[29] This primarily dealt with land ownership and exploitation of natural resources—approaches the Indians knew little if anything about. "Much of New England's authority in continental affairs from 1763 down to the Revolution stemmed from its early and united adherence..." to being selective in who was a citizen and allowed to be part of the community—in other words, insular.[30]

New England, with a milder climate, greater gender parity, and tighter immigration controls, prospered in ways the Southern colonies did not. In fact, "despite attracting the fewest emigrants, healthy New England became the most populous region in English America."[31] An export cash crop, such as existed in the South, did not exist in New England. Fish however became a commodity and contributed to the rise of income inequality. "For want of a plantation staple, like tobacco and sugar, New England avoided the trap of a plantation economy: the highly uneven distribution of skill and income as a labor-intensive crop polarized the population into large numbers of impoverished workers exploited by an elite."[32] Strangely enough, New England also prospered by providing most of the raw material (wood based fuel) needed to develop the sugar plantations in the West Indies as profitable ventures.

The Mid–Atlantic and Southern states took their guidance from their more commerce minded ancestors who settled Jamestown and places like Christiana, Delaware, in the hopes of creating mercantile opportunities in the New World. In these colonies one was apt to find less ownership by the lower members of society who tended to be tenants on vast estates reminiscent of Europe. Names such as Carter, Penn, and Livingston, among others, created family dynasties that oversaw enormous tracts of land for decades. Another major difference in cultural attitudes between the three major regions in the colonies concerned slavery. Largely, the anchor regions, New England, and the South, had opposite views of the practice of slavery; New England opposed it (although some did own slaves) while the South embraced it. In the British colonies the patterns of the slave economy without question became most entrenched in the South. Here the agricultural pursuits and land-owning patterns lent themselves well to vast armies of workers. Naturally, for the plantation owner, the lowest possible cost for labor ensured the highest profit on sales of the commodity harvested. As is also well known, questions of racial slavery went well beyond the economic aspects and dwelt on the very notions of humanity, personhood, and citizenship. For America, this question seemingly culminated in the Dred Scott decision of 1857—a decision quickly reversed by the Civil War.[33]

New colonies, like South Carolina, which was first inhabited by Europeans in the 1670s who fled Barbados due to overcrowding and disease, would become bulwarks for the institution of racial slavery. South Carolina was a Crown colony in the 1720s. South Carolina's neighbor to the south, Georgia, did not permit slavery when it was settled in 1733 as a buffer to Spanish Florida. This prohibition did not last long and by 1751, when it became a Crown colony, slavery was entrenched.

The Mid–Atlantic was divided over the practice. Racial slavery, as is well known, became the measure against which all aspects of American life was defined as the decades passed after 1789. At the Constitutional Convention in 1787, the Civil War in 1860–1865, and the Civil Rights Era in the 1960s, and even into the first quarter of the twenty-first century, slavery and race provided the constant, never-ending narrative which identified American attitudes about government, citizenship, and the notion of American exceptionalism.

By 1760, slavery had existed almost as long as the colonies had; the first enslaved Africans having arrived in 1619 in Virginia; a year later, or shortly after, they arrived in Jamestown.[34] The practice could be said to date to Columbus who enslaved native Caribbean "Indians." And of course, the Spanish were hardly more accommodating in their treatment of South American populations. By 1518, less than thirty years after Columbus arrived in the Americas, the Spanish were forced to start importing enslaved Africans due to the rapid decline of Native Americans who succumbed to European diseases.

By 1710, with the advent of the British Empire, English colonists had developed a sense of pride in being English with all the rights that appellation conferred. Especially when compared to Spanish and French colonists, the English felt superior. Foremost among their claims were all the rights and privileges associated with the English nation. This meant the unwritten English constitution, or the common law heritage. This was far more advanced than many areas of Europe. This early identification of the colonists as simply Englishmen living abroad would provide one aspect of the sense the colonists felt in the 1760s of having been betrayed of their rights by Parliament.

As colonial America became more settled politically by the first decades of the eighteenth century, the outlines of what could be called an awareness of the intellectual segments of life were becoming more apparent. Science, literature, art, and law were all areas that Americans began to not only copy Europe but in fact begin to advance uniquely American interpretations of. As Europe eased into the larger movement known as the Enlightenment, Americans responded with variations alongside traditional European responses to the challenges of the rapidly evolving eighteenth century. Arts such as architecture and theater also saw a blossoming throughout America, with each region, especially in design and furnishings, contributing its own unique influence.

Learning also led to bookstores, printing presses, libraries, learned societies, and other aspects which were not always viewed in a welcome manner in the seventeenth century, especially in the religiously dominated colonies. As an example, Benjamin Franklin offered European printed versions of the classics (Greek and Roman), titles generally frowned upon as heathen. Today, these titles, and many others in the public domain, are easily found for free on the internet.

Similarly, the rise of formal education advanced with the eighteenth

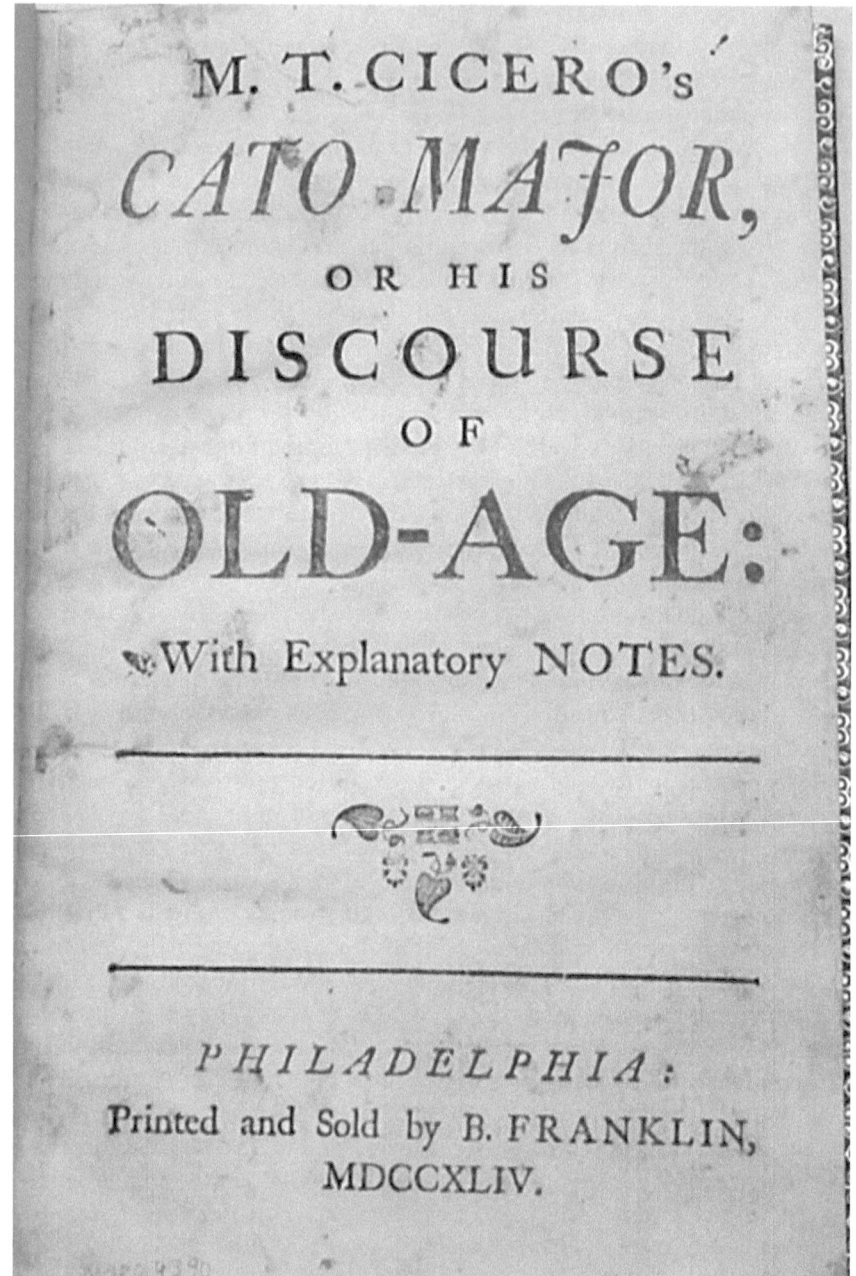

One of the earliest printings in the colonies of a major classical writer. In this case, a work by Cicero, printed by Benjamin Franklin in 1744. Morristown NHP. Lloyd W. Smith archival collection. MORR 9390.

century. Whether the one-room schoolhouse or the college lecture hall, education was making a strong showing in the colonies. The historians Charles and Mary beard have written:

> If, on the whole, the colonial college was narrow in its intellectual range, it need not be supposed that the discipline offered was correspondingly thorough in every case or that a deadly uniformity ruled all classrooms.[35]

As is generally known, only white men, usually of some means, were permitted such an extended undertaking. Furthermore, in keeping with the principles of Enlightenment Europe, many established schools, or those just founded, were beginning, however tentatively, to loosen the grip that organized religion had on the curriculum. As with so many other aspects of mid-eighteenth-century colonial America, Benjamin Franklin was a major force in this transformation. Yet, even with all the force of Franklin and other reformers, "collegiate education of the eighteenth century, both in the mother country and the provinces, immersed the students in theories and dogmas that had little or no relation to creative intelligence or independent thinking."[36]

Crevecoeur

The most perspicuous observations of the American colonies during the 1760s came from a Frenchman who fought in the last great battle of the French and Indian War. Although French gentry by birth, J. Hector St. John De Crevecoeur was fascinated by the English and spent a considerable amount of time while growing up visiting relatives in Britain. Ironically, the Frenchman who adored England fought against the British in the French and Indian War after making his way to American in the early stages of the conflict. Crevecoeur was an accomplished soldier and engineer who was seriously wounded in September 1760 at the epic battle at Montreal, where the French lost control of Canada. After his recovery and release from military service he went to New York, looking to start a new life in America. In 1765 Crevecoeur became a naturalized subject of King George III and took up residence in New York. Two years later in 1767 he was part of "a surveying and exploring party that went over the Appalachians and down the Ohio River to St. Louis, up the Mississippi to the Great Lakes at the present-day site of Chicago, and returned to New York...."[37] During the return journey, Crevecoeur spent time with upstate New York tribes.

From virtually the beginning when Europeans discovered America, it became shrouded in a mythos which endures in an altered manifestation to this day. When active colonization began in 1607, the initial observations of

America came under scrutiny, but nonetheless remained intact. As historian Daniel Boorstin has written:

> When the intellectually and spiritually mature man of Europe first settled in America, he was forced to relive the childhood of the race, to confront once again the primitive and intractable wilderness of his cave-dwelling ancestors. In America he became an anachronism. This quaint juxtaposition of culture and barbarism—the Bible in the wilderness—which characterized the earliest settlement of the continent, has left a heritage of conflict and paradox for our own time.[38]

As late as the 1760s, America was as much myth as fact to the European mind. Some of this misunderstanding was grounded in prejudice, some in ignorance, and some in the willful fantasies of gullible Europeans. The myth of America was in some measure as responsible for the ultimate conflict between America and Britain as any policy debates. In fact, the ignorance and misunderstanding of the colonies by Parliament were the cause of much of the disastrous legislation which was produced between 1765 and 1775. There were some colonists who were just as invested in various American myths as their European counterparts.

In short, the myths generally revolved around the new, virgin land and the ideal of the noble savage—especially as it applied to Native Americans. There were elements in Europe where the belief that colonists could somehow render themselves noble, as the native-born Indians, without the detrimental impacts of modern (eighteenth-century) society. Writers and thinkers never tired of attempting to define that special "something" about America. Writers and thinkers such as Rousseau, Buffon, and of course Benjamin Franklin (parading around Paris in a coonskin cap), all wrote and acted as though America was some Eden which not only produced virtuous people, but also created new people thorough the cleansing power of its pure society. These and many more were indicative of the efforts to explain the New World to the Old. Thomas Jefferson became so incensed at the naïve way many Europeans portrayed America that he wrote his *Notes on the State of Virginia* in 1785 in part as an antidote to some of the nonsense.

Two French classics about America were written by Hector St. John De Crevecoeur, who published in 1782 but who wrote in the 1760s and 1770s; and another by Alexis de Tocqueville, who wrote and published in the 1830s. These two writers were in the vanguard of authors who struggled to represent the essence of the American mystique to the wider world. It could be argued Tocqueville had a slightly easier task as the United States was well established when he wrote, as opposed to Crevecoeur who wrote during the tumultuous period of America's creation. His first work, *Letters from an American Farmer*, dates from 1769 and was based on information gathered during the 1760s. "In the half century after 1782, *Letters from an American Farmer* enjoyed only a moderate fame in the United States but in Europe went into edition after edition … it provided two generations of Europeans with their chief impressions of the American colonies."[39] During the nineteenth century when travel became move regular to the United States, Europeans began to explore more earnestly their "cousins" across the Atlantic. Therefore, the types of books written by Crevecoeur or Tocqueville became less popular. More people were able to make the trip to the new world and see for themselves what all the talk was about. Even with greater travel, writers such as Charles Dickens wrote widely circulated travelogue-type books about America.

Understanding how Americans saw themselves, and how other populations saw Americans, is vital to our own understanding of the crucial period of the 1760s. America, it was believed, literally re-created a man. From being downtrodden by his lot in life, a journey to America, experiencing the redeeming qualities of a new brotherhood, the European everyman became somebody. "He begins to forget his former servitude and dependence; his heart involuntarily swells and glows; this first swell inspires him with those new thoughts which constitute an American."[40] And again, this theme is clear, "The American is a new man, who acts upon new principles; he must therefore entertain new ideas and form new opinions."[41] Almost like a religious revival, America makes a man born again.

This is an important observation given that while it provided Europeans their first and lasting impressions, it was their first and lasting impression based on the famous question that Crevecoeur asked, "What, then, is the American, this new man?"[42] (See Appendix 1) This is probably one of the most important questions ever presented. Crevecoeur knew he had an audience, and he knew the question was more rhetorical than answerable. America was whatever the reader wanted it to be. And that was the point. In America, everything was new. While ancient Europe nominally put patterns of society upon the American scene since the first settlement in 1607, those patterns never quite fit. The rawness of the land dictated otherwise. Plus, the distance from Europe allowed for a mitigated application of European patterns to accommodate the realities in the colonies.

Whatever motivated Crevecoeur to write, and to write such panegyrics for the American way, may never fully be known. His life and conduct are generally perceived in basic outline, however, there are significant gaps and questions concerning nearly every phase of that life. He was French but passed himself off as English, was he a loyalist or patriot during the Revolution; why did he wait to publish his works until a decade after he compiled them; why did he try to return to Europe in the middle of the Revolution via New York—the British headquarters; why is his service in the French and Indian War so under-documented; why did he abandon his family? Historian James Myers, Jr., speculates he may have been a French spy for nearly two decades.[43]

The concept of the farmer, the man of the earth, was the chosen profession of numerous writers who wanted to instantly evoke the rural kinship of American life. As we will see, John Dickinson hid his identity behind the façade of a farmer to promote his ideas concerning colonial taxation in 1768. Dickinson, and others, sought to show that a humble farmer, someone without much formal education if any at all, could present simple, common sense ideas without the burden of too much thought. Therefore, the arguments they were making against Britain would have naturally been accessible to the "average" American. Other writers, less well known than Crevecoeur, who worked within this genre were John Woolman, William Bartram, and Moreau de Saint-Mery. All these men worked within the concept of the new America which created the new man—the man who could never have existed in depleted, tired, Europe.

Crevecoeur's first letter (he called his essays "letters" to effect a rustic touch—as would Dickinson) lets his readers know the intent of his writing—"they cannot therefore fail of being highly interesting to the people of England at a time when everybody's attention is directed toward the affairs of America."[44] The topic Crevecoeur picked, America, was to be studied through the eyes of the humble farmer, America's true aristocracy. As Crevecoeur described a farmer, he was a "humble American planter, a simple cultivator of the earth...."[45]

According to Crevecoeur, the first glimpse of America for an immigrant when arriving by ship was awe-inspiring. Much like later immigrants recording their first glimpses of the Statue of Liberty, Crevecoeur wrote, "what a train of pleasing ideas this fair spectacle must suggest; it is a prospect which must inspire a good citizen with the most heart-felt pleasure."[46] Crevecoeur continued:

> It [America] is not composed, as in Europe, of great lords who possess everything and of a herd of people who have nothing. Here are no aristocratic families, no counts, no kings, no bishops, no ecclesiastical dominion, no invisible power giving to a few a very visible one, no great manufacturers employing thousands, no great refinements of luxury.[47]

Such was the impression the colonies made in the 1760s on one who sought to explain them to his fellow Europeans. In short Crevecoeur concluded, "we [America] are the most perfect society now existing in the world."[48]

This endorsement begs the question, why did the colonists ultimately revolt? If America was perfect, what drove a small band of wealthy, educated men to take such umbrage to British efforts at raising revenue? The short answer would be that Crevecoeur was simply out of touch with a society he thought he knew so well. However, there is no doubt something more troubling here. Crevecoeur, and others like him, while having good intentions, were too willing to mask the hardships and intense debate already working its way through America's elite.

Like many American movements, those of the 1760s took shape with America's leaders who felt threatened by proposals coming out of Britain, which in the 1760s meant some of the early tax bills. Although most of the taxes would have impacted all classes of society, America's leaders sought to amplify the damage which the tax proposals would have had on society overall. It was not difficult to convince the public at large that their interests were compromised. Many of America's leaders saw the proposed taxes as both an economic problem and a sovereignty problem. Americans had advanced to a point where colony-specific liberty had become something very real. What America's elite found most fortuitous, consciously or not, were the writings of people like Crevecoeur who unwittingly partnered with the fears of America's leaders by producing works that sold the greatness or uniqueness of America that was attainable by all. Thus, side by side, the confluence of two separate modes of thought worked to unify two disparate branches of American society. Crevecoeur and others emboldened the lower classes by uplifting the farmer, the menial laborer, to an equal level with the elites; the new American left "behind him all his ancient prejudices and manners, receive[d] new ones from the new mode of life he has embraced, the new government he obeys, and the new rank he holds."[49] Ironically, while Crevecoeur and those similar to him were breaking the ancient bonds of law and government, America's elite, during the 1760s, demanded a return to the outlines of ancient liberty as they understood it. "[L]iberty [for the white man] was a privileged status that depended upon the power to subordinate someone else."[50] In many ways, the resulting revolution was about who would control not only the future, but the past as well.

Crevecoeur was not a simpleton writer. He was an extremely talented observer who fused his talents to create what is today considered a literary masterpiece. Always recognized as important, Crevecoeur has moved beyond the simple manner and language he employed to be studied for the messages within his messages, something his contemporaries had no notion of while he portrayed a sentimental landscape and society that has ever since type-cast America as a land of the humble, hard-working, commonsense farmer and laborer; he is now more seen as someone who, not fully rejecting what he wrote, nonetheless was not fully convinced by what he wrote either. In other words, his thinking was malleable; his readers were not. This earned him a large readership and inspired other writers to follow his approach as indicated.

Crevecoeur can easily be dismissed as naïve or simplistic in his relationship with observations he gleaned during the 1760s and 1770s, and no doubt there were those at the time who felt that way about his work. However, Crevecoeur's approach served their need as it helped put the so-called average American along with elites in the American experiment in representational government. Crevecoeur provided a bridge between two distinct groups of Americans who would split into political parties in the 1790s—Thomas Jefferson's agrarian concept and Alexander Hamilton's mercantile, industrial concept. There is no evidence Crevecoeur consciously sought to straddle this gulf, but he did, nonetheless. And it is a legacy we live with to this day, however permutated that gulf has become.

The genre of writing wherein the American psyche is given more credit than due was over a century old by the 1760s. The plot and storyline were well established. The evolution of the North American continent to a majority British holding had been accomplished. Hence the storyline could only get stronger and more dignified with independence.

CHAPTER 3

The Era of the French and Indian War

Between the turn of the eighteenth century and 1760 the colonies and Britain, while generally prosperous as pointed out, could nonetheless not avoid the most relied upon tool of diplomacy of that period: war. In the decades leading up to the French and Indian War in the 1750s, the colonies and Britain fought in several smaller, yet linked, conflicts involving the French, Spanish, and Native Americans. Each conflict centered on territorial claims in North America and securing the allegiance of the Native Americans. The shifting loyalties exhibited by all parties were a consequence of the immense amounts of money to be generated from future trade in the equally immense areas of land. The dawning realization of patterns of wealth set off a frenzy of diplomatic activity culminating in the French and Indian War and indeed ultimately in the American Revolution.

The Seven Years' War was a colonial war fought by France and England over control of North America. It was an extension of the European War of Austrian Succession. The stakes were high from the start with the potential rewards in the form of future mercantile interests in a promising landscape. Both England and France understood the wealth beyond the agricultural aspects extended to trade with the Indians and even to appropriating their traditional sources of communal wealth: fur.

Some colonies saw the situation beyond the Appalachians with little interest. They did not support the British although they provided some money and supplies to the army before General Braddock's defeat in July 1755. Enough settlers though saw the enticing lands as too much to pass by—Native Americans in the way or not. Britain saw the potential for future conflict and hoped to prevent altercations by keeping forces available to deter colonists from interfering with natives. This policy would prove fruitless.

The colony of Pennsylvania bore the brunt of the fighting and destruction of the French and Indian War. While fighting raged in unsettled territories (eventually becoming Ohio, Indiana, Illinois, and Michigan) Pennsylvania saw the greatest loss of any of the existing colonies. Britain also relied "heavily on its craftsmen and its industry for war material and on its farmers to feed the troops."[1] Pennsylvania was the entry point to the riches of the Ohio River Valley and thus was the crossroads of belligerent activity.

The Ohio Territory was not the only venue where the British and French came to blows in America during the Seven Years' War. For decades, as in Ohio, the two antagonists had traded recriminations and occasional bloodshed over Nova Scotia. A British territory populated by French speakers who saw themselves as French, by 1755 the situation had become untenable. The British had decided on a plan to remove, forcibly, the French from Nova Scotia and rid the outpost of a potential enemy. The Acadians, as they were known, were expelled in a series of moves since retold in countless heartbreaking stories, poems, and later, films.[2] In all, some 6,000 French inhabitants of English Nova Scotia, some families in residence for generations, were forcefully relocated. Aside from the "success" of removing the French from Nova Scotia, the overall British policy in America against the French was failing before the intervention of William Pitt. The arrival of Pitt as Secretary of State in London changed everything. John Dickinson, finishing his law studies in London, was aware of the sorry situation of the quasi-war in the American colonies: "I hope our affairs in America will be managed better this year than were the last, and that by this time you begin to find advantage of having a supreme commander, whose authority, knowledge, and address may turn out united force against the common enemy.[3]

New Secretary of State William Pitt in 1758 dramatically increased the scope of the French and Indian War after several years of defeat. He poured resources into the effort and promised the colonies they would be reimbursed for their contributions. In addition to money and equipment, 20,000 soldiers and sailors were sent to America. Aside from the period of the American Revolution, it was the largest armed force to appear in North America. Three new commanders were tasked with taking three major French sites: Fort Duquesne; Ticonderoga; and Louisbourg. Ticonderoga would be the only French fort to survive the British offense.

The decades of turmoil between England and France preceding the French and Indian War were the prelude to a decades-long conflict that ultimately ended with American independence. The potential riches of North America provided adequate enticement to keep both adversaries sufficiently engaged in the contest to control America for nearly seventy years prior to the French and Indian War starting. Similarly, like most endless wars, one side usually is victorious for a time only to be vanquished later.

Chapter 3. The Era of the French and Indian War

Like a tennis ball, victory bounces from one side to the other side with consistent regularity. Indeed, although the French ultimately lost the war(s), they more than redeemed themselves during the American Revolution by ensuring Britain's final defeat in the colonial wars for North America.

The British had the French and Spanish under nearly constant surveillance during the decades prior to the outbreak of war in the 1740s and 1750s. However, Spain was not much of a threat; overall, "Spain was a liability, requiring French armies to defend it; and the Spanish colonies were at the mercy of the Dutch and English fleets."[4] Britain was concerned about the land claims made by their erstwhile enemies and competitors for dominance on the North American continent. While Britain did not initially have the financial inclination to push beyond the Appalachians in the 1750s, they at the same time did not want their rivals to gain too much power in an area of potential future expansion. Even without official British directives, some American traders had established themselves deep into the Ohio River Valley by 1747.

Neither France nor Britain were going to allow the vast untapped riches of North America to pass by without a fight. Both Virginia Governor Robert Dinwiddie and the Governor of New France, Michel-Ange Du Quesne de Menneville, Marquis de Duquesne, knew this, and both were willing to press the issue, especially Dinwiddie. Dinwiddie "was the most watchful sentinel against French aggression and its most strenuous opponent."[5] As governor of Virginia, nominally the leading colony, he knew firsthand the enormous wealth potential lying just beyond the populated portions of his colony.

> In the spring of 1754, war had not yet become inescapable but only possible. Dinwiddie and Duquesne had escalated minor skirmishes into a major colonial war; after this had been done, another complex series of events escalated this colonial conflict into a general Anglo-French war.[6]

Land speculation offered not just the chance at riches, it provided an outlet for career-minded men with families who could make use of skills such as surveying, exploring, farming, hunting, and trapping.

Officials in both Britain and France, however, saw no need for undue alarm. That would come a few years hence when William Pitt poured nearly every available pound, soldier, and sailor into the contest. What exacerbated the problem for both England and France was the lack of an ambassador in either London or Paris during much of 1754 when matters were being pressed in America by both Dinwiddie and Duquesne.[7] It was in 1754 that the death of Joseph Jumonville and the British defeat at Fort Necessity (with George Washington in command) which set the diplomatic levers in motion. As late as May 1756, no movement had been detected by the English public concerning war. Writing to his father on May 10, 1756, a young John Dickinson, in London studying law, observed, "The public affairs of Europe continue as they have been a great while, that is, many things talked of, but nothing done."[8]

The British and French did meet briefly to discuss North American issues in early 1755—it proved pointless. Within a year, war had been declared. Dickinson, writing in a letter to his mother on June 6, 1756, noted in an understated comment: "As to public affairs, there is nothing new except his majesty's declaration of war against France..., which has not made and is not likely to make the least alteration in the face of affairs."[9] As we know that declaration of war created a huge alteration in the face of affairs impacting France and England and more specifically Dickinson himself. It would be the French and Indian War which would make John Dickinson famous and establish his reputation. It would culminate in another event which made Dickinson equally famous, his not signing the Declaration of Independence. For now, as a young law student in London, all of that seemed completely improbable. Dickinson was clearly well informed, as presumably the English public was as well, on events in America. Dickinson expressed apprehension "of returning to one's country groaning under the double miseries of war and discord...."[10]

England by this point had more colonists living in America than the French and more territory under active use. The Canadian boundaries were murky after the Treaty of Aix-la-Chapelle of 1748 (ending the War of Austrian Succession) but without question the real prize in the colonial struggle was the vast and fertile Ohio Valley.[11] The French had hoped to link their possessions via the Mississippi—thus linking New Orleans and Canada in a vast longitudinal empire. France however proved too weak and financially insecure to accomplish this goal.

A Wider Conflict

It is often thought that the French and Indian War was strictly an American affair concerning theaters of war and areas of impact. It is equally forgotten that the French and Indian War and the Seven Years' War and the War of Austrian Succession were virtually one and the same. The British, under the leadership of King George II, had a significant handicap in that George was also the Elector of Hanover in Germany where much of the War of Austrian Succession was being fought. As such, he was exceptionally vulnerable to attack on mainland Europe and thus required significant investment, which potentially drained valuable resources away from the fighting in America. The king and his ministers were forced to keep a wary and constant eye on events in Europe.

The dominant army in Europe in terms of size, France was always within striking distance of Germany and the Hanover lands. This continental European aspect along with the Far East components of the war are often cited as leading to the French and Indian War being viewed as the first true global war. The European components of the French and Indian War were interwoven with much complexity resulting from centuries of European dynastic intrigue. The back and forth world of European diplomacy and war, and the French and Indian War, stood at the apex of centuries of death and destruction in the seemingly endless attempts of the belligerents to control fates of citizens and nations alike at home or across the globe. The eighteenth century, with an added extra decade on either side, transformed the world into the modern in ways which linger with us to this day. The eighteenth century, more than any previous century since the fall of Rome impacted a greater percentage of the global population which has lasted until the twenty-first century.

Winston Churchill, writing in the 1950s, stated that during the period from 1688 to 1815, "three revolutions profoundly influenced mankind. They occurred within the space of a hundred years, and all of them led to war between the British and the French."[12] Churchill's sentiment (his ancestor would have a major role early in the transformative century) shows that the French and Indian War and the peace in 1763 were mere laybys in the seemingly never-ending struggle between France and Great Britain. The sheer destruction of over a century of war essentially put matters right back where they started. The one great loss of over a century of struggle between England and France were the colonies of North America. Churchill recorded this one measurable as having "Separated the English-speaking peoples into two branches, each with a distinctive outlook and activity, but still fundamentally united by the same language, as well as by common traditions and common law."[13]

Dynastic Wars

Although it may seem somewhat incoherent to have a section on Continental European problems in a book about 1760s America, in fact it was a seminal part of the intellectual agitation that roused the early Founders' thinking. Indeed, the colonial problem by 1760 was entirely the making of decades of Continental European political agitation. Ever since the accidental discovery of the New World in 1492, European power politics had an element of colonial competition surrounding every decision they made.

The struggles for dominance that plagued the European continent for a millennium simply expanded geographically to the western hemisphere.

It was completely natural for the colonists in North America to be sucked into this vortex of struggle for power. In fact, it was as natural as could be. Colonists, given their geographic distance from Europe had the luxury of miles to insulate their debates until they were ready for a wider audience. In this regard, America truly was the new world, continuously laying the groundwork of a new system of government drafted on the concepts of the old.

Over nearly a century, starting in 1688 with the English Glorious Revolution, England and France waged four difficult wars over the fate of their empires. The first phase from 1689 to 1697 proved a stalemate. The second part, from 1702 to 1713, which saw the creation of Great Britain, also saw the British best the French on several fronts. The third iteration of the protracted colonial struggle lasted from 1738 to 1748 and did little more than set the stage for the final or closing act in the contest—the French and Indian War of 1754–1763 (known as the Seven Years' War in Europe).[14]

While the French and Indian War, the American Revolution, and even the later Napoleonic Wars are well known to have involved Britain and France, the carnage between the two powers dated to the beginning of the eighteenth century with what most, given its title, would never consider having involved Britain and France—the War of Spanish Succession. It is easily argued that all history is reduction, cause, and effect. As such, the start of the eighteenth century with the War of Spanish Succession inaugurated a century of destruction that has defined the world we live in today. Without going into burdensome detail, it will be enough to understand that this conflict dealt specifically with European power politics on the continent; although the Spanish overseas empire was up for grabs and Spain, of the three major powers, had proven by 1700 that the Americas were indeed a fabulously lucrative investment well worth fighting for.

In brief, the last Spanish Hapsburg monarch, Charles II (partly a victim of centuries of inbreeding), died without an heir in 1700. The French, already invested in the dynasty through marriage, sought to advance their claim. Britain, while not connected by such ties, still did not want to see France expand her territory in Europe. By the Treaty of Partition of June 1699, King William III of England and King Louis XIV of France agreed to split the Spanish Empire between a French prince, Philip, duc d'Anjou, the grandson of Louis XIV, and a German prince, the Archduke Charles, son of the Holy Roman Emperor Leopold.

Louis XIV, before formal war was declared, entertained the idea that he could return England to the Catholic faith. Louis dreamt that upon the death of former King James II, then living in exile in France, he (Louis) would support the cause of the former King's son, James III. As a Catholic, the potential James III would reverse the contours of the 1688 Glorious

Chapter 3. The Era of the French and Indian War 37

Revolution which sent James II into exile and brought the Protestant William III to the English throne.

Louis XIVs fantasy died a quick death (although the dream of a Catholic Stuart on English throne would not end until 1746 with the battle at Culloden). The English Parliament made it a crime to espouse the cause of the Catholic Stuart family, providing for the eventual accession of the Protestant Queen Anne (daughter of James II) in 1702 following the death of William III. The War of Spanish Succession nearly devolved into a war of English succession given William's early death in 1702. The second grand alliance he created ensured Anne would be secure and be the monarch to oversee the subsequent War of Spanish Succession against Louis XIV's never-ending wars of diplomacy.

As with all well devised plans, they rarely go as anticipated; such was the fate with the Treaty of Partition. In a surprise move, the feeble-minded King Charles II of Spain rallied before his death and in a period of brief sanity left a will leaving his entire empire to the French prince. King Louis XIV, sensing his good fortune of not having to split the Spanish Empire two ways, "graciously" accepted the last will and testament of Charles II as authentic and ignored the Treaty of Partition he signed with William III of England. William III, for his part, was unsure if it was worth a fight to contest the will of the late Charles II. As fate would have it, William III died in 1702; the new monarch, Queen Anne, and one of her senior advisors, John Churchill (soon to be the Duke of Marlborough), felt the ceding of the Spanish Empire to the French prince Philip as per the late king's will to be unwise. Under Churchill's command, the English set out to challenge Louis XIV and his interpretation of the last will and testament of the late Charles II. John Churchill was already a well-regarded and eminently competent general. His leadership during the War of Spanish Succession only added to his fame. The battle of Blenheim, in 1704, was his most famous victory. Churchill's unquestionable victory over the army of King Louis XIV at Blenheim in Germany began the new century with an English win over the French. Thereby would begin over a century of near continuous warfare between England and France. As the century advanced, the prolonged conflicts became more global in scope with much more at stake than territory or trade with Europe. The eighteenth century, as John Churchill's descendant Winston would write, became the century of world war.

The battles of Blenheim and Rock of Gibraltar were the two major and deciding engagements of the War of Spanish Succession, even though the War raged for almost another decade until 1714. Louis XIV, growing older and nearing the end of his reign, attempted to procure a peace settlement throughout the first decade of the eighteenth century, but failed. His country was starving and broke; his armies were unable to win, and chaos or worse threatened. By 1711, four years before Louis' death in 1715 (English Queen Anne died in 1714), the War of Spanish Succession finally officially ended with the signing of the Treaty of Utrecht on April 11, 1713. As the historian Will Durant has written, as the result of the War of Spanish Succession, "between France and England in America a balance was established which would hold till the Seven Years' War."[15]

The Treaty of Utrecht of 1713–1714, through a series of small treaties, allotted the remains of the Spanish Empire equitably among the royal houses of Europe. This allowed the British to focus more on their overseas empire without the pressing concerns of an immediate European conflict over inheritance beyond the one just ended. One of the outcomes of the Treaty of Utrecht was to position England for involvement in greater trade opportunities worldwide. This would help make England wealthy ahead of an anticipated next round of warfare with France.

Between the Treaty of Utrecht in 1714–1715, and the outbreak of renewed hostilities between France and Britain by 1750 in Europe, which was soon to arrive in the colonies, Britain maintained a cold war with Spain for almost two decades. At stake in this struggle were the lucrative trade opportunities, specifically trade in the New World. This meant colonial North American trade which included enslaved Africans. It was during this period that slavery expanded greatly in North America with the subsidence of a shooting war in Europe. This interval of active warfare laid the foundation for near continuous conflict from 1750 forward. In the immediate response to the trade competition, Britain and Spain did come to a low-level war called the War of Jenkins Ear. Britain declared war on Spain on October 19, 1739. While the war was officially with Spain, it did not take long before France, through the French-related King of Spain, became involved in the conflagration that erupted into the War of Austrian Succession, the French and Indian War, and the subsequent iterations through to the early nineteenth century. There is no separating out these conflicts as though they happened in a vacuum. The world was literally changing faster than any one person could control.

During the oddly named War of Jenkins Ear, which had an on again, off again, lifespan in the 1740s (the conflict accomplished little of significance) between Britain and Spain, George Washington's half-brother Lawrence gained considerable fame fighting alongside the British Admiral Edward Vernon (who lent his name to the future Washington estate—Mount Vernon). Lawrence was more of a role model to young George given their father's early death. No doubt Lawrence's stories of military valor and adventure during war with Spain impacted young George. George would keep a portrait of Lawrence in his study at Mount Vernon his entire life (a home created by Lawrence in 1743 on land inherited from their father).

Chapter 3. The Era of the French and Indian War

The peculiar circumstances which saw the advent of the War of Jenkins Ear became all too real when that useless conflict was absorbed into the War of Austrian Succession. Again, like the War of Spanish Succession, it seems an unlikely conflict to involve Britain, and ultimately the colonies. Yet, it serves to highlight how interconnected European power politics were. The War of Austrian Succession ignited upon the death of Charles VI in 1740, who left his empire, although not necessarily his title, to his daughter Maria Theresa. She immediately became a target of the new Prussian king, Frederick II (the Great—and a nephew of George II of Britain), and thus once again Europe was etiolated by the destruction of war. It was a threat of a Franco-Prussian alliance that George II feared, and which drove Britain in the direction of greater involvement to secure the king's family seat of Hanover in Germany. The lines of interconnectedness are easy to lose sight of. The War of Austrian Succession and War of Spanish Succession forty years earlier were nearly fought over the same reasons. The same royal families were involved, as were the motivations. The one difference was that the War of Austrian Succession would spill over to colonial America and set the colonies on a course to independence.[16]

The major reason France was not able to fully engage the English in America militarily prior to the 1750s was the defeat of the French—under King Louis XIV—at the hands of John Churchill, the first Duke of Marlborough, at Blenheim in 1704 during the War of Spanish Succession. The French loss, while stinging, did not annihilate the French army. Rather, the defeat was significant enough to cause the French to focus more on continental European issues from a military perspective instead of overseas. Naturally, overseas military actions were immensely expensive, as the British found out in 1759. The French thus allowed the British more leeway in North American affairs before they engaged militarily by 1756.

The War of Austrian Succession proved mostly fruitless. Historian Francis Parkman, writing in the nineteenth century, commented: "Both nations were tired of the weary and barren conflict, with its enormous cost and its vast entail of debt. It was agreed that conquests should be mutually restored."[17] Only one major British victory occurred in North America. In 1745 the British captured Louisburg on Cape Breton from the French.

The War of Austrian Succession ended with the Treaty of Aix-la-Chapelle in 1748 in which it was agreed "each side should restore to the other its conquests."[18] This provision, while allowing for peace, angered many American colonists who had fought for Britain during the conflict. It helped set the stage for 1756 and the French and Indian War. As Francis Parkman wrote, "peace returned to the tormented borders; the settlements advanced again, and the colonists found a short breathing space against the great conclusive struggle of the Seven Years' War."[19] Beyond the sacrifice was the debt some of the colonies incurred during the war, especially Massachusetts. Indeed, "a spirit of discontent with the mother country went abroad and, after this sacrifice of colonial interests, never wholly died out."[20] This feeling of abandonment would linger until the Revolution.

North America and the larger world served as the natural battlefield for the Seven Years' War. With Europe exhausted from the War of Austrian Succession and with little territory to be gained or enhanced by further fighting among the powers, the scene shifted to colonial possessions in the New World, or parts of the world new to Europeans. This did not mean however that Europe was war and battle free. The major powers found it in themselves to continue, with much the same results as a decade before, the ruinous approach to diplomacy that had plagued Europe for centuries.

This had the effect of draining resources away from Europe to address the surrogate battles raging in North America most specifically. Here, unlike in Europe, the contest had only two participants: France and England. Russia, Austria, and Prussia had little interest in the colonial arguments raging on the other side of the globe. Other than provide support with material or money or occasional troops, Frederick the Great, Maria Theresa, and Catherine the Great had no interest in the seemingly barren wilderness of North America.

While the War of Austrian Succession raged on the continent, the French saw a possible opening. In North America, the British had a near undisputed claim to their coastal colonies. However, beyond the Appalachians the situation was much different. The lawless and unclaimed (by European standards) lands west of the mountains the French saw as an opportunity to challenge the British and establish a link between their Canadian territories and their holdings in what is today Louisiana. This challenge was too much for Britain to outright ignore and in 1755 it sent General Edward Braddock to confront the French in the vast Ohio Valley. George Washington earned great fame by bringing some organization from the disastrous losses incurred by Braddock and his unfortunate death. For four years, the British suffered grievously in the Ohio Valley, enduring stinging defeats.

The 1748 Treaty of Aix-la-Chapelle had left the area west of the Alleghanies unaccounted for. This left enterprising ministers, and adventurers, in both France and England uninhibited by any legal framework. Significantly, as mentioned, it was two men in America who sought to exploit this oversight. One, Michel-Ange Du Quesne de Menneville, Marquis de Duquesne, was French Governor General of New France. The second, Englishman Robert Dinwiddie, was Royal governor of Virginia. Both men agitated their respective governments for action in the "no man's land" west of the Alleghanies. It was Dinwiddie who entrusted the

Chapter 3. The Era of the French and Indian War

twenty-two-year-old George Washington with patrolling the region. Dinwiddie was a major shareholder in the Ohio Company, which sought to exploit the Ohio Valley region. Dinwiddie was a promoter of the Ohio region when even some in the government felt the area was French territory and best left alone. Dinwiddie chose a course of deliberate confusion about title to the Ohio area and always concluded with priority being given to the British argument. This strategy eventually would lead the British into a war they struggled to avoid. Dinwiddie made the case of French invasion of the Ohio Company territory real enough that the British convinced themselves it was happening on a large-scale basis. The French did indeed desire a series of sites to ensure communication between Canada and New Orleans, their southernmost outpost. However, Dinwiddie took these desires out of proportion. Governor Duquesne of Canada (New France) was not without blame either. Both men obfuscated and painted their opponent in the most sinister way possible. Their complementary strategies worked. "From greed, incompetence, or imperialism, but in any case, from private motive, they had succeeded in involving their governments in a shooting war."[21]

The early stages of the French and Indian War are well known for the role George Washington played, first as a defeated colonist who attempted to deal with the French at the behest of Governor Dinwiddie only to hopelessly lose in the process, and then, to save half of British General Braddock's army after he (Braddock) was killed trying to initiate conflict before the war officially began, again, at the behest of Dinwiddie. Washington exhibited the same uncanny characteristics he would rely on twenty years later in the American Revolution—being soundly defeated only to redeem himself soon after.

Driven to action by Canadian Governor Duquesne, the French began to enter the upper Ohio River Valley by 1753. Some felt with their greater power they could even attack and acquire the colonies of Pennsylvania and Virginia from the British. No one seriously believed that the Pennsylvania and Virginia colonies were in any real danger of becoming French. The fear lay in the damage the Indians, agitated by the French, could cause to frontier English settlers. For decades prior to 1754, the French agitated the British settlers throughout New England by prompting their Native American allies to attack and harass the British rather than by direct military engagement. The annals of New England are filled with gut-wrenching stories of attack and reprisal by the Native Americans and the British (and French, although they seemed to handle relations with Native Americans better) settlers. London was not insensitive to this carnage, but clearly set the blame on the French for inciting Indian passions against the British overall. In part due to this potential threat, an unknown Virginian, desperate for glory and fame, made his way during the winter of 1753 to try and counter

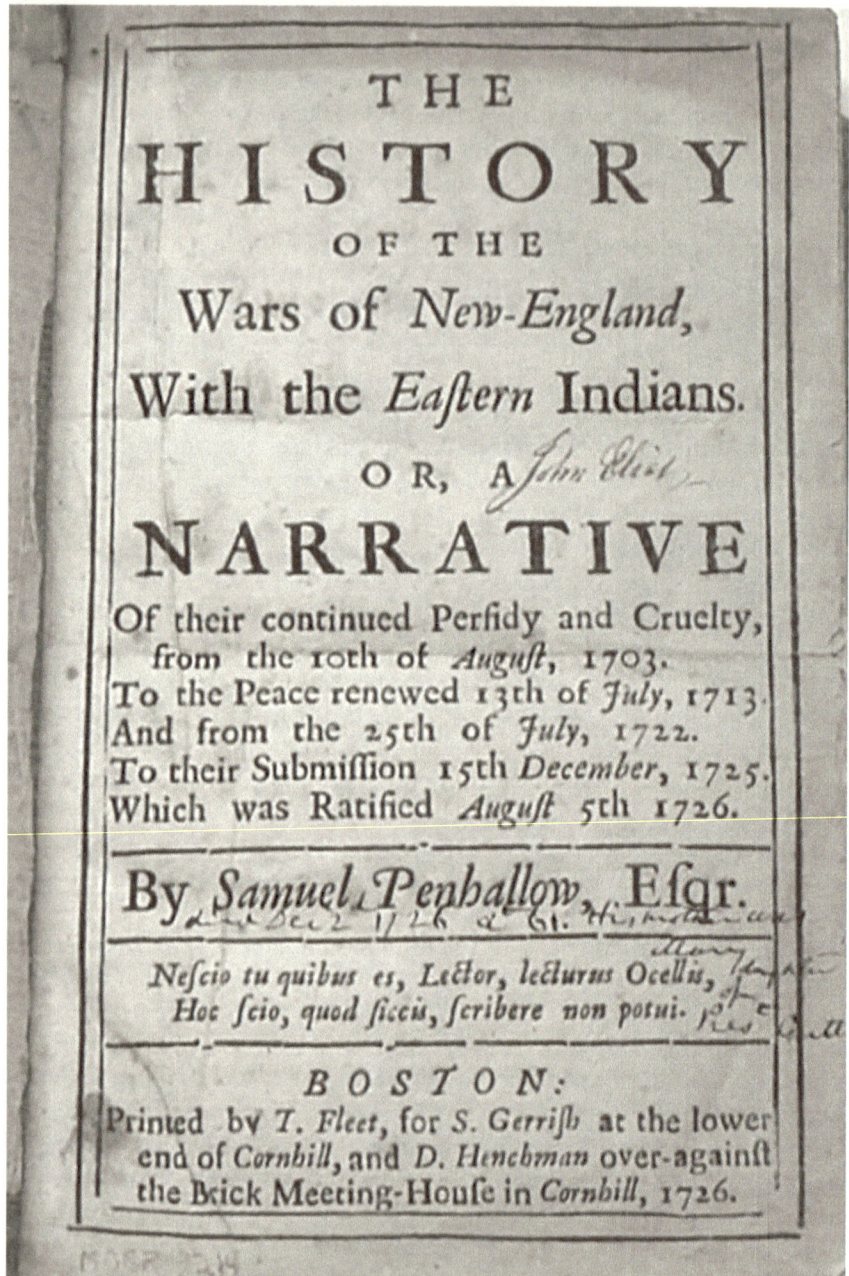

As early as 1726 works were being published about the conflicts between colonial settlers and the Native Americans. Morristown NHP. Lloyd W. Smith archival collection. MORR 9214.

Chapter 3. The Era of the French and Indian War

the advances of the French. The unknown young man, George Washington, was on a special mission from Virginia Governor Dinwiddie.

Young George Washington, through exposure to his half-brother Lawrence's family connections, came to embrace the upper-class English pedigree of the Fairfax family. Lawrence's father-in-law, William Fairfax, was a veteran of the War of Spanish Succession and provided an endless assemblage of anecdotes to his son-in-law's half-brother George. After Lawrence's death in 1752, George became more restless than ever. Having spent three full years surveying some of the new lands to the west, he felt his talents could be used for better purposes. It was at this point that Washington's future started to come more into focus. Petitioning Virginia Governor Robert Dinwiddie for a role in helping to challenge the French incursions in the Ohio Valley, he relied on his work surveying Fairfax lands in the same general areas to help convince Governor Dinwiddie that he knew the area well and would prove an asset to any expedition.

It is fair to say that Washington at this point was a proud Englishman and an even prouder and ambitious Virginian. As a younger son he could be expected to be more responsible for making his own way in the world, as opposed to his oldest brother, who stood to inherit the bulk of their father's estate. As such, by necessity and character, young George formed early opinions on his future eminence. Even he could not imagine where fate would lead him though. Enamored of the Virginia aristocracy that he was born into, he probably started to mimic some of their habits. Historian Stephen Brumwell wrote that "it is possible that George may have deliberately imitated the speech patterns of his mentors, … cultivating an English accent."[22]

Young Washington, barely old enough to drink by modern standards, proved his inexperience by stumbling into an ill-conceived attempt at negotiations with the French at Fort La Boeuf (modern day Waterford, Pennsylvania). Delivering a letter to the fort's commander Jacques Legardeur de Saint-Pierre, from Governor Dinwiddie, Washington received a reply that he (Saint-Pierre) would not abandon the fort as Dinwiddie's letter demanded. This trip was fortunately documented in a journal Washington kept about the journey.

Washington's Journal

Major George Washington (Virginia militia) began his "Journey to the French Commandant" in a simple way:

> On Wednesday the 31st of October 1753 I was commissioned and appointed by the Honorable Robert Dinwiddie Esqr. Governor & etc. of Virginia to visit and deliver a letter to the commandant of the French forces on the Ohio….[23]

It was a very matter-of-fact type entry. Straight and to the point. There was no room left for interpretation or equivocation.

Young Washington set out on a mission of courage and recklessness at the beginning of winter in 1753 in support of his home colony and in support of his ambition. The journal is brimming with observations consistent with a student and practitioner of the occupation of surveying, which Washington considered his vocation at the time. Into the mix the young major included observations on military expediency in relation to sites for the building of forts. He was traversing land that England had informally ceded to the French via the 1748 Treaty of Aix-la-Chapelle; however, there were those in the colonies, like Governor Dinwiddie, who saw it as foolish to write off the vast Ohio Valley without a challenge. The official British policy held that the costs involved in securing the territory were too great to incur—much like France saw the situation.

Washington's journal was also filled with his interactions and reflections on the Indian tribes he met with. This was likely his most extended formal encounter with Native Americans in his young life. He recorded in detail conversations he had with the mostly French aligned tribes. Through the guidance of these tribes, he was able to locate the remote forts more easily in the vast western reaches of Pennsylvania. His first formal encounter with the French was during a brief stay at a house used as a headquarters for Captain Joncaire prior to his arrival at Fort Le Boeuf. During dinner on Washington's first night with Joncaire, December 4, 1753, the wine flowed freely, and Washington wrote that the French exposed their designs to him:

> They told me it was their absolute design to take possession of the Ohio and by G[od] they would do it, for though they were sensible, that the English could raise two men for their one, yet they knew their motions were slow and dilatory to prevent any undertaking of theirs.[24]

Washington also gathered valuable intelligence on the troop strength throughout the region. This adventure helped to fine-tune his awareness of the basic aspects of military preparedness and observation, two skills he would employ twenty years later against his current British command structure.

On December 12, 1753, Washington arrived at Fort Le Boeuf near Lake Erie and met with the commander Le Gardeur de Saint-Pierre. He was treated with the upmost of hospitality and respect. However, Saint-Pierre rejected the demands of Governor Dinwiddie, which Washington had presented to him. Washington found Saint-Pierre "an elderly gentleman and has much the air of a soldier."[25] Tactically, Dinwiddie may have made a mistake by sending the young, completely inexperienced Washington on a trip which clearly required an understanding of foreign policy and the intricacies of colonial competition among Europe's great powers.

Washington returned to Williamsburg in January 1754 after his failed mission and wrote his journal which was published as *The Journal of Major George Washington* in newspapers in Maryland and Massachusetts. The journal also appeared as a pamphlet in London. Washington's name became known far beyond Virginia. Four months later in April 1754, with a new commission as Lieutenant Colonel in the Virginia militia, Washington returned to the Ohio Valley with a force of 160 soldiers. Governor Dinwiddie was not about to accept the French rejection of his request to leave the area and essentially hoped Washington could provoke an incident to elevate the matter to the level of armed conflict. On May 28, 1754, Washington succeeded in Dinwiddie's plan to lure the French into combat. Near the present-day site of Uniontown, Pennsylvania, Washington, and his troops engaged the French. While a victory for Washington, the French commander Joseph Coulon de Villiers de Jumonville was killed. The French insisted this was an assassination as they claimed Jumonville was on a diplomatic mission in the region. Effectively, Washington's actions can be argued to have started the French and Indian War. The historian Jared Sparks later wrote as much when he commented, "this obscure skirmish began the war that set the world on fire."[26]

One month later, after harassing, and being harassed, by the French, Washington built a small defensive position called Fort Necessity. Within a month of the building of the Fort, the French attacked in part to avenge the death of Jumonville. It was not much of a fort physically and Washington and his soldiers were bested by French and Indian soldiers on July 3, 1754. Under the command of Louis Coulon de Villiers, brother of Jumonville, the French engaged Washington and his troops at Fort Necessity. The fort itself proved its worthiness in the daylong battle which itself was a complete soggy mess due to constant rain. Outnumbered, Washington surrendered and returned to Virginia. On July 17, Washington arrived back in Williamsburg and resigned his commission in the Virginia militia. The defeat at Fort Necessity resulted in not only a disastrous defeat for the British, it heralded the future alliance of the Indians with the French against the English, an alliance that would have an impact long after the French and Indian War had ended. The Indians would always be more adversarial to the English going forward. Historian Francis Parkman wrote, "without wise and just treatment of the tribes, the French would gain them all, build forts along the back of the British colonies, and, by means of ships and troops from France, master them one by one, unless they would combine for mutual defense."

After Washington's defeat, Dinwiddie tried to raise money again from the Burgesses, with minimal success. "Here was one cause of

The Night Council at Fort Necessity. The Miriam and Ira D. Wallach Division of Art, Prints and Photographs: Print Collection, The New York Public Library. New York Public Library Digital Collections.

military paralysis. It was reinforced by another. The old standing quarrel between governor and assembly had grown more violent than ever; and this as a direct consequence of the public distress, which above all things demanded harmony."[27] He then reached out to the other colonies. Similarly, he received a tepid response. New York offered five thousand pounds to Virginia, Maryland gave six thousand, while New Jersey offered nothing. Massachusetts provided money and troops to aid in the efforts against the French as well. Massachusetts governor William Shirley was an ally with Dinwiddie against the French and met with Washington twice to talk strategy. So naturally his colony was inclined to offer some support.

The defeat at Fort Necessity, while not moving the colonies to organize more, prompted the British to mobilize a force under the command of General Edward Braddock in the spring of 1755. The French, upon learning of the Braddock expedition, similarly outfitted their own force. Strangely, both fleets arrived off the American coast simultaneously and became confused in the fog and rain.

By the spring of 1755, recovered from illness and disappointment, Washington decided he had to return himself to the scene of action without

Chapter 3. The Era of the French and Indian War

delay, with or without an official appointment. Washington indeed returned to the scene of action, which was now in the hands of the British Regular army, without a rank or pay in the service of British commander General Edward Braddock. Outside of Fort Duquesne, present day Pittsburgh, General Braddock's force, including Washington, engaged a force of French and Indian soldiers on July 9, 1755, exactly a year after the Fort Necessity defeat. It was not long before firing started, and the opening salvos of the larger French and Indian War were heard. Braddock's expedition proved a disaster except for George Washington. In the ensuing battle, Braddock was killed. His death left a natural vacuum in command in the British line. Washington, without rank or portfolio, took charge of the chaos and organized a successful retreat. As a result of his heroics, he was commissioned the rank of colonel in the Virginia militia and charged with patrolling a 350-mile swath of land with 1,500 soldiers.[28] He became famous for a second time—both times for maintaining order during a defeat.

Washington continued in his role throughout the difficult year of 1755 for the British and in February 1756 met with the overall British commander in North America, Massachusetts Governor William Shirley. During the discussions of broader strategy goals, Washington pressed Shirley for a royal commission. Shirley was noncommittal on both strategy and the promotion within the British army. The year 1756, much like 1755, was an awfully bad year for the British army. Without resources, without strategy, and lacking effective political leadership in England, the British seemed on the verge of capitulating to France. It was an especially difficult time for Washington as he struggled to make some sense of his orders and to hope that he could earn the respect his rank, he felt, warranted.

In February of 1757, Washington met with the new overall British commander, Lord Loudoun (John Campbell), and encountered similar equivocation from Campbell as he encountered a year earlier with William Shirley, concerning strategy and his promotion. Washington found these encounters frustrating. As with Shirley, he received no solid commitments from Campbell. He would spend the rest of 1757 much like 1756, fruitlessly trying to stem the tide of French victory in the Ohio Valley through any means possible.

It is important to remember that Washington was only twenty-five years old at this point. He had no real grasp of colonial affairs beyond intuition and it is indicative of the lackluster approach to the overall military campaign that the British let a twenty-five-year-old novice have such an extensive portfolio in the conflict. Washington himself may have sensed this too.

After recovering from a second severe bout of dysentery in late 1757, Washington returned to active service in March 1758. The strategic situation was little improved for the British on the ground, although at Parliament in London the outlines of a major infusion of money, material, and troops was taking shape. Unfortunately, for Washington, he would not be on active duty to partake in the benefits which ultimately would bring victory to the British cause.

Upon Washington's return to active service in March 1758, he was again sent to the Forks of the Ohio (present day Pittsburgh) to confront the French at Fort Duquesne. The French, through intelligence, were aware of the designs on the Fort and rather than lose the strategic site, burned, and destroyed the area, rendering it unusable by the British in the immediate future. Washington, despondent over the continual setbacks, resigned his commission in December 1758 and returned to Virginia.

Less than two weeks after his return, Washington wrote to Richard Corbin expressing his desire for a promotion to Lieutenant Colonel in the British army. Washington wrote:

> …you gave me some room to hope for a commission above that of a Major…. Knowing this, I have too sincere a love for my country, to undertake that which may tend to the prejudice of it. But I could entertain hopes that you thought me worthy of the post of Lieutenant-Colonel and would favor me so far as to mention it at the appointment of officers, I could not but entertain a true sense of the kindness.[29]

Washington received no commission and returned to Mount Vernon to rent it from his widowed sister-in-law who was the current owner of the estate through her late husband Lawrence. To add insult to injury, Washington suffered through yet another severe bout of dysentery which no doubt added to his already depressed feelings.

His career in the French and Indian War ended uneventfully and just before the efforts of the new policy imposed by Secretary of State William Pitt would shift the war decisively in Britain's favor. The overwhelming commitment of resources, especially money, by Secretary of State Pitt to the French and Indian War was crucial to the defeat of France. Why this is so important is because it was the money that the British spent which led directly to the rise of John Dickinson and the nascent beginnings of American resistance to British rule. It also is indicative of the perspective which Britain's leaders, especially the new monarch George III, had towards the purpose and role of revenue raising plans. There was no denying Americans were the main beneficiaries of Britain's victory in the French and Indian War. Yet, they were the first to protest that contributing to that victory on a monetary scale was "unconstitutional." For Washington though, the next phase of his life was about to begin in January of 1759, when he married Martha Dandridge Custis.

CHAPTER 4

Escalation and Victory

By the end of 1758, the British Secretary of State William Pitt had made a momentous decision. Under Pitt, Britain dramatically increased spending on the French and Indian War. In fact, they marshalled one of the largest armies ever for such a distant conflict. Realizing "that isolated inroads into French territory would bring no decision" in the North American war, he gave orders to devote all available resources to the American campaign.[1] Fighting a global war, Britain under Pitt could have left the French alone in North America and tried for a treaty and hoped for the best. With dwindling resources and flagging public opinion, Pitt sent a massive army and naval force to North America to rid the American colonies of France once and for all. This expenditure for the invasion would largely drive the need for taxation in the 1760s. The British invested so much because of the potentially enormous benefits from the fertile land in areas still unsettled in the American interior (areas beyond the existing colonies). The future benefits were simply too enticing to ignore. Pitt devised a plan of offense "along the whole frontier from Nova Scotia to the Ohio."[2] By early 1759, there were "20,000 British regulars in the North American theatre, aided and abetted by 25,000 locally raised troops."[3] His plan was audacious and successful. 1759 proved the wisdom of Pitt's thinking, with victories along a vast corridor within the North American Continent.

In February 1759, a fleet of over two-hundred and fifty vessels, fully manned and provisioned, set out from England to Quebec. Major General James Wolfe (who would be killed in the fighting) began his expedition to Quebec via the St. Lawrence on February 14, 1759. The great armada found little or no resistance on the journey. The French were convinced the British armada of 1759 would suffer the same fate as the Spanish Armada of 1588. It was not to be. The English captains expertly navigated the difficult waters leading to Quebec.

On September 13, 1759, the battle for Quebec began. The English had regular troops, the French a mixture of Indians, regular, and local conscripts. By the end of June 1759 William Pitt's vast military surge was gathered before Quebec, the seat of French power in what we know as Canada and at the time was New France. Historian George Wrong, writing in 1918, described the tension:

> Nature had furnished a noble setting for the drama now to be enacted. Quebec stands on a bold semicircular rock on the north shore of the St. Lawrence.... Its currents change ceaselessly with the ebb and flow of the tide which rises a dozen feet, though the open sea is eight hundred miles away.... In every direction there are cliffs and precipices and rising ground.[4]

The winter of 1759–1760 saw the British prepare as best they could in the cold for the spring assault. The French sensed the end was near but enjoyed the calm that came with winter. Through the spring and summer, the British overwhelmed the French at Quebec and finally Montreal. Quebec would fall to the British by the end of September 1759. Then Montreal, in September 1760, fell to the British. Canada thus went from French to British in less than a year. The French surrendered on September 8, 1760. France ceded everything east of the Mississippi except New Orleans to Britain, and to Spain New Orleans and other sites. The Treaty of Paris of 1763 secured a recognition of British claims in North America to all the land east of the Mississippi River. It was truly Britain's moment in America.

The siege of Montreal should not be completely memorialized as total victory. No victory is obtained without sacrifice and terror. British soldier John Baldwin experienced the battle and witnessed firsthand that war is not always glamor, no matter how hard we try to erase the pain. In a diary he kept (written over a printed copy of *A Political and Satryrical History of the Years 1758 and 1759*), Baldwin captured the brutality of war, both intentional and unintentional. In one entry, Baldwin wrote of the dangers of firing cannon, "One of the cannon in our battery broke and wounded the gunner and four men more."[5] In another entry Baldwin posted via a N.B. (by the way) statement, "There was twenty-one or twenty-two killed. Eleven of them was taken and after was killed, scalped, and chopped and stabbed and prodigiously mangled."[6] Amidst the carnage, Baldwin did have moments to rejoice, writing at one point, today "a sixty gun ship came in and joined our fleet which was very rejoicing."[7] This was an example of the elation of soldiers who found Britain's defeats in Europe restored by the victories in America. While the Seven Years' War in Europe was less than rewarding for Britain,

> Overseas, by contrast, the war was proving a glorious triumph for Britain with success against France in America, Africa, and Asia. In 1760 the final conquest of Canada was imminent, and Britain's mastery of the sea had been confirmed by Admiral Sir Edward Hawke's defeat of the French navy at Quiberon Bay late in 1759....[8]

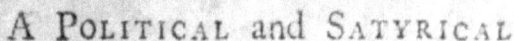

Journal of John Baldwin written over *A ... History of the Years 1758 and 1759*. Morristown NHP. Lloyd W. Smith archival collection MORR 12118. Photograph by Steve Newfield.

Pitt had engineered a stunning string of victories, he "not only won Canada, with its rich fisheries and Indian trade, but had banished forever the dream and danger of a French colonial empire stretching from Montreal to New Orleans."[9] While the French were largely victorious through 1758, the fall of Fort Duquesne in that year showed the effectiveness of British Secretary of State William Pitt's aggressive policy toward the war (hence the renaming of Fort Duquesne as Pitts-borough or Pittsburgh) and the effectiveness of the enhanced British military policy in the region.

Britain overwhelmed France in North America between 1758 and 1760. Sheer numbers of troops, ships, and material, sent as part of Prime Minister Pitt's new policy, effectively ended French resistance. Marquis de Vaudreuil, Governor of New France, surrendered to Sir Jeffrey Amherst, the British commander. Britain made an enormous investment in North America and were not going to easily let it go as their position would show over the decade of the 1760s.

Fittingly, the last battle of the Seven Years' War and the French and Indian War was fought in Europe, the battle of Saxony in 1762. The Peace of Fontainebleau (ending the European component of the War) was signed on November 5, 1762, by England, France, Portugal, and Spain. The February 10, 1763, Treaty of Paris (ending the American component of the War) confirmed and further identified territorial gains and losses. In terms of North America, France lost Canada to England, Spain lost Florida to England, and Spain gained Louisiana from France. The Germans signed a similar treaty a week later near Leipzig ending their participation in the European war.

A sermon was delivered in Boston on the fall of Quebec which lends credence to the jubilation felt among the Americans. The sermon, preached by Samuel Cooper, was delivered before Thomas Pownall, Captain-General and Governor in Chief of the Massachusetts Bay colony on October 16, 1759. Cooper began: "No one can be insensible how largely your Excellency partakes in the universal joy, occasioned by the late happy success with which it has pleased Heaven to crown his majesty's arms in North America, particularly in the reduction of the capital of Canada...."[10] Cooper addressed the governor directly by stating:

> You have had the joy to see your incessant cares and endeavors for the interior welfare of our province, and the security of its exposed territories, happily succeeded. A respectable fortress, constructed under your excellency's eye, and well garrisoned, has given His Majesty the firm possession of the important country of Penobscot; a part of the province till now commanded by a savage enemy, the scourge and terror of our eastern frontier.[11]

A

SERMON

Preached before His EXCELLENCY

THOMAS POWNALL, Esq;

Captain-General and Governor in Chief,

The Honourable His Majesty's COUNCIL
and House of REPRESENTATIVES,

Of the Province of the

Massachusetts-Bay in *New-England*,

OCTOBER 16th, 1759.

Upon Occasion of the Success of His Majesty's Arms in the Reduction of

QUEBEC.

By SAMUEL COOPER, A. M.

Pastor of a Church in *Boston*.

BOSTON : NEW-ENGLAND ;

Printed by GREEN & RUSSELL, and EDES & GILL, by Order of His Excellency the GOVERNOR, and both HOUSES of ASSEMBLY.

Title page of pamphlet of sermon by Samuel Cooper. Morristown NHP. Lloyd W. Smith archival collection MORR 11013. Photo by Steve Newfield.

What to Do with Victory?

"The series of wars that ended with the Peace of Paris secured the opportunities and set in action the forces that have planted English homes in every clime and dotted the earth with English garrisons and posts of trade."[12] Some have referred to 1759 for Britain as the *Annus Mirabilis*—a miracle year. "[T]hat the Peace of Paris marks an epoch than which none in modern history is more fruitful of grand results. With it began a new chapter in the annals of the world."[13] However, it was not inexpensive, and in this fact lies the most immediate cause of the American Revolution fifteen years later. This was something Pitt could never have envisioned. Historian Gordon Wood has written: "In 1763 Great Britain emerged from the Seven Years' War … as the greatest and richest empire since the fall of Rome."[14] Wood neglected to add that along with the riches was a mortgage the likes of which was never seen probably since the fall of Rome. "By 1763 the war debt totaled £137 million; its annual interest alone was £5 million…."[15]

Whatever the source of Pitt's efforts to enhance the war in North America, he did. The true motivation of Secretary of State (acting as Prime Minister in all but name) William Pitt's expansion of the North American War in the late 1750s may never be truly known. As Britain was fighting a two-front war—one on the Continent converging around the king's ancestral home of Hanover, and one along the almost incomprehensible vastness of the American theatre. This space ran from Nova Scotia to the Mississippi and Ohio Rivers to the west and east into the Caribbean. The success Britain was having on the Continent no doubt contributed to Pitt's feeling of enhanced power.

There is no doubt of the success of Pitt's approach. The unquestionable string of victories from 1759 to 1760, with the fall of Montreal, were truly momentous. "All, and more than all, that France had lost England had won. Now, for the first time, she was beyond dispute the greatest of maritime and colonial powers."[16] Sober minds, however, began to question the value for the money spent almost from the very beginning. Thinkers on both sides of the Atlantic wondered aloud not only how Britain would pay for their investment, but what exactly they were going to do with the new territory now unencumbered by French threats? With no clear policy articulated by London, thinkers were free to prognosticate at will. While we tend to see the ending of the French and Indian War and the Seven Years' War in a positive light for America—and it was—it was however near total devastation in Europe:

> All Western Europe was exhausted. Prussia most of all, where boys of fourteen had been conscripted, and farms had been devastated, and merchants had been ruined by the stifling of trade. Austria had more men than money, and had lost

vital Russian aid. ... France was bankrupt, her colonies were gone, her commerce had almost disappeared from the sea. England needed peace to consolidate her gains.[17]

At the time of her greatest triumph, England faced a revolt from within. It was against this backdrop of devastation and destruction that England, the lone victor along with the colonies, began to assess the dire consequences of war. What money existed was held by citizens, and taxation was one measure considered to start the process of revitalization.

In Britain, a writer known as "Cato" asked the seemingly simple question of whether or not the new territory "will operate towards the prosperity, or the ruin of the Island of Great Britain?"[18] The governmental aspects of overseeing such a vast expanse without the luxuries of modern communication systems seem incomprehensible today. Yet, that is precisely what Britain attempted. At the root of this attempt was taxation; money, revenue, was necessary for government functions. Further exacerbating the growing chaos was the arrival of a new king, George III, who sought to impose more of his own perspective on the North American situation than either of his predecessors. There was also the clash of perspectives engendered depending upon which side of the Atlantic one resided. In Britain, there was jubilation that they were victorious on two fronts against multiple enemies. From their perspective, they ruled the world—and in a certain measure they did. Living in the colonies, especially in North America, the perspective tended to be a bit more parochial. There was certainly pride in being part of the British empire, but the benefits of that membership on a local level were what was of immediate concern. In the North American colonies, this meant unlimited opportunities, or so the colonists thought, in the Ohio River Valley.

Cato argued much as though one could argue against excessive wealth with individuals—how much is too much? Cato pointed to the example of Spain in South America, warning that unlimited wealth only led to eventual problems, as it did with Spain by 1700. Cato even wondered why Britain stopped at the Gulf of Mexico when they could have conquered the entire Western Hemisphere. In hindsight we know that Cato was most prescient.

Cato cautioned the British people relative to their over-enthusiasm in acquiring victory in America and Canada over France. Victory in any war will bring jubilation, as much for victory as for the end of the war. England in 1760 was no different. After a particularly martial several decades in the eighteenth century, the nation had every reason to expect some very hard-won peace. Most did not contemplate governing and managing the vast territories acquired in America; some probably did not even know exactly where some of the areas were. Yet, in the general excitement of victory those concerns seemed small. England had a new king, a new outlook, and was for the moment master of a vast chunk of the world.

> In 1763 Britain ended the war in possession of all North America east of the Mississippi River, buttressing the fifteen old colonies along the Atlantic seaboard from Newfoundland to Georgia. The problem of how to organize and control the new territory loomed large in the public mind....[19]

Cato warned his fellow Englishmen of the potential impacts, soon to be realized, of administering such a vast territory with antagonism still high between settlers and Indians. The financial impacts of governing this new territory were significant as well. Cato acknowledged that the territory acquired was bound to produce unintended consequences: "The territory acquired is so immense, that it must make the time of acquisition a remarkable era of this government, and produce a great change in our situation and circumstances as a society."[20] As the philosopher Francis Bacon wrote in the early seventeenth century in defining an empire, "it is a thing rare, and hard to keep."[21]

Ostensibly, Britain was not fighting a war of territorial expansion in North America, although that was what they ended with. Britain was concerned more about security in the vast Ohio Valley regions and sought to minimize French influence there among Native Americans. Within this area west of the Appalachians and east of the Mississippi lay an area of vast potential. Yet, after 1763, the British decided to restrict settlement in this region to avoid conflicts with Indians. The settler community, including many investors, felt this misguided and thought the British instead should provide protection to American settlers and investors from hostile Indians.

For nearly five years, both France and England seemed content to allow matters to somehow work themselves out in North America with neither side forming a winning strategy. It was under William Pitt that England devised the winning plans that allowed Britain to claim the territory Cato wrote about. That territory was so vast that Cato admitted he did not even know its extent. Given this lack of information, it was highly likely his commentary could suffer for not being a full analysis of the problems associated with the acquisition of territory. The problem, or one of them, as Cato saw it, was the vast nothingness, and the impact that nothingness would have on the Native Americans:

> [O]ur late acquisition may be justly called mere earth. Nay, though we had all that the Indian possess behind, as which we shall very soon have, it will be the same thing; for they seem upon the eve of either dwindling into nothing of themselves, or being exterminated by us.[22]

Tellingly, it was the British government that showed more interest in the Native American. American colonists and settlers saw them more as hinderances to settlement and historical mythology has carried forward that viewpoint.

The territory Britain acquired was larger than the island of Britain itself. Theoretically, this meant England itself could be depopulated and reconstituted in America. Cato also warned that even if everyone would not ultimately leave England, those that did would have the potential to create a society to rival and possibly move beyond England.

One of the first consequences of Britain's victory, aside from revenue generation, was the decree that went directly against the mercantile efforts of colonists. Land speculation was nothing new by 1760. Many colonists had formed companies to purchase land from Indian tribes.[23] Ambitious Americans like George Washington, with extensive knowledge of the Ohio frontier from his work with the Fairfax family, had begun to invest heavily in the region. After the French and Indian War, Britain issued proclamations against such activity until it could be determined the best course to pursue relative to land allocations and to relations with the Native Americans. Britain was concerned to limit any negative interactions between the colonists and the Indians. Unfortunately, the colonists ignored these directives and continued to settle the region and to buy and sell land.

Albany Plan of Union

Amid the carnage and mayhem of the early years of the French and Indian War, and the endless frustrations of the young George Washington, a bright moment of hope emerged. Under the erstwhile leadership of the British Board of Trade, a recognition of their vulnerability in North America led them to call for a gathering of the colonies. As such, they sought to bring the colonies together to enhance defense and protect trade. The effort, while fruitless, identified the need for greater cooperation between the colonies on a variety of issues. It was one of the first times colonial leaders looked beyond their colony boundary to consider how their neighbors' concerns would impact their own.

In the summer of 1754, as Britain and France careened toward war in America, there occurred an odd congress of representatives nominally chaired by Benjamin Franklin. Known as the Albany Congress, Franklin promoted his Albany Plan of Union during the gathering which has often been seen as a precursor to the larger gatherings that would occur twenty years later in Philadelphia. Franklin proved to be a champion of greater colonial cooperation. It was a month before the start of the Albany Congress when news reached most of colonial America of the defeats suffered by George Washington, which prompted Franklin to draw his famous "Join or Die" cartoon to encourage colonial support.[24] It was also Franklin's draft plan that became the basis for the ultimate proposal which the Albany

Congress developed and presented to the colonies. Benjamin Franklin described the gathering of 1754, when he was forty-eight years old, as an attempt to find a mutually agreeable system of defense for the Americans and the Native Americans. As he described in his autobiography (written sporadically between 1771 and his death in 1790):

> In 1754, war with France being apprehended, a congress of commissioners from the different colonies was, by an order of the Lords of Trade, to be assembled at Albany, there to confer with the chiefs of the Six Nations concerning the means of defending both their country and ours.[25]

Franklin continued that he came upon an idea for a greater collaboration of the colonies "for defense, and other important general purposes."[26] He was not the only delegate to consider the wider union of the colonies for the common interest. It was a reasonable suggestion which, although it had its supporters, was rejected throughout the colonies. Franklin saw the 1754 plan as having negated the need for the American Revolution had the proposal succeeded with the individual colonies. The Plan was principally drawn by Franklin, which included an executive position chosen by Britain and would likely have been an effective advocate for the colonies overall.

Calling the Albany Congress a precursor to the 1774 Philadelphia congress is probably a bit too generous for the Albany gathering, given that it did not occur under the stress that would accompany the meetings during the 1770s. Nonetheless, the Congress represented an attempt to reflect on the governance of the colonies and provides some interesting parallels. In England, the Earl of Holdernesse, an official in the foreign service, wrote as early as August 1753, that "it may be greatly conducive to His Majesty's services, that all his provinces in America, should be aiding and assisting each other, in case of any invasion."[27] The impetus for the congress was French incursions in colonial America in the Ohio River Valley. While their fellow colonists were fighting and dying nearly 500 miles to the west for a diametrically opposed cause, colonists gathered for one of the first all-colonial meetings to occur. A letter was sent "to colonial governors instructing them to correspond with each other on matters of defense and warn their legislatures of the urgent need for mutual military assistance."[28]

Trade in the Ohio Valley and beyond was far too valuable to leave to the French without a fight.[29]

> A map that pinpoints colonial towns obscures and distorts much of the reality and movement of America in 1763. Activity pulsed along trade networks as well as in towns and cities, and trade networks reached across Indian country as well as across the Atlantic.[30]

Trade was ever present and was foremost on the minds of Americans and Europeans equally. No country could seriously cut itself off from all external relations. It was absurd to even contemplate it. The French and Indian War ushered in the age of trans-Atlantic trade unlike anything before. Identifying the globalism which marked the world of the 1760s, historian Colin Calloway wrote:

> Gentlemen in Paris and London wore hats made of beaver pelts from the lands beyond Hudson Bay; Indians on the northern Plains carried guns from Birmingham. Slaves from West Africa labored in fields in West Florida wearing textiles from West Yorkshire. Products and profits, people and plagues, news and fashions traveled the shipping lanes and the traders' paths.[31]

There was a desire on the part of the British, and Americans, to try and secure promises of Indian allegiance should war occur with France. At the end of the Congress, no such indication was forthcoming. The failure of secure pledges of support would soon prove detrimental to the British position in their war with France. The colonies would reject the proposal.

In his biography of Benjamin Franklin, author Walter Isaacson simplified down to two reasons for the Albany gathering, "meeting with the Iroquois confederation to reaffirm their allegiance and discussing among themselves ways to create a more unified colonial defense."[32] Defense is a term and mindset that arises nearly as frequently as taxation. The colonies were as disjointed in 1754 as they would be in 1774 at the start of the Revolution. It is stunning to think of what might have been had the colonies looked to their greater good rather than their individual sense of sovereignty. In most instances, that sovereignty was enveloped in the aspirations of a handful of men who led the individual colonies. As such, these men saw the colony as an extension of their social, political, and business undertakings. No doubt these men (and their families) acted with great deference to the role of the monarchy and within British colonial traditions, but they were also self-serving in a way that we find hard to imagine today.

In the report that Stephen Hopkins presented in 1755 to the Rhode Island legislature, he specifically stated before anything else the proposed Plan was for the common safety and defense of British northern colonies.[33] Massachusetts governor William Shirley echoed the themes of defense and mutual interests in his letter to the Massachusetts delegates attending the Albany Congress. Shirley found common cause with the geographically linked colonies a major point of benefit when it came to the Albany Plan and to larger geo-political issues as well. Shirley had a large view of the colonies and his approach was not a one-man lone voice. Others felt the need for more colony-wide cooperation. There is no way of knowing, but it seems likely, given the ultimate problems encountered, that a Shirley-type plan would have greatly enhanced the colonies' efforts to face Britain from a united perspective during the American Revolution. All the governors who sent representatives sounded similar themes.

The Connecticut governor, Thomas Finch, was just as straightforward as Shirley, telling his fellow officials:

> [you] are commissioned ... in behalf of His Majesty's Colony of Connecticut, to meet the Commissioners, appointed by His Majesty's other governments in America, at Albany ... to consult proper measures for the general defense and safety of His Majesty's subjects in said governments....[34]

Interestingly, Finch referred to the other colonies as "other governments." This only highlights the separateness that each colony felt towards its neighbors. Each colony was its own separate government. Nominally affiliated with the other colonies only through geographic ties and suzerainty with Great Britain.

On July 9, 1754, the Congress opened by cataloging a long list of French incursions into British North America. The opening communication outlined the history of English and French activities. The Treaty of Aix-la-Chapelle of 1748 being the defining aspect of recent French-Anglo relations. The Congress wrote that "since the Treaty of Aix-la-Chapelle, [France] made this Northern Continent more than ever, the object of its attention."[35] Furthermore,

> that it is the evident design of the French to surround the British colonies, to fortify themselves on the back thereof, to take and keep possession of the heads of all the important rivers, to draw over the Indians to their interest ... to be in a capacity of making a general attack upon the several ... [colonies].[36]

As the intentions of the French to oppose the English in America became clearer, the British Board of Trade attempted to organize a meeting of all the colonies in Albany, New York, for June 1754. It was the Board of Trade initially, indicating the financial rewards of the Ohio area, not the military, which was the more concerned over the French actions. The Albany Congress was a British attempt to draw the colonies closer together, not an American one—which could be one reason why it failed in every colonial legislature.

The draft of the Albany Plan of Union stated in the preamble, July 10, 1754:

> That humble application be made for an Act of the Parliament of Great Britain, by virtue of which, one general government may be formed in America, including all the said colonies; within and under which government, each colony may retain its present constitution, except in the particulars wherein a change may be directed....[37]

Any move by Parliament in this direction would have greatly impacted the individual governance of the colonies much to the detriment of the ruling families and the methods they employed to maintain their rule. However unorganized or unrecognized this rule may have been, nonetheless it was a rule and the colonial leaders felt too much was at stake personally to desire a change in the system as it currently existed. No single colony could have confronted the French during the War, yet the colonies were unable to come together as was seen in the failed Albany Plan, which had the backing of King George II. Yet, victory in the French and Indian War benefited the colonies. Still, the colonies were unwilling to acknowledge this benefit.

The Albany Plan of Union that was approved by the Albany Congress was passed by a near unanimous vote (see Appendix 7). However, not one colony accepted the Plan in their legislature when delegates took the draft home for consideration. Not only did the separate colonies reject the Plan, but so did Parliament, even though "since Charles I had established the Committee of Foreign Plantations, British governments had been concerned to develop a plan of union…" for the colonies.[38]

The Plan turned out to be something too remote for the colonies to consider. Voluntarily turning over some aspect of their separate power to a central authority was out of the question for the individual colonial legislatures to even contemplate. The individual colonies at this point saw themselves as just that, individual. This would naturally prove a barrier too far in terms of uniting for the common defense or common benefit.

The Albany Plan of Union sprang from the desire on the part of several colonists to seek greater representational security measures at the outbreak of the French and Indian War. Often seen as a proto- or incipient attempt at forming a nation, the Albany Plan instead was a proposal intended to be implemented by Parliament for the consolidation of British North America. The Plan would have maintained the separate, unique governing platforms of each colony while administratively bringing the colonies more closely together. This would also aid in colonial security. Fearing a loss of their independence and identity, no colony supported the plan and consequently Parliament never acted on it. The opposition was indicative of the trouble the colonies would have twenty years later at the start of the American Revolution. Stephen Hopkins, future signer of the Declaration of Independence from Rhode Island, supported the Albany Plan, and argued against those who saw the Plan as a loss of identity or autonomy.

Stephen Hopkins of Rhode Island reported back to the Rhode Island legislature on March 20, 1755, seven months after the Plan had first been introduced to that body. Hopkins chided the lawmakers for taking so long to not act to protect the colony and the colonies overall. Hopkins was one of the stronger supporters of the Plan and saw greater strength for the colonies through closer governmental cooperation.

Above all, this points to the descent into war as a crisis of American leadership. The colonists, who dominated the individual colonial legislatures, uniformly balked at the requests of the royal governors, much like they would balk at Franklin's Albany Plan, the tax overtures, as with General Washington begging for supplies during the Revolution, and the Continental Congress begging for donations. The list, several decades long, led directly to the Constitutional Convention in 1787 which was the one successful effort to get the states to come together and produce something.

It should not be forgotten that the Native American population was inextricably linked to this Congress too. Both Britain and France, the major European powers in North America by 1750, were vying for the support of the native tribes. The tribes became inevitable pawns in the power politics being directed from London and Paris. In particular, the upstate New York coalition known as the Six Nations were highly sought after in terms of their support. Their organization and governmental framework, power, and influence, made them ideal partners in any attempt to be a power in colonial affairs. It remained to be seen whether the Six Nations would work with individual colonies or try and work on behalf of the British in colonial affairs as one unit.

The failure of the Albany Plan of Union sprang from multiple causes. Naturally, the colonies were jealous of their unique individual political liberties; the recommendations were complex relative to implementation and enforcement; and the British government itself had reservations about the power allotted to the Board of Trade should the Plan of Union be ratified. Internal British politics would negatively impact colonial relations for the next quarter century from 1754. This infighting ultimately doomed British control of colonial North America.

It is no surprise that the colony of New York was instrumental in trying to lead the colonies to promote the Albany Congress. The king (George II) was supportive of the plan and his ministers made every effort to ensure the colonial administrators knew this. Still, even with the monarch's support the Albany Plan was rejected. Aspects of the Plan which may have caused alarm in the colonies revolved around calls for each legislature to raise money for a general fund for "paying the charge of levying troops to make up the complement of regiments" necessary for defense.[39]

Pontiac's Rebellion

While pre–Revolutionary American history is often considered the forgotten period of American history, a subset of that forgotten period

Opposite: **Even after the failure of the Albany Plan of Union, essayists were promoting efforts to get the colonies to understand the value of a collective approach to defense. This anonymous tract dates to 1757. Morristown NHP. Lloyd W. Smith archival collection. MORR 9230.**

PROPOSALS

For Uniting the

ENGLISH COLONIES

ON THE

Continent of *America*

So as to enable them to act with Force and Vigour againſt their Enemies.

LONDON:

Printed for J. WILKIE, behind the *Chapter-Houſe*, in St. *Paul's Church-yard*.

M. DCC. LVII.   [Price 1s.

is even more forgotten. With the great victory over France in the French and Indian War, Britain should have had a period of relative quiet to consolidate its gains. While this in some minor way did occur, it was not long before the elements of war were again threatening to consume British North America. The uprising known as Pontiac's Rebellion arose over resentment of Native American tribes to the presence and policies of the British following their victory over France. The Indians, having lost their French partners, attacked the British in 1764 throughout the Great Lakes region in what became known as Pontiac's Rebellion. This move further intensified racial animosities for decades to come and highlighted the need for large size security forces in the region which meant the need for Britain to raise revenue. There was no way the colonies could individually deal with confrontations with the Indians and they proved incapable of working together for fear of losing their identity or sovereignty. The Indians, without their French partners and protectors, had no reliable European contact in North America. The presence of the British, and of their colonial settlers progressing westward, ensured a conflict would inevitably occur.

After the transfer of power between the French and English, the Indians, longtime enemy of the English, felt conflicted. "[F]rom the Indians anything might be expected" towards the English as they sought to move into former French territories.[40] In fact, "notwithstanding outward expressions of assent to the new order of things, a deep-rooted dislike on the part of the Indians for the English grew after 1760 with great rapidity."[41] This was certainly one aspect of their victory the British badly miscalculated. They anticipated the Indians, former enemies, would suddenly transition to partners; perhaps not friends as such, but tolerating one another.

"Englishmen celebrated 1763 as a victory for liberty, but Indians saw Britain's victory as a threat to freedom."[42] With the defeat of France, their allies, the Native Americans were ostensibly vanquished through the same measures as France; this included the 1763 Treaty of Paris which shocked most tribes once they learned what it contained. From the perspective of the Indians, whose land was primarily impacted by the Treaty, they felt betrayed. They did not give their land to the French to be surrendered to the British. The Indians thus felt they lost one partner (France) to one who had even less concern for their claims (Britain). When the British failed to create the types of partnerships with the tribes that the French had, the Indians further felt let down. Naturally, the never-ending arrival of settlers did little to alleviate their apprehension.

Simply put, the British were ignorant of Indian diplomacy and failed to learn it. They generally held attitudes which were antagonistic of the many unique tribes whose land they now claimed as their own. Deprived of their sense of purpose and struggling to adapt to a non–French overlord, the multiple tribes began to consider reprisals against the British. This outlook acquired a spiritual dimension as many tribes struggled to adapt to the new British regime without the supplies once provided by the French.

The initial friendly relations between the British and the Indians would lead to the British letting their guard down in the early stages of the uprising inspired by Pontiac. It was not uncommon for British soldiers to have Indian mistresses who often acted as agents for the various tribes. Over five hundred British personnel (and just as many settlers) were killed in the early stages of the uprising before it became organized by the various tribes throughout the Ohio Valley. The British settled on a strategy of total war against the Indians in response to the sporadic uprisings. This plan, much as with the surge of emphasis against the French a few years earlier, was doomed from the start as it was impossible to generate what the soldiers needed, much less the money and materials, so soon after the end of the war with France.

Pontiac was principal chief of the Ottawa tribe. While his center of power was the area around present-day Detroit, his influence extended much further into the Ohio Valley to the south and west and east into areas of the Northwest Territories. He was a charismatic leader with considerable leadership and strategic skills. As historian Frederick Ogg wrote:

> He [Pontiac] saw that, unless the tide of English invasion was rolled back at once, all would be lost. The colonial farmers would push in after the soldiers; the forests would be cut away; the hunting grounds would be destroyed; the native population would be driven away or enslaved.[43]

Pontiac devised a strategy to take on the British and remove them from the lands he and his people called home.

During the winter of 1762–1763, before the Paris Peace Treaty was formalized, Pontiac set in motion his elaborate battle plan virtually without any knowledge on the part of the British. "A simultaneous attack, timed by a change of the moon, was to be made on the English forts and settlements throughout all the western country."[44]

The man whose name is forever affixed to the uprising did lead one attack. May 7, 1763, was the date determined by Pontiac for the overall coordinated attacks to begin. By some conveyance, the British were alerted to the plot and the initial attack at the fort at Detroit was averted by an overwhelming display of British power before hostilities even began. A week later Pontiac laid siege to the fort in a display of overt warfare. For six months Pontiac struggled to subdue the fort. There was little actual fighting and Pontiac endeavored to enlist the French at every opportunity. The French however had no appetite for further warfare with England, especially after the Paris Peace Treaty was formally signed by this point. By October 1763, Pontiac sued for peace with absolutely nothing gained by him at Detroit.

However, other tribes, inspired by his message, had far more effect in spreading terror throughout the Northwest Territories. As historian Frederick Ogg has written:

> Scores of pioneer families, scattered through the wilderness, were murdered…; traders were waylaid in the forest solitudes; border towns were burned and plantations were devastated. In the Ohio Valley everything was lost except Fort Pitt, …; in the Northwest, everything was taken except Detroit.[45]

Pennsylvania bore the brunt of Pontiac's Rebellion, seeing ferocious raids deep into the colony. This prompted the colonial legislature to raise money and troops internally. This caused tension between the large eastern communities and the sparsely settled and completely vulnerable western settlements. Although the debate was acrimonious, the colonial legislature did in fact raise taxes and fit out a force of over one thousand troops to face the Indian onslaught.

Throughout the summer of 1763 small battles erupted throughout the region, each one more horrific than the previous. The intense distrust and dislike solidified into the hatred with all its ill consequences. Among those consequences was smallpox, a dreaded disease among Europeans and a devastating disease among the Indians. The British made attempts to introduce the virus to the native population with terrifying consequences.

By the end of the summer in 1763, "[d]isease, shortage of supplies, and the separate agendas of individual tribes undermined the Indian war effort."[46] It would not be until 1765 that all the fighting subsided.

Amid the carnage, an overwhelming force of British regulars eventually subdued the Indians without much further bloodshed. Pontiac himself survived to be a rambling old man with little influence but a steady core of admirers. He did enter into an agreement of peace with the British, but it was mainly for diplomatic showmanship. Except for the city bearing his name, Pontiac was all but forgotten until he was resurrected in the twentieth century for the name of an automobile company.

The rebellion, such as it was, convinced the British that a much larger permanent force was necessary in North America than originally planned. This naturally would cost money and that led the British to devise new means to raise revenue, including taxing the colonies.

The French and Indian War was the fulcrum upon which American relations with Britain reached their apogee and began their descent. The war defined the sequence of events which culminated in yet another war and ultimately the loss of the American colonies.

Conclusion

The two chapters thus concluded have dealt with a period in American history which set the stage for the American Revolution. Without the involvement of the French, Native Americans, the Spanish, and various other Europeans, throughout much of the eighteenth century, the colonies would have never reached the point of revolt by 1775. Revolt was not an organic act, it was the germination of decades of grievances and policy development which generally had the past, rather than the future, as its guide. Even with an understanding of the French and Indian War and all that entails, the picture is not complete. There were enormous factors within society in America that churned the colonies to war and most of those revolved around the expanding concepts of government.

The global nature of the conflict was seen in the fact that Britain also won territory from Spain—who entered the war in the final stages against Britain—in Cuba and the Philippines. In the Treaty of Paris of 1763, Britain gained all of Canada and all land east of the Mississippi to include the Ohio River Valley. France ceded New Orleans to their allies the Spanish, which forty years later Napoleon would sell to President Jefferson after having reclaimed it from Spain, along with a vast swath of interior North American land. In a final swap, Spain reacquired Havana and Manila in a trade of Florida with the British.

It is hard to overstate the role the British victory in the French and Indian War had over the future American Revolution. The British debt incurred was astronomical. The British people (in England) were paying hefty rates of tax and it was not at all unreasonable to expect the colonists to start to pay more to help lower the overall debt. Until the 1760s, the American colonists had paid little in direct tax to Britain and had consequently grown prosperous. They naturally had grown jealous of their prerogatives and system of social and governmental life; each region enjoying its own unique peculiarities. Like the British, they were not prepared to give this up without a fight. The colonists also were perplexed by British attempts to prohibit settlement west of the Appalachian Mountains. The colonists, not the British, saw the Native Americans as a hinderance to development and resented British policy keeping them from pursuing their push westward. The British wanted more time to draft a plan for the region while the colonists were impatient. They wanted access and protection. The Ohio River Valley was just waiting for exploration and exploitation. For the colonists, it seemed their birthright.

Although relatively few settlers were beyond the unsettled portions of the established colonies, most felt it their inherent right to have that option available to them. Land speculation was a growing industry, with investors in every colony including some of the most common names from the Founding Era. The native population was seen not so much in conflict with these attempts unless they started to actively pose an impediment. Ideally, settlers saw the Indians as partners and enemies only as a last resort. After all, the Indians had extensive knowledge of the land and resources that the settlers coveted. In most cases settlers saw cooperating the best course of action. However, after the French and Indian War, when the Indians still sided mostly with the French, the British sought to limit interaction between settlers and Indians much to the settlers' annoyance. Americans felt the British made the western territory (Kentucky, Ohio, Tennessee) French and Indian free for the benefit of Americans by winning the French and Indian War. When the British tried to restrict access to prevent hostilities, Americans felt betrayed.

The French and Indian War, aside from producing a British victory, generated several positive emotional enhancements that accrued to the benefit of the colonies overall. The colonists learned they had a vested interest as a colony rather than colonies. In other words, the separate colonies began to see themselves in a unified way unlike seeing themselves as purely separate colonies with only self-interest to guide them. A young John Adams saw this as the defining feature of the American colonies; America united was the future of the British Empire.[47] The War opened the American west in a way only dreamed of in 1750. The possibilities seemed endless. No European power except for Britain stood in the way of westward expansion—only the Native Americans.

Finally, the French and Indian War kept Britain from an already planned revenue enhancement scheme aimed at raising taxes in the colonies and simultaneously plan for the use of the new territory acquired. With the end of war, Britain felt it could go ahead and begin the process. The final decision was made in 1764 when Britain decided to explore revenue enhancement measures.

The relationship, in theory, between Britain and the colonies was symbiotic. It did work occasionally, and when it did, it was greatly beneficial for all concerned. "[T]he colonists benefitted from the mother country as a protected market for the produce of their farms and plantations, while the British manufactures increasingly relied on colonial consumers."[48] Especially prior to the French and Indian War, the "free colonists enjoyed a higher standard of living than did the common people in Europe."[49]

One consequence of this prosperity was the relative rise of the power of women. "In vain, old-fashioned newspaper writers denounced an erosion of patriarchal power that allegedly left husbands ruined by their newly aggressive wives."[50] This gender imbalance and growing materialism became a target for the Great Awakening revivals sweeping America during this period. That, however, is another story.

CHAPTER 5

King George III and the Rise of American Resistance

Next to John Dickinson, few today have a reputation so tarnished from the Revolutionary generation as King George III. Like a piece of cheap silver, George III seems to defy attempts to polish his image. As might be expected, he was not all bad. In fact, when he ascended the throne in 1760 at the age of twenty-two, he seemed a relief for his subjects (including those in America). He was young and had a growing family. He radiated confidence, youth, and energy; not only for himself but for the monarchy and Britain. In fact, the quintessential American, Benjamin Franklin, in England as the agent for Pennsylvania, felt the new king represented a new age in the relations between the colonies and England (he would turn out to be accurate, just not in the way he thought). Even after three years as monarch, Franklin still had the highest admiration for George. Writing to William Strahan on December 19, 1763, Franklin gushed:

> I am of opinion that his virtue and the consciousness of his sincere intentions to make his people happy will give him firmness and steadiness in his measures and in the support of the honest friends he has chosen to serve him; and when that firmness is fully perceived, faction will dissolve and be dissipated like a morning fog before the rising sun, leaving the rest of the day clear with a sky serene and cloudless. Such after a few of the first years will be the future course of his Majesty's reign, which I predict will be happy and truly glorious. A new war I cannot yet see reason to apprehend. The peace will I think long continue, and your nation be as happy as they deserve to be.[1]

George III took his role seriously. He "was one of the most conscientious sovereigns who ever sat upon the English throne."[2] He was a studious student of statecraft and as such he factored prominently in the story of the colonial experience during the 1760s. More than either of his two most recent predecessors (both named George as well) George III's actions would impact the colonists in ways which would not be overcome. Helpless to deal with the situation, he played big and lost bigger. And in the process, he forever doomed his reputation in the historical memory.

In a preface to the 1972 biography of King George III, Charles, the current Prince of Wales, wrote that "perhaps Americans will soon come to see the true George III without bias and traditionally held opinions."³ The biography of George III, by John Brooke, was part of the McGraw-Hill American Revolution Bicentennial Program. The idea, aside from a much-needed overview of the monarch's life, was to try and allow Americans an opportunity to understand the man who, above all others, had come to represent all that was not American. Regardless of our differences, the one thing that could bring Americans together was the tyranny of Great Britain and especially of King George III. "In the mythology of American history King George III is the would-be tyrant whose wicked plans were foiled by the courage and resistance of the American people. He is the scapegoat for the act of rebellion."⁴ After nearly two hundred and fifty years, the American appetite for "us v. them" thinking is as strong as ever. If anything, the bicentennial in 1976 showed how insecure America was with her independence and power.

King George III. The Miriam and Ira D. Wallach Division of Art, Prints and Photographs: Print Collection, New York Public Library Digital Collections.

Oddly, George III was heir to a dynasty—Hanoverian—which worked to develop the constitutional monarchical system which is today admired by those nations which still have monarchies. George, as Prince of Wales, was taught nearly exclusively in the emancipation theory of the House of

Chapter 5. King George III and the Rise of American Resistance 71

Hanover which saw itself as restoring the ancient English liberties which the Stuarts had menaced during their reigns in the seventeenth century. The Prince of Wales was taught a heavy dose of traditional Whig history; the Whigs were generally associated with the anti-royalist side of the political spectrum against the more royalist Tories. George was not a monarch who favored the "divine right of kings."[5] At first glance this might be strange given that George was soon to be the third member of the Hanover dynasty. Yet this observation does show how and why as king George was somewhat taken aback by the early claims of the colonists that he (King George III) was depriving the colonists of their ancient liberties and freedoms. As far as George was concerned, the colonists must have been confused. Was not the House of Hanover, his ancestral home, the guardian of English liberty? Indeed, Britain, under the Hanovers, would "eventually ... produce a system of government which has had no rival in the modern world for flexibility, honesty, and efficiency."[6]

George's father, Frederick, Prince of Wales at the time, the son of King George II, was something of an intellectual where the Royal Family was concerned. He pursued the arts and sciences much to the dismay of his militaristic father. Young George likely received his appreciation for such pursuits from him. Architecture, music (he was an outstanding harpsicord and flute player), poetry, and history, all competed for his attention. Frederick and his son both inherited the outlook of the overarching social phenomena of the time: the Enlightenment. George came to the throne when the predominate intellectual movement in modern times was taking aggressive hold of traditional institutions and patterns of life. The Enlightenment poured into Europe the greatest spirit of human thought since the so-called Dark Ages. Whether a fervent adherent of the philosophical tenants involved, it would have been difficult for a public figure not to have been influenced, even indirectly, by the profound ecumenicity of the thought patterns which emerged from nearly every nook and cranny of the Western world. (George would provide pensions to several influential thinkers, including the Scotsman David Hume.) While it is easy enough to argue that George III was not an enlightened ruler, it is similarly accurate to say that he was not a regressive one either. Indeed, one tangible element of George's immersion in the learning environment of the time was his massive book collection, which became the nucleus of the British Library and is still accessible for research to this day. Rarely however is the voice, or the words and the thought, of King George III utilized. He is analyzed, but rarely utilized. Putting a context, or dimension, to George is almost anathema it would seem. For a man who would have one of the longest reigns in English history—regardless of his health—so little is heard from him, rather than about him. Generally, what we read is a synopsis of what an author sees as the most salient aspects George's life and career as they interpret it—without hearing from George himself.[7]

George III, rather than the arrogant philistine we depict him as, was, in the 1760s anyway, the quintessential English gentleman of learning, pedigree, and manners. Historian John Brooke has written, "King George has good claims to be considered the most cultured monarch ever to sit on the throne of Great Britain."[8] George III was someone thrust upon the stage after the early death of his father and became king in 1760 after the death of his grandfather, King George II. The grandson as mentioned was someone who looked to art, culture, and science. As befitting a future monarch, George, as Prince of Wales, actively pursued those subjects of study which would benefit him and his nation. During his long reign (1760–1820), George III would found the Royal Academy; the King's Library (which became the nucleus of the British National Library much as Thomas Jefferson's library was the nucleus of the Library of Congress); and studied science with the aid of a variety of scientific instruments which are today seen in the science museum. He also maintained an observatory and was a patron of famed astronomer William Herschel.

Frederick's death in 1751, when George was thirteen, forever changed the dynamic for the sensitive and somewhat shy boy who suddenly became Prince of Wales. He was thrust into a role as heir apparent for a grandfather (George II) whom he barely knew. The king had hated his son Frederick, George's father, and consequently saw little of his young grandson George. When the king's son Frederick died, and his grandson became his heir, the king made little effort to tutor the future monarch beyond naming him Prince of Wales. This defect left the new Prince of Wales with little or no exposure or understanding about being a king. His lessons in the classroom were one thing, but they could not substitute for observing a king and spending time with his grandfather. The elderly and headstrong monarch was as distant from his grandson as he was his late son, Frederick.

Furthermore, it was feared the old monarch might die before the young George reached his majority, thus generating a power struggle within the increasingly powerful Parliament for control of the government before the future king came of age. Given all his advantages as the new Prince of Wales, he still faced the emotional burden of having succession thrust upon him. "They were so concerned about the heir apparent that they forgot the growing boy."[9] His childhood was dramatically cut short, and he was thrust into the role of heir apparent with much learning to make up.

Although young George, as the Prince of Wales, was expected to inherit the crown someday, he had little early contact with King George II. Primarily due to the frosty relationship between George II and his son

Chapter 5. King George III and the Rise of American Resistance

Frederick, Prince of Wales, young George, before his father's death, saw his grandfather infrequently. One of the earliest letters by young George to his grandfather reads:

> I hope you will forgive the liberty I take to thank your Majesty for the honor you did me yesterday. It is my utmost wish, and shall always be my study to deserve your paternal goodness and protection. I am with greatest respect and submission.... George.[10]

Allowing for the requisite tone of the language in the eighteenth century, this letter does have feeling and an awareness by the eleven-year-old George that he is not just any child writing to just any grandfather.

It is both easy and difficult, after two hundred and sixty years, to analyze the childhood of George. He is forever an object of fascination given his later slide into the figure of mad King George. Trying to plumb the depths of the later King George by trying to understand the early pre–King George is an academic pastime for some scholars. For our purposes, which are relegated to the 1760s, it is enough to say the young George had a fraught relationship with his grandfather which was only exacerbated by the unique status he was born into: heir to the English throne.

The rival political camps struggling for power with George II now sought to influence the new, impressionable, Prince of Wales. First among the items on the agenda for the new heir was education. At first, George received a mixture of instruction on statecraft and leadership. He was not well served initially and was often more confused than educated. It was not until John Stuart, the 3rd Earl of Bute, was appointed George's private tutor to oversee all aspects of his education that the young boy began to see his world (admittedly he lived in a bubble as Prince of Wales—he suffered the ill effects of having limited knowledge of the outside world beyond the Court and never fully grasped the expansive nature of life) and his future started to take shape.

One reason George III has suffered so badly in the court of public opinion is that his early writings were never widely published and made available to an audience. While not academic, the voluminous early works show George as a studious, serious young man of reasonable intellect and someone who gave much thought to his role into which he was born. The future king wrote, and indeed even after his accession to the throne, on a variety of topics related to statecraft and good government—and taxes and revenue, topics forever associated with him. As Jeremy Black described it: "From his period as prince, he brought a potent mix of determination, commitment and sense of self-righteousness, and a difficult mix, for himself and others, of self-confidence and self-doubt."[11]

The most stabilizing influence in George's early life was the Scotsman, the Earl of Bute. Bute provided a safe harbor for George although not without self-advancement for himself. Ensuring that the future monarch was properly educated was his greatest achievement. As the first English-born Hanover king it was vital that George learned the English perspective of the British constitutional monarchy. Compared to his father, grandfather, and great-grandfather, George had the most thorough, and thoroughly English, education.

During his preparatory period as Prince of Wales, the future George III was a dedicated pupil. As such, part of that learning involved taxation and government theory and practice. His future role as a constitutional monarch meant his position was not to be supreme in the sense that the early Stuart monarchs attempted. In an early, although undated extract, George, probably as Prince of Wales, wrote concerning the nature of government:

> When men first began to form themselves into societies, the equality subsisting in the state of nature ceased, the weakness of the individual was felt no more, the aggregate body became sensible of its force; this produced wars and contention....[12]

Here George sought the essence of society—the coming together for the greater benefit, including defense. George continued: "Here then we see the beginning, and real foundation of the laws of nations, some kind or other of which appears even amongst the most barbarous people, though often formed on erroneous principles."[13]

George made an argument for law in general being the adhesive which pulls together the various strands of social centrifugal forces. These forces, all pulling in their own self-interested way, can only work towards that self-interest in as far as the law would permit. George wrote:

> Law in general is mere human reason, in as much as all the world is governed by it, and the political, and civil laws of each nation, are the particular cases in which this human reason is applied. Political laws form government, municipal laws support it, in either case, they should be relative to the nature of the government intended, or already formed.[14]

While a sweeping approach to the richness and power of law, George nonetheless envisioned law in its grandest, most ecumenical sense. Law is government, law maintains and fortifies. Rather, his future was reminiscent of the Glorious Revolution of 1688 which brought William of Orange to the English throne through his marriage to Princess Mary Stuart.

Through his studies young George actively sought examples from English history of kings and queens and nobles which could guide his learning and hopefully his future reign. George elaborated on the three most common forms of government: "The greatest principle of a republican

Chapter 5. King George III and the Rise of American Resistance   75

government is virtue, in monarchy, honor, and in despotic states, fear."[15] As the Prince of Wales' guide in his studies the Earl of Bute became not only mentor and friend, but eventually Prime Minister under George III. Bute "directly and indirectly had a bigger influence over the course of his life than any other person."[16] The internecine struggles within the Court itself caused enough angst to render even the sturdiest boy grief, much less someone as predisposed to introspection as young George.

Bute was widely distrusted in British government circles due to his Scots heritage. George and Bute's relationship would have far-reaching consequences during his first decade as monarch. To keep his closest friend and ally nearby, the new king appointed Bute Secretary of State. This placed Bute, and the new George III, in direct opposition to William Pitt, the mastermind of the French and Indian War strategy that brought victory to Britain. Additionally, it created unwanted political frictions when Britain least needed them. With a new king and a significant victory to make the most of, Britain needed political stability. Unfortunately, it got political chaos resulting in destruction of its global empire with the loss of the American colonies. Had George appointed more ministers in the tradition of Pitt, the 1760s, and indeed the 1770s, may have been handled much differently. "The best hope of political stability at the outset of the new reign lay in an alliance between Bute, the minister of the King, and Pitt, the minister of the House of Commons."[17] Tragically for George, this was not to be. John Brooke has written, "Pitt bears a heavy share of responsibility for the political confusion of the early years of King George III's reign."[18] Pitt and his followers, confident in their approach considering the war they successfully managed, objected to Bute, and by extension the king, at nearly every turn.

The increasing power of Parliament which preceded the Hanover dynasty and doomed the Stuart dynasty, found the Hanoverians receptive to adopting a comfortable mix between Parliament and the monarchy. Had George III not been so vilified, and so obstinate himself—perhaps because of the vilification during his lifetime—the American colonists may have been able to work with Parliament and the king to produce an amicable settlement to the quickly developing crisis during the 1760s. The confusion over the colonies boiled down to a legal struggle which was debated on the battlefield instead of a courtroom or other governmental venue. The rapid and unequivocal reaction from the colonists to the revenue measures caught many in Britain off guard. The crisis with the colonies, over representation and taxation, was an outgrowth of the internecine conflict between the king and Parliament as a continuing evolution of constitutional monarchy. The colonial problem, from this perspective, sprang from the decades-long maturation under the Hanovers of the relationship between king and Parliament. In fact, the colonists would often toggle between blaming the Parliament and the king, depending on which villain most suited their immediate needs. Yet, "alone among the great European monarchies, [the Hanoverians] could boast that they held their crown by the free and deliberate consent of the elected representatives of their people."[19] How could the king view himself and his policies as tyrannical? The young Prince of Wales, George, wrote:

> As no society can subsist without government, the union of all the powers of individuals gave birth to the political laws; such a union of power can never be expected without a perfect agreement of the wills....[20]

George, Prince of Wales, and Money

When George, son of Frederick, Prince of Wales, succeeded his late father as Prince of Wales and heir apparent to his grandfather, King George II in 1751, the young George was already starting his studies. In his early writings on taxation history, one element was clear concerning English tax policy: it was inconsistent. The history of English taxation pointed to the need to formalize tax policy. George referred to many of these early tax schemes as raising revenue by "arbitrary means."[21]

George wrote of the dangers of money in a republic arguing that while an assembly of leaders may work out of passion for their principles, once that passion is impacted by money, the leaders then "have nothing but profit in view; for whenever corruption grows strong enough here to suspend the laws, this state is irretrievably undone."[22] George was idealistic yet thoroughly practical. He saw the weaknesses in human nature because he too was human and experienced many of the same temptations. However, as a monarch, he knew his role was more than just being the average virtuous citizen or subject. This outlook created a rigid sense of duty that George eventually came to expect in others before he lost his exalted view of humanity. This is one contributing factor in his prosecution of the American Revolution. He saw it as a matter of virtue not just for himself, but for the colonists as well. George simply could not countenance, in the early part of his reign, the notion of colonists questioning, much less fighting, Britain.

George often viewed himself as the Patriot King. This idea was described by Viscount Bolingbroke as "a monarch who was virtuous, impartial and powerful enough to override parties...."[23] In many respects, young George was taught to see himself, as part of a system of government, not the government. This was an approach well in keeping with the Whig conception of monarchy as viewed by the Hanoverian monarchs who preceded George III. As such, George was part of the lineage, which was his birthright, but also responsible for nurturing that viewpoint. He would not be a monarch who ruled because of divine inspiration, but he was to be a monarch who would rule as part of the government of Great Britain, albeit at the top. As historian Jeremy Black has written:

> As a result of his political upbringing, George saw himself, and his constitutional role, as acting out of national, rather than sectional, interest, and retained that conviction and goal throughout his reign, while being unwilling to take such a charitable view of others.[24]

Assuming the Throne

George III came to the throne in his twenty-second year. Even before his accession there were high hopes for his eventual reign. In a sermon preached after the English victory in Canada, the Rev. Samuel Cooper noted, speaking of George, Prince of Wales:

> With joy the British nation beholds a bright pledge of its future happiness, in the royal progeny of our gracious King, particularly in the heir apparent now arrived at full age. We also in these Western extremities of his dominion, partake in this joy, as we largely do in his paternal care and protection, and the benign influences of his government.[25]

This was a year that saw an upsurge in a *Pax Britannica* type consciousness of world events from the British perspective. George was the first Hanoverian king to speak English as his primary language, and he was the only eighteenth-century-born king, and the first to view England as his primary interest (as opposed to the family ancestral lands of Hanover in Germany). George III had no interest whatsoever in the Hanover lands in Germany and effectively abandoned them.

Following the victory over the French at Montreal in the fall of 1760, George, with the nation, naturally looked forward to a return to peace. As the new monarch, George faced the added pressure of the debt incurred with victory over the French, which cast a shadow over the general feeling of joy and relief. George was by inclination opposed to debt and extravagant displays of wealth. His desire to see the debt reduced would put him on a collision course with the American colonists.

During the 1760s, as the tensions with the American colonies reached a crisis point, George, as a still relatively new king, faced the added internal pressure of poor advisors. Unlike his immediate predecessors, George I and George II, George III took a more hands-on approach to governing. The first two Georges, having both been born and raised in Germany, were more content to allow the party system in England to establish and execute policy with limited oversight from the sovereign. George III however, who was born and raised in England, felt more of a duty and affiliation to and with the English people. He also felt a greater understanding of England overall and its systems. This was no doubt true, with some glaring deficiencies.

For George III, an understanding did not equate to a functional working capacity of the British system. This led to frequent personnel changes in crucial posts necessary for advising the king on policy. In addition to the inexperienced new king, the government was left with a new set of ministers by the time of the Stamp Act crisis. Political turnover had created a less-than-ideal assemblage of leaders—certainly nowhere near the level of Secretary of State (Prime Minister) William Pitt. All this internal consternation was occurring during the greatest threat the British faced since perhaps 1588 with the Spanish Armanda—the break-away of the North American colonies.

George distrusted political parties. In Britain at the time the two dominant parties were the Tories and the Whigs. George saw the two-party winner-take-all approach of governing as a waste of effort. "George's virtues were governmental rather than political, and he saw others in the same light."[26] The real goal should not be party victories, but victories for Britain; victory for all Englishmen. "The balancing act of a ministry ... was threatened by the redefinition of political groups greatly hastened by George. He saw himself as able to appeal to all groups."[27] This redefinition started immediately with George's perspective on the Seven Years' War and the French and Indian War.

With England ascendant on the world stage, George and Britain could have prosecuted the war further, especially with Spain, to acquire more land in the Western Hemisphere. Much of that land south of the North American colonies was ruled, however tenuously, by Spain. The Spanish were no longer the threat they once were. Gorging on two centuries of South American gold and silver had produced an exhausted kingdom with wholly inadequate monarchs. The War of Spanish Succession (see Chapter 3) was one in a succession of wars fought by England and continental Europe in part for greater control of the vast overseas network of colonies accumulating to Britain and France, and the over-extended Spanish.

The Stamp Act crisis was the beginning of the charade in the colonies whereby leaders would attempt to pit the king against Parliament, and vice versa. Almost as a child will occasionally try to play one parent against another to achieve its wishes, so the colonial leaders attempted to appeal to either the king or Parliament as they gauged their arguments. "Many American critics of the Stamp Act sought to assert a direct relationship with George which he, constitutionally, could not allow to exist."[28]

Initially, the colonists too wondered; after all, they were Englishmen with all the inherent rights that citizenship conferred. The colonists were also aware of the reputation of the young monarch and of his family's reputation. In this seeming dichotomy, the colonists found their first sustained arguments against the English monarch with the German heritage.

The Business of the Revenue: Taxation

Without a sound system of revenue collection, or taxation, organized government would cease to exist. Indeed, if taxation is left out of the equation of starting a government it would likely never begin. The example of the American states under the Articles of Confederation need only be looked at to understand this imperative.

Government taxation has been a part of life since there have been governments. Some of the earliest examples of writing that exist record the paying of taxes and other revenue payments to a government. "Taxes have waxed and waned over the centuries. In western Europe, the centuries that followed the end of the Roman Empire were marked by a reversion to more rudimentary systems of revenue generation … that inhibited both economic development and effective government."[29] So engrained were taxes by the time of the Roman Republic that Cicero commented, "Revenues: the sinews of the state."[30]

As a monarch, George was not unaware that governments functioned on money. That money had to come from somewhere.[31] A significant amount of his learning involved studying past reigns to understand the purpose, meaning, and execution of revenue-generating legislation. George looked at English history from before the Norman Conquest of 1066. George began one study:

> We are told in general that the Saxon kings had levies of money and personal services towards repairing cities, castles, bridges, and for military expeditions, such levies were called Burghbote [a type of infrastructure repair], Brigbote [bridge or pathway repair], and Heregeld [for military upkeep].[32]

Modern (in the eighteenth-century) usage of terms such as taxes and tallages "were Norman words applied to most impositions, though levied in a very different manner from what they are at present...."[33]

The quintessential passage in George's study, as would ultimately impact the American colonies, was his assertion concerning the right to taxation policy. George wrote:

> The right of laying impositions has been affirmed by some to have made formally part of the prerogative while others deny it, but by an Act of the 25th Edward I taxes can be laid upon the subject without the consent of the Lords and Commons in Parliament.[34]

Under this Act (late thirteenth century) the monarch has the right to tax their subjects without the consent of Parliament. Naturally, this was not an efficient policy. Even George himself thought it unwise to try and raise revenue outside of Parliamentary involvement. George also admitted that until Queen Elizabeth I the history of taxation was complicated and not well understood due to poor record keeping and the fact that some monarchs "had recourse to illegal and arbitrary methods of levying money and the produce of such taxes is either totally unknown or variously represented."[35] George felt that studying the history of English taxation would provide a greater understanding "of the power of the Prince, and the wealth of the nation during the dark areas of our history."[36]

George argued that the revenue of the Crown had lost its power in part due to an effective mechanism in the law to allow for the monarch to hold the money:

> The hereditary revenue of the Crown having been by many grants and alienations transferred into the hands of private subjects, it became necessary for private contributions to supply the place of it, besides war, marriages of the Royal family and various things of the same nature demanded extraordinary supplies from the subjects, the patrimony of the Crown not being sufficient to answer these demands even in good reigns and never enough to satiate the desires of avaricious and tyrannical monarchs.[37]

For George, the inherent right to tax British subjects, wherever they lived, was beyond question. His studies confirmed this a decade before the colonists rose in revolt. George saw the colonists revolting not just against him, but against the entire pedigree of English history. That would have been a difficult position for George to abandon.

In a futile effort to stabilize his government, George enticed William Pitt, the master of the French and Indian War, to reenter the government to provide a cohesive strategy. In a July 29, 1766, letter, George wrote to Pitt,

> I have signed this day the warrant for creating you an Earl, ... as I know the Earl of Chatham [Pitt] will zealously give his aid towards destroying all party distinctions, and restoring that subordination to government which can alone preserve that inestimable blessing, liberty, from degenerating into licentiousness.[38]

Pitt tragically was not able to "restore that subordination to government" George so earnestly desired.

In a September 1766 diary entry, George wrote:

> If a due obedience to the law, and the submitting to that as the only just method of having grievances removed does not once more become the characteristic of this nation, we shall soon be no better than the savages of America, then we shall be as much despised by all civilized nations as we are as yet revered for our excellent constitution....[39]

Strikingly, George was writing about adherence to legal principles at the same moment that the Americans were starting to make the same argument more formally and cogently about the British policy towards the colonies. There was one law, but two conceptions of that law especially concerning how it related to American policy. Still, it does beg the question, had the Americans been given the chance to debate the taxation policy with British leaders, what might have been the outcome? What if the courtroom, instead of the battlefield, had been the venue for determining American grievances?

The Genesis of a Revolution

One of the early policies passed by the Grenville ministry in 1763 was the Proclamation of 1763. Parliament was convinced that a major part of the problem in America impacting defense was the continuing movement of settlers west into Indian lands. This occurred at both the individual colony level and as part of formal British policy. The 1763 Proclamation sought to reverse the earlier settlement policy by restricting western lands by forbidding "settlements upon any lands within the said colonies which may interfere with the Indians bordering upon them."[40] While this was a policy easy to declare in England, it was much less easy to acknowledge in America where for decades many families had undertaken the arduous task of settling in the vast lands beyond the Appalachian Mountains. Added to the human migration was the enormous investments made by land speculators both big and small. The 1763 Proclamation would prove another unwelcomed intrusion on colonial affairs which would aggregate around the issue of Parliamentary representation.

In his gathering with colonial agents, Prime Minister Grenville saw the meeting as "a precedent for their being consulted before any tax is imposed upon them by Parliament."[41] Grenville saw a protocol for working with colonists in taxation policy. Had Grenville's response been more widely accepted, the trials and difficulties of the next few years might have been avoided—presuming both sides acted in good faith. Grenville was absolutely convinced that it was "highly reasonable they [the colonists] should contribute something towards the charge of protecting themselves...."[42]

American prosperity was not an unknown fact by 1765. American success was the work of a diverse body of immigrants whose status was claimed by Britain as the "mother country." By 1765, this was indeed the case; however, England was far from alone in claiming a lineal descent to the founding era of the colonies. Spain, France, Sweden, and Holland, all could claim in varying degrees the title of founding nation to a multitude of areas along the Atlantic coast and points south, west, and north. It was the good fortune of Britain that she subdued other nations' claims to North America by 1765. Furthermore, Britain had invested more in time, treasure, and personnel over the course of the seventeenth and eighteenth centuries and rightfully expected the participation in the upkeep of the empire to be assented to by those who benefited most.

Although the sugar and stamp taxes were designed to be broad-based and evenly distributed, Americans saw the implementation as containing elements which would more intimately impact one region over another. This, they argued, would render the taxes as more onerous on some and less so on others. Those impacted tended to be the merchants and men of business who utilized more broadly the types of items covered by the taxes. They were caught in the middle, literally middlemen, in the cycle of producer, exporter, importer, and consumer. For those who had invested and benefited from the existing systems, suddenly changing the calculus was too much to ask. "The Sugar Act was thus made out to be, even from the point of view of English merchants, an economic blunder; but in the eyes of vigilant Bostonians it was something more, and much worse than an economic blunder."[43] By attempting to show that English merchants would be as impacted as American merchants, American leaders sought to bring the resistance to the sugar tax as close to home as possible. American merchants rightly sought to show the impact of the tax not only upon themselves, but upon the entire system of commerce as it had developed over the previous several decades. The British leaders failed to recognize that the tremendous advance in American mercantile policies signaled a leap in economic advancement which went undetected by American and British officials. The money pouring in from the system as it existed could only work in an environment which was elastic and capable of expanding and contracting as necessary to meet the demands put on the policies. The sad fact was that neither American or British officials had the foresight to grasp the changing realities in the economic relationship that existed between America and Britain. When the taxation policy was implemented by Britain the Americans struggled to understand the new dynamic and resorted to the time-honored cry of tyranny. The eighteenth century had not produced leaders versed in the nuances of international finance. These concepts of finance and international trade, which became standard over the next century and more, were simply not recognized in 1765. The fiscal territory being established by successful American merchants and dealers was not fully understood, if even recognized, by those who were making it. In modern terms, we understand a regulated economy on both domestic and international planes, but in the eighteenth century, while they were unwittingly functioning at a high level of international money exchange, the

Chapter 5. King George III and the Rise of American Resistance 83

participants were less than versed in the evolving intricacies of what was for all intents and purposes international finance.

The Bostonians, whose city was the scene of the most egregious violence and by default the center of American resistance, saw the imposition of taxes as the start of a slippery slide into further British tyranny. How accurate that perspective was is debatable. British ministers and members of Parliament certainly proved a willingness overall to work with the colonies to determine an appropriate level of tax, or donation, or payment in kind to help offset the tremendous costs Britain incurred with the French and Indian War and Pontiac's Rebellion. Over the decade prior to 1765 the British national debt more than doubled and was continuing to hemorrhage money beyond any historical parallel. From the British perspective, and most well-meaning colonists, financial input from the colonies was appropriate in theory. In principle, a mechanism needed to be worked out in the evolving relationship between the colonies and Britain. As we know, this was not to be the case.

Among the multitude of problems Americans faced with finding counter arguments to the sugar and stamp taxes was the seemingly simple matter of language. Attempting to recycle language used to oppose a colonial governor over a topic did not ring as true when transposed to argue against Parliament. "[M]oderate terms could hardly be trusted to cope with the serious business of Parliamentary taxation."[44]

Before the American Duties Bill was passed by Parliament in 1764 (a package of taxes that originally contained the Stamp Act), British politicians had a full slate of issues to deal with domestically. Treason trials were pending for printing damaging and obscene materials, debate on a domestic cider tax, among other issues, sought the attention in the minds of members of Parliament as they contemplated American and colonial taxation. It has been pointed out that in addition to the problems with America over taxation, George faced a political crisis in Parliament and within his cabinet. One crisis at a time was more than enough for George, but two simultaneously was overwhelming. Writing to Lord Egmont on January 11, 1766, George expressed his frustration: "all I desire is that they [his ministers] will act firmly till the arduous business of the American colonies is over, then I can stand upon my own feet."[45] Of the three Hanoverian monarchs of eighteenth-century England, George III experienced the most difficulty in maintaining a quality ministry with competent advisors and administrators. George's ministers share in the blame for the American fiasco as much as Parliament or George himself. Britain, with their victory in the French and Indian War, stood alone as a world power. It was a moment of great triumph that required great leadership to take full advantage of the opportunities presented. Unfortunately for Britain, strong leadership, visionary leadership, was not forthcoming. The political factions selfishly sought power and influence over the young inexperienced king, and this had dramatic effects over the next two decades.

Writing to Lord Northington, the Lord Chancellor, on February 3, 1766, George commented:

> I am more and more grieved at the accounts of America. Where this spirit will end is not to be said. It is, undoubtedly, the most serious matter that ever came before Parliament; it requires more deliberation, candour, and temper than I fear it will meet with.[46]

A week later, in a memorandum dated February 10, 1766, King George III wrote:

> Lord Rockingham this day came and complained to me as if he was accused of having wrongly stated my opinion on the Stamp Act; I told him I had on Friday given him permission to say I preferred repealing to enforcing the Stamp Act; but that modification I had ever thought both more consistent with the honour of this country, and all the Americans would with any degree of justice hope for.[47]

George was willing to talk about the Stamp Act, perhaps even compromise, but ultimately felt the poison unleashed by the more radical-minded Americans precluded such an approach to the taxation impasse.

Added to this was the unsteady leadership of George III (who exhibited his first signs of mental stress by the mid–1760s) and his ministers and it became clear how the British leaders could have stumbled into a major problem with American taxation. With the repeal of the Stamp Act George faced his greatest challenge as a ruler. At that moment, the great victory of 1760 over the French began to crumble and he knew it was not going to have a good outcome. For the next eighteen years, until the Treaty of Paris in 1783 recognizing American independence, George would be transfixed and stymied by the American problem.

Opposition to British taxation was nothing new in 1765. It did not suddenly spring into life. The colonists had long sought workarounds to British taxation plans. This was:

> demonstrated programmatically by contravention of such trade laws as did not suit them, it had been shown more directly in the weakening of royal government, as the elected assemblies deployed the power of the purse and other weapons to encroach on the authority of governors and their subordinates.[48]

In addition, several untimely deaths of political leaders created great unease among ministers and Parliament. After suffering from a months-long illness himself, George III feared for his own life, going so far as to prepare regency paperwork should he become incapacitated. The most infamous

Chapter 5. King George III and the Rise of American Resistance   85

component of the tax scheme, the Stamp Act, was postponed a year until 1765 to allow for adequate time to explain it to colonial agents in London. After the agents unanimously rejected the proposal, Parliament offered to let them recommend alternatives. The American agents however refused to consider any alternatives. The contours of the larger, later debate in America were quickly drawn. The Americans foresaw a loss of what sovereignty they possessed, while the British foresaw the loss of their sovereignty. If any moment can be said to be a starting point leading to American independence, this was it. Both sides naturally held to principle yet understanding that compromise was necessary. Unfortunately given the slow transportation of communications across the ocean, tempers, rather than cooling, could simmer and stew to a boiling point.

On February 6, 1765, after a year delay, debate began in Parliament on the postponed Stamp Act. Within a week news from America arrived of agitation in the colonies over the proposed tax, stamp or otherwise. Some in Parliament questioned the wisdom of moving forward under such circumstances; however, the vast majority, including George III, urged moving forward.

The Parliament was willing to listen but much less inclined to accept the premise of questioning Parliament's right to tax. This was one of those pivotal moments in history when events could have benefited from the full attention of all parties involved. Unfortunately, Parliament, and George III's ministry, were dealing with significant internal upheaval and had little time to spare on the American question—especially a question challenging their rights to legislate.

Jared Ingersoll, Charles Grath, Richard Jackson, and Benjamin Franklin, the four colonial representatives, met with British government officials, specifically Grenville, to discuss options to the stamp tax. Grenville stood firm on the belief that Parliament could tax the colonies while the agents wavered and suggested the colonies offer a donation in lieu of taxes of their own accord, rather than at the behest of Parliamentary legislation. This created a unique situation which both sides sought to strengthen for their own cause. The optics of the basis of the revenue drove both parties to attempt to further narrow their reasoning. This brinksmanship certainly could not go on forever, and eventually Parliament rejected the agents' logic. Parliament, not the colonies, got to determine taxation policy. "The marvelous growth of the colonies in population and wealth, much commented upon by all observers and asserted by ministers as one principle reason why Americans should pay taxes."[49]

The colonies had enjoyed a light tax burden for decades and many of those were avoided. They had invested much time and energy in the political development of their respective colonies and colonial leaders were not about to relinquish this fact, as they saw it, without an argument. Being left to create a semi-independent government allowed each colony to create its own unique aspects of social, economic, and political qualities that made a unified response to Britain so problematic. Being against a new tax was not enough, reasons had to exist to compel Parliament to review its policy. For Britain, the government saw the colonies as one, not individually. The colonies saw themselves just the opposite. The tendency would hamper the American cause for the next twenty-five years.

The Townshend Duties of 1767 fulfilled the declaration made in the Declaratory Act that Parliament could oversee the colonies in all legislative matters. The Townshend Duties went further than the Sugar Act or Stamp Act in part because Britain now had to maintain a larger army in the colonies for possible enforcement of the new taxes. The Townshend legislation included language punishing the New York Assembly for not paying its share of the expenses for quartering British troops in private American homes (an issue that would eventually find its way into the Declaration of Independence and the Bill of Rights as the third amendment to the Constitution).

The Townshend Duties received a reception in the colonies like that of Britain's previous attempts to impose revenue-generating measures. By 1767, the Americans had over two years of debating, writing, and thinking about America's place in the empire. The two sides could not have been further apart by this point.

It was likely no surprise when the Townshend Duties generated an outpouring of government themed literary productions unlike anything in the preceding decades. Going forward, Americans would write about their struggles at an unprecedented level through to 1789, the year the new government established by the Constitution came into being. The output during the twenty-plus years was staggering. One of the first "page turners" was John Dickinson's *Letters from a Farmer in Pennsylvania*, which began appearing in December 1767. They were an immediate bestseller as they "explicitly denied the right of Parliament to lay any taxes on the colonies, whether internal like the stamp taxes or external like the Townshend port duties."[50] Dickinson forcefully argued "any tax infringed the rights of American subjects because they were not represented there [Parliament]."[51] By mid–1768 the situation was spiraling quickly out of control with hardline rebel patriots daily goading Britain and Britain in response deciding to send more troops, especially to Boston. Calmer heads on both sides urged caution but to no avail.

The Townshend Duties struck at a complicated time in Britain. Continuing internal political crises meant that "the ministry was not able to give America the attention it deserved."[52] It was clear to British leaders that

Chapter 5. King George III and the Rise of American Resistance

if they acquiesced on taxation, the Americans would, contrary to all the claims they had made thus far, try and carve out more and more exemptions due to non-representation in Parliament. Naturally, carrying this logic to its extreme would mean American independence, something no one in Britain could contemplate in 1768. Given that, Parliament, and the ministers, kept working on plausible compromises within the limits imposed by internal political disarray.

By early 1769, inaction left both sides wondering what to expect next. George III and his ministers were against coercion and force and contemplated supporting a repeal if the Americans would cease with their violence and associated fiery rhetoric. By late 1769 Parliament had agreed to repeal the Townshend Duties but left in place a tax on tea. Although like the stamp tax, the tea tax has become a part of American historical lore—currently with many seaboard communities celebrating annual tea parties reminiscent of the infamous one in Boston; in 1770 there was not a great upswell of emotion over the tax. Political agitation, and mob activity in America continued to burn the fire hot. It would not take long for the fire to spread.

CHAPTER 6

The Stamp Act and a Congress

Overview

The colonial economy was land-based, and legislation over the decades formalized this through law. Law, custom, tradition, all these elements, upon which colonial wealth resided, were threatened by the stamp tax. "Both supporters and opponents of the Stamp Act understood that it was a measure to deliberately use taxation to change colonial institutions and to shift the trajectory of the North American economy."[1]

More than just a tax, more than just an attempt to raise revenue after a very costly war, the stamp tax was "an effort to reform both Britain and its empire."[2] There was clearly an effort by Parliament to attempt to reorient the colonies back to British standards and by extension to look forward. Britain had amassed the largest empire by 1765 and they realized centuries-old colonial policy would no longer work, after decades of somewhat weak oversight wherein most of the colonies-imposed legislation placed many executive and administrative functions within the colony and not Britain. "The American ruling classes had already wrested the government from the royal authorities by 1765; their uprising was designed to preserve what they had, rather than to gain something new and untried."[3] In June 1765, at a meeting in Boston, the legislature drafted the following:

> The House of Representatives of this province, in the present session of the general court, have unanimously agreed to propose a meeting, as soon as may be, of committees, from the house of representatives or burgesses of the several British colonies on this continent, to consult together on the present circumstances of the colonies, and the difficulties to which they are, and must be reduced, by the operation of the acts of parliament....[4]

This worried many ministers in England who saw the efforts as an early prelude to separation, if not independence. This troubling development created divisions within the British government as to the future of the empire. By controlling what was needed (paper) to enact the colonial policies, Britain could reassert some functional aspect of their depleted power. "The regulations the Stamp Act placed on the colonies would reduce land speculation by raising the cost of buying and selling real property, discourage litigation by taxing most legal papers, and curb colonial civil society by revising the cost of newspapers that fanned the flames of political opposition."[5]

On a scale rarely seen, Britain faced two momentous turning points in 1764: money and leadership. "These two forces, political reorganization and the enormous national debt, prompted Parliament to devise the Stamp Act."[6] The Stamp Act was not as well thought through as it could have been. Parliament, consciously or not, ended up targeting two of the most powerful interest groups: printers and lawyers.

> It is difficult to imagine a parliamentary action more ill-conceived than the Stamp Act. By placing the heaviest tax burden on the two groups [lawyers and printers] most capable of directing public opinion, the British government kindled flames of resentment and nationalism that it could never quench.[7]

As the Stamp Act would target paper, the primary ingredient of the printing press and the legal profession, Parliament made two extremely powerful enemies nearly overnight. Printers were a powerful force in society in the America of the early 1760s. "When the [stamp] tax took effect, there were twenty-two newspapers printed in colonial British North American."[8] Nearly half of these were associated with America's most famous printer, Benjamin Franklin. Printing and publishing had made him a very wealthy and influential man early in life. This wealth allowed him to pursue his multiple interests, most notably science and diplomacy, throughout a long and productive life.

A stamp duty was nothing new in colonial America. At the start of the French and Indian War two colonial assemblies, Massachusetts, and New York, passed stamp tax legislation to defray the costs of the war on each colony. Ostensibly, the difference between these stamp taxes and the one the British passed in 1764 was the government imposing the tax. For all the arguments made during the 1760s, the true issue was not the tax per se, it was who was passing, and imposing, the legislation. American lawyer and Connecticut's colonial representative to Parliament Jared Ingersoll admitted as much when he wrote, "America can and ought to contribute to its own defense. We, one and all, say the same on this side of the water, we only differ about the means."[9] For the colonists, those who voted, the idea of representatives, whom they could not vote for, passing tax legislation they had no control over, was simply too much. While it is often portrayed as a mass uprising, the American opposition to British policy was intricately choreographed between those who voted, generally the more affluent, and those who could not vote, the less affluent, but were nonetheless impacted by some aspect of the tax. A less affluent non-voter could still purchase a newspaper which would have been taxed. "Colonists were incensed, contending they should not be taxed by a political body to which they did not send representatives."[10] While this thinking was popular, it was a similar situation in the colonies between those affluent who voted to send representatives to colonial legislatures, and those less-affluent who could not vote and consequently did not have a voice in sending representatives to colonial legislatures.

While the American colonists clearly felt their inalienable rights were being violated, they had difficulty in pointing to an actual law or prohibition against taxation within the British legal canon. The literature is conflicted to say the least on taxation of the colonies and we will see how John Dickinson in his *Letters from a Farmer in Pennsylvania* will twist and turn to find some actual law upon which to pin his argument about Parliament's taxation of the colonies. Any argument the colonists wanted to make could be supported in part with something they could find in British legal precedent, even if they had to journey back into the mists of time—when English law was anything but stable. In fact, some American colonists no doubt accentuated this lack of specificity and purposefully kept aspects of the argument unclear to enhance their opposition. Ambiguity was an asset in colonial America during the 1760s when the written war against Britain was being waged.

The mob violence directed at the stamp tax collectors in the colonies was vicious and at times conjured up what today we might see in a horror film. The violence and lawless reactions were endlessly promoted by the newspapers which continued publishing during the period the tax was briefly in effect. Tax collectors, and their supporters, bore the brunt of the violence although on occasion it spread to those suspected of supporting the tax, such as government officials. Psychologically, the violence could be attributed to the dislocation many who composed the mobs felt to the American social tapestry. Then, as now, financial, and cultural isolation created an incendiary mixture which only needed a slight effort to ignite the toxic brew. Certainly, there was more than one reason why violence became the American weapon of choice against the British. This method of resistance would be fine-tuned throughout the 1760s, with the newspapers providing a means to broadcast the events and keep feelings at a simmering temperature.

The outcry against the Stamp Act was a major miscalculation on the part of Benjamin Franklin, friend of printers. Although Franklin forcefully

THE

General Opposition

OF THE

COLONIES

TO THE

Payment of the Stamp Duty;

AND THE

Confequence of Enforcing Obedience
by Military Meafures;

IMPARTIALLY CONSIDERED.

ALSO

A Plan for uniting them to this Kingdom,
in fuch a manner as to make their Inte-
reft infeparable from ours, for the future.

In a LETTER
To a MEMBER of PARLIAMENT.

LONDON:
Printed for T. PAYNE, at the *Mews-Gate*.
M.DCC.LXVI.

[Price One Shilling.]

The General Opposition of the Colonies to the Payment of the Stamp Duty, 1766.
Morristown NHP. Lloyd W. Smith archival collection MORR 11089.

testified before Parliament on the topic of the stamp tax, he initially believed the best course of action was acceptance. He had no idea of the outrage it would generate. "An ocean away from the scenes of public and journalistic uprising, Franklin underestimated the colonial opposition occasioned by the economic restraint on the press, its advertisers, and its audiences."[11] Franklin saw the law as the law and urged submission to violence. His stature in the American mind at this point mattered little as violence continued to be the main method of resistance. As historian Ralph Frasca has written: "The aristocratic republic of Virginia was intensely jealous of the slightest encroachment on its rights by the Crown or its representative."[12] The Virginia House of Burgesses had accrued and finessed its power since 1620. As a Crown colony it had a limited and defined area within which local government could operate. And within that defined area, the Burgesses made the most they could. This even amounted to rejecting to a call for funding from Governor Dinwiddie for the purpose of building strategic forts along the Ohio to halt the momentum of the French in the area. It is stunning to think that the members of the Burgesses, all eminent figures in Virginia, would, on principle, deny money for their own self-defense simply because the governor represented the Crown. This is precisely what the members of the Albany Congress of 1754 ran up against when they tried to bring the colonies together to face the growing French threat immediately before the start of the French and Indian War. Dinwiddie had the express permission of King George II for measures to stop the French in the Ohio Valley and provided funds for such expeditions. Yet, the colonists themselves, who benefited most directly and immediately from stopping the French, refused to participate financially.

The colonial legislature of Connecticut published a remonstrance against the proposed tax when they learned of the rumors. Language like what they wrote would end up in the Declaration of Independence twelve years later:

> Not to be subjected to laws made without his consent ... lodged in the hands of Representatives, by them elected and chosen for that purpose ... for if the privilege of not being taxed without their consent be taken from them, liberty and freedom are certainly gone with it.[13]

The largest issues at play during the time, and twelve years later, were just what exactly did rights, liberty, freedom, and similar language mean? It is easy to say that the Americans defined those concepts by the winning of the War for Independence. Yet that is hardly the answer if the current news stories are anything to go by. Even in the twenty-first century, rights, freedom, liberty, all still are undefined. So how does a historian, or anyone else, go about defining these terms? Whatever is determined, consistent application of definition must be maintained. The colonists, while striving for a coherent approach to concepts of freedom struggled with a fluid concept of liberty, freedom, and the associated themes we attribute to the Founding Era.

Naturally, the whole issue of taxation was woven into this atmosphere. Taxation was *the* topic above all topics in colonial relations between Britain and her far-flung colonial system. Taxation engaged at all levels, from the yeoman to the lord. Taxation touched every aspect of life and allowed the monarch to function the government. Eventually, it was taxation which allowed the new American government to function, as necessary. However, in the 1760s, this was still far in the future and a world away from the political realities facing the colonies in 1765.

On March 10, 1764, Thomas Whately of the British Treasury introduced into the House of Commons "a series of resolutions [formally known as 5 George III] providing for the raising of revenue in North America and the West Indies to aid in meeting the expense of defending these areas."[14] With the sealing of the Treaty of Paris in 1763, Britain was forced to come to terms with its new empire. What a decade earlier had been the colonies arranged north and south along the eastern seaboard of North America now extended unequivocally westward to the Mississippi River; an overall distance which more than doubled their North American holdings. This accumulation of territory was no doubt daunting. Given the amount of resources poured into the struggle during the French and Indian War for the area it is small wonder that Britain needed to find revenue sources quickly. The demands of Secretary of State William Pitt, while they produced victory, left the British pubic with little appetite and less cash for fresh taxes.

Yet, it was taxation that made the whole system work. Even though it was taxation that enabled victory and kept the system running, not everyone was quick to see a new tax as the best solution to the North American financial problem. Part of the trouble too was officials simply trying to wrap their heads around the enormity of the land involved. Some felt Britain needed to understand the new area in relation to the existing colonies and move from there. Better yet, perhaps the colonies could be convinced to raise their own tax, but that involved a host of complicated political and legal issues no one wished to engage.

The proposed stamp tax on the colonies was not unknown before it was enacted. Many colonists feared some type of tax was going to be called for after the French and Indian War and a stamp tax was just one of numerous revenue streams available. A stamp tax was in place in Britain itself by 1694. Indeed, one of the first taxes conceived by the Americans after independence was a stamp tax. It was nothing new as a concept and paper products were widely accepted as something carrying a tax. Therefore, when the rumors started to arrive in the colonies of a tax on stamps and other paper, colonists began to realize their worst fears.

Many colonists who had early knowledge of the proposed tax warned Parliament that they would see a blanket tax as unfair and uneven as some colonies would naturally wind up paying more than others due to population and assorted economic factors. Benjamin Franklin was one colonist who cautioned British ministers about proposed taxes. Individuals like Franklin saw the possibility of developing a system of colonial taxation through a colonial parliament or congress also recognized that such a move, "demanded exceptional perspicacity as well as the good faith of persons in public life on both sides of the Atlantic. Unfortunately, such perspicacity and such confidence were wanting."[15]

Members of Parliament, those with vision, were not insensitive to the realities. There were those in the British government and those advising the government who suggested letting each colonial legislature vote on the proposed Stamp Tax to have the tax be more authentic and organic. Lord Grenville openly discussed postponing the Stamp Act implementation to allow the colonies to respond to the idea of the tax.

Connecticut had a more straight-forward idea: "they suggested that a tax on the importation of Negroes or on the export of furs might be a more satisfactory form of imposition."[16] Pennsylvania's plan was more technical while Connecticut's would impact different regions of the country disproportionately. Jared Ingersoll, the London agent for Connecticut was likely the source of the plan much like Franklin for Pennsylvania.

This was not to be as indignant ministers felt the absolute right to legislate for the colonies without their input. There was little that could be done to ameliorate the situation that was over two centuries in the making. Even during the French and Indian War, attempts were made by the British to have the colonies contribute to a defense fund. It proved less than successful, and no doubt offered a learning moment for the colonists who, a decade later, tried to get the colonies, now self-styled states, to contribute to the general war fund for the Revolution. It would be a lesson that would need to be relearned for the next thirty years forward from 1755.

Arguments over taxation broke down around two concepts, internal and external taxes. What the colonists at first found difficult to accept was the notion of an internal tax, a tax generated within the territorial confines of the thirteen colonies. The Stamp tax was just such an internal tax. The colonists generally felt Parliament could however impose an external tax, such as on shipping or import/export related revenue generating schemes. This too however would eventually soon run afoul of American sensibilities.

Throughout 1764, the debate volleyed back and forth between the varying interpretations of taxation within the empire. The stamp tax (internal) and the sugar tax (external) were both measures that were part of the 1764 Revenue Act, but the stamp tax is the one that has come down through history as the more onerous and the one that has been remembered. In general, the colonists did not oppose taxation in theory; rather, they opposed what they viewed as specific taxation on colonial America. The British responded that indeed, a tax proposed was a specific American tax but that it benefited only America. The British saw themselves as limiting or targeting the tax rather than imposing a tax empire-wide. Many in Parliament found the rising argument over the internal/external taxation differentiation, which the colonists themselves argued to convince the Parliament that a tax was not just a tax, to be compelling.

Three issues conspired to keep North American defense at the top of priorities after 1763: (1) Pontiac's Rebellion; (2) the presence of the French in the West Indies within easy striking distance to America; and (3) the Spanish in the Louisiana territory.[17] Any one of these was sufficient cause alone, never mind when combined with the other two threats. Without question, from the British perspective, a ready military force was needed in North America. Alone among the threats facing the American colonies, one can be wholly attributed to the American design. While the French and Spanish were largely beyond the control of the colonists, the issue of Native American relations were not. The insatiable desire of colonial Americans for land led directly to the escalation of Indian wars. Britain's attempt to mitigate this was completely appropriate. "In dealing with the natives, they [Americans] had showed a violence, ruthlessness and lack of scruple to which the constant danger of an Indian uprising must largely be attributed."[18]

Both the colonists and British ministers genuinely had reasonable arguments. Britain, in addition to specifically explaining the focus and intent of a proposed tax, pointed out that the Americans were eager to venture deeper and deeper into the uncharted lands newly won in the 1763 peace treaty. This required a military force due to lingering Indian hostility from the French and Indian War. Some Americans felt this was a role they could undertake themselves, although few believed this to truly be the case. The colonies were far too fragmented politically and economically in 1765 to even consider a joint undertaking of such proportions. Even a decade later, after declaring independence, the colonies were far from unified.

The Sugar and Stamp Acts represented the first step in a reorganization of colonial policy by the British government. After their victory in the French and Indian War and the Seven Years' War, Britain was the undisputed world power. This would have been an ideal time to re-evaluate the policies impacting their growing empire. The arrival of a new king coincided with the victory gained and provided yet another ideal part of the colonial equation impacting governance of the colonies. Everything from taxation, the judiciary, and defense were identified as areas which needed review by 1764. Historian David Lindsay Keir has written:

> At the close of the Seven Years' War, the need for reconstructing the system had become plain. During the war, the incoherence and inefficiency of the defensive system of the colonies, the evasion of trade laws, and the prevalence of trading with the enemy had all been constant sources of anxiety.[19]

The Stamp Act Congress and Colonial Reactions

As early as 1765, as resistance to the Revenue Act of 1764 was spreading, the colonists began to formulate the idea of being loyal to the Crown while resisting, indeed even claiming no fealty, to Parliament. The stamp tax overall was debated in the colonies for two years, from the spring of 1764 when it was first learned about until the spring of 1766, when news of the February 1766 repeal reached America.

By 1765, two major colonies, New York, and Virginia, were arguing that Parliament had no authority to tax the colonies and they were under no obligation to any tax imposed on them. It was during this period too that colonists, concerned about their material wealth and the threat of losing it to the tyranny of Parliament, began to refer to themselves as "enslaved" by Parliament. The imagery of slavery would be a potent refrain (and completely ridiculous) up to and during the actual conflict during the 1770s. It was during this period too that the references to ancient rights and liberties being transgressed by Parliament began to appear.

Every colony debated throughout 1764 and 1765 on the efficacy of Parliament taxing (either internal or external) the colonies. In Pennsylvania, John Dickinson, not yet famous, helped write the colony's response to the Stamp Act tax. Made public on September 21, 1765, it declared taxation by any group not representative of the citizens to be unconstitutional. While various approaches and attitudes surfaced throughout the period, by the end of 1765, "The Stamp Act produced an all-but-unanimous reaction: Parliament had no right to tax the colonies."[20] In total, "during the period of the Stamp Act crisis, fifteen formal statements of colonial rights had been issued."[21] Pennsylvania favored Franklin's plan of raising revenue "through interest-bearing bills of credit."[22]

The first organized, serious violence which would become a hallmark of the pre–Revolutionary period had occurred in August of 1765 in Boston, two months before the Stamp Act Congress. To what degree the fiery unauthorized Virginia Resolutions contributed to the mob violence is debatable, although it is certain it could not have hurt the mob's cause. The most significant violence occurred when a more organized and energized mob attacked

Chapter 6. The Stamp Act and a Congress

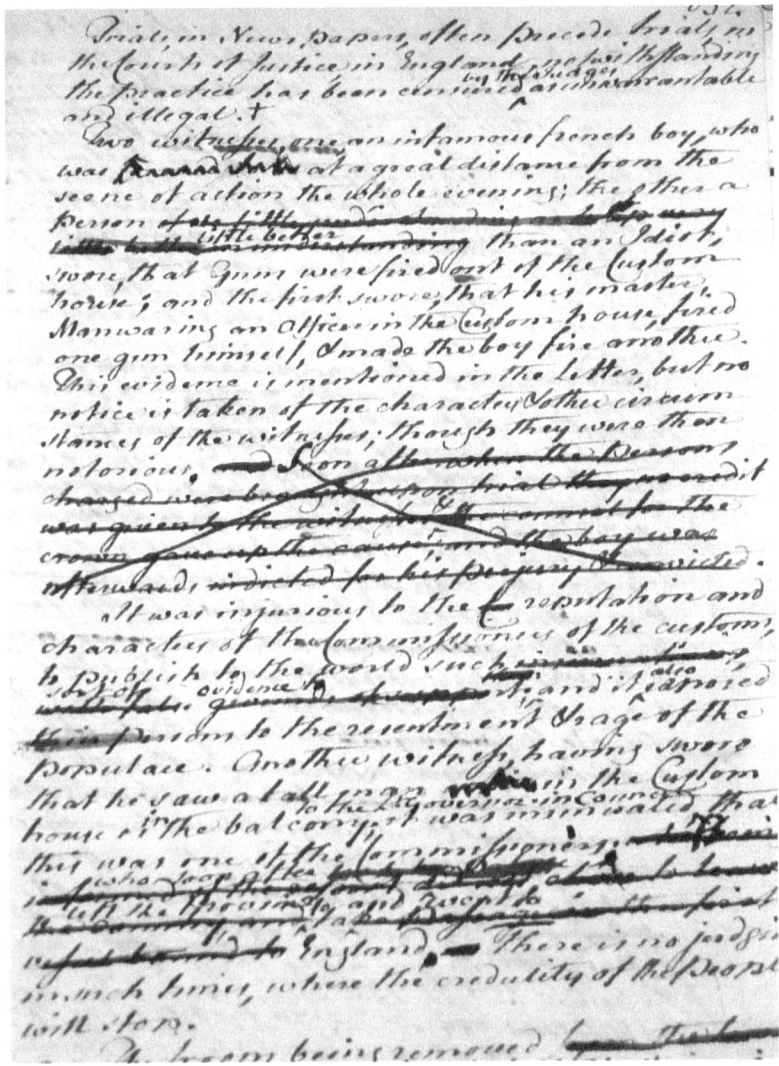

Manuscript page from Thomas Hutchinson's *History of the Province of Massachusetts Bay*, Volume 3. Morristown NHP. Lloyd W. Smith archival collection MORR 12093.

Lieutenant Governor Thomas Hutchinson's splendid mansion in Boston. Although he was personally opposed to the tax, the mob did not stand on formality and destroyed or stole his large collection of furnishings before destroying his house. No one was ever held responsible for the lawlessness.

Thomas Hutchinson (Massachusetts Lt. Governor from 1758 to 1771; and Governor from 1771 to 1774) will always be remembered as a Royal

Governor due to the destruction of his mansion in Boston on August 26, 1765. What is not as well remembered was that Hutchinson attended the Albany Plan Congress as a delegate and was also a historian and pamphleteer.

> Nowhere had the Stamp Act come into operation on the due date of 1 November.... The choice between military enforcement and concession was discussed in the press, and since complete repeal would be an overt surrender to mob violence, the most popular form of concession being mooted was the face-saving device of suspension.[23]

The proceedings in the Virginia House of Burgesses for May 1765 have become the stuff of legend. The delegate Patrick Henry has been ascribed any number of potent verbal exhortations during debate. Unfortunately, in those pre–C-SPAN days, no one knows exactly what he did say. However, what he did say was bordering on treason as understood, if not fully treasonous. It was not written down for full public consumption until well after the events portrayed (and American independence safely secured). This led to wild variations as to what Henry uttered. Naturally, with independence achieved, looking back at the seminal events in the run up to the Revolution there was certainly cause to remember the historical record in the best way possible. This meant allowing full rein to Henry's "remembered" comments.

Language was a powerful weapon and certain Americans excelled in a new type of fire-breathing rhetoric which was to become a hallmark of the Revolutionary period. Americans would write, and they could write very well and with effect. In fact, this language is with us to this day as many of the famous words—spoken and written—form the basis of much of our learning of the Revolutionary Era.

Patrick Henry is unquestionably the most remembered American figure from this time. The Virginia Resolves, introduced by Henry on May 30, 1765, cogently laid out the premise of Americans having the same rights as native-born Englishmen and that primary among these rights was the right to be free from taxation imposed by an authority which the citizens had no say in choosing. Furthermore, they could not participate directly in this authority either.

The Virginia Resolutions passed by the House of Burgesses "asserted no more than that the first adventurers and settlers of Virginia brought with them and transmitted to their posterity all the privileges as if they had been born and were then abiding within the realm...."[24] Patrick Henry's most treasonous action item was not included in the official resolutions as confirmed by the Burgesses. In fact, even at the time of his utterances, the reporting was suspect. As the historian Laurence Gipson has written:

Chapter 6. The Stamp Act and a Congress

Patrick Henry addressing the Virginia Assembly. The Miriam and Ira D. Wallach Division of Art, Prints and Photographs: Print Collection, The New York Public Library. New York Public Library Digital Collections.

> The importance of what seems to have been the Henry resolutions—as distinguished from the official Virginia Resolves—lies in the fact that they were erroneously accepted throughout the colonies as the actual ones adopted by the House of Burgesses.[25]

The leaders in Burgesses, Peyton Randolph, Richard Bland, Edmund Pendleton, and George Wythe, ensured Henry's theatrics were not in the official version of the proceedings of the Burgesses. His histrionic theatrics were published in unofficial versions which circulated through the colonies and beyond—much to the dismay of nearly everyone.

News of the Virginia Resolves (passed in May 1765) reached London in August.[26] The general feeling was that the Resolves were a release of anger that did not represent a significant opposition to the Stamp Act. However, it became clear over the next several months, as reports came into London, that a major problem was at hand in America. By fall, stories of violence erupting in the colonies created a sense of urgency in Parliament that some remedy was needed before events spiraled out of control. Haste was imperative as the Stamp Act was scheduled to go into effect on November 1, 1765. The unavoidable slow pace of communication of the mid-eighteenth century once again proved a major factor in the escalation of events.

The reaction to the inaccurate Henry-inspired Resolutions being printed was twofold. While most responsible leaders rejected the unquestionably treasonous language, privately they rejoiced at the tone taken against Britain. The Resolutions reached fever pitch by July 1765 as news of a colony-wide congress was being planned for later that fall. The colony of Massachusetts sent out the original call for such a congress and suggested New York as a meeting place due to its midway location. Nine colonies sent representatives, making for twenty-seven attendees of the Stamp Act Congress—not in attendance were New Hampshire, Virginia, North Carolina, and Georgia.

The Stamp Act Congress convened on October 5, 1765, and after nearly two weeks of meetings, the Congress fashioned a closing statement, or declaration. Most colonial governors considered the congress illegal. John Dickinson, the most well-known attendee, was chosen to prepare a draft statement of the Congress, sort of a closing summation. Dickinson's resolution was grounded in English law, not some abstract theory on the rights of man. John Dickinson squarely staked out a position with his first entry into political writing as someone who looked to law, human law, to lay the foundation of his argument. Dickinson was not subsumed with the airy "rights of man" or "natural rights" concepts. Positive law guided Dickinson in his approach to British policy and the evolving American policy. The goal was to send the declaration to Britain. First and foremost, among the declared intents was that Americans, indeed all colonists, were entitled to the same benefits as Englishmen residing in England, namely, of not being taxed by a government in which they have no representation. Yet, overall, the Stamp Act Congress' declaration was mild compared to the original version of the by now well-known Virginia Resolutions containing Patrick Henry's histrionics. Historian Carl Becker has written: "No one was likely to be profoundly stirred by the declaration of the Stamp Act Congress, ... when the spirited Virginia Resolutions were everywhere well known."[27]

Resolved

John Dickinson, as the main author of the Stamp Act Congress Resolves, left the power of Parliament over the colonies an unanswered role. Clearly, they had a role, but what was it? "Not one of the Dickinson drafts contained a really clear statement of the power of the British legislature; they revealed considerable confusion on the subject."[28] As colonists, what exactly was their legal status? And who would determine and enforce that status? If judged by the reaction to the Stamp Act, a line had clearly

Opposite: Title page of pamphlet of the Proceedings of the Stamp Act Congress. Morristown NHP. Lloyd W. Smith archival collection MORR 9859.

AUTHENTIC
ACCOUNT
OF THE
PROCEEDINGS
OF THE
CONGRESS
HELD AT
NEW-YORK,
IN MDCCLXV,
On the SUBJECT of the
AMERICAN STAMP ACT,

———

MDCCLXVII.
[Price One Shilling.]

been crossed. However, the question remained, by whom, and when, and how, was that line determined? William Blackstone, in his highly influential *Commentaries on the Laws of England*, wrote that America was dependent on Parliament. As historian John Jezierski phrased it:

> In the *Commentaries* Blackstone classified the American colonies with Ireland since they both had been acquired by conquest or treaty. Unlike Ireland, however, the common law of England had not been made the rule of justice in the American colonies. Since they also were distinct though dependent dominions, the colonies were subject to the control of Parliament, but only if specifically mentioned or included under the general wording of the King's dominions. The American colonies, therefore, though *distinct* dominions, were *dependents* as an inferior upon the British Parliament....[29]

Clearly there was concern on the part of the colonists over the issue of taxes. While it is understandable that taxes are never a popular topic, they are nonetheless a prerequisite for a functioning government, especially in terms of providing defense. The stamp tax was ostensibly to help offset the costs of the French and Indian War and Pontiac's Rebellion. These were massive investments on the part of Britain and they predictably sought American participation. The petitions sent by the colonies:

> Emphasized the economic distress of the colonies, some the willingness of the colonies to contribute to the British Treasury if requested to do so in a regular constitutional manner, but none admitted that Parliament had a right to levy the proposed tax and most of them asserted vigorously that Parliament had no such right.[30]

Chapter 7

The Ink War on the Stamp Act

If the 1770s would be remembered for open warfare with Britain, the 1760s would be remembered for the ocean of ink deployed by both sides in the debate over revenue. Ink and paper were the weapons a decade before firearms and bayonets.

Although both American and British writers published essays, by far the largest number came from America. Many essays were published both in America and Britain and enjoyed wide readership. Most of the writers went on to become famous Founding Fathers, while some suffered historical obscurity.

American Essays

Before John Dickinson became the voice of American resistance, Boston resident James Otis wrote movingly and knowledgeably about the rights of the British colonies. Otis was born in 1725 in the small village of West Barnstable. Graduated from Harvard in 1743, he was admitted to practice law in 1748. The brother of the noted author Mercy Otis Warren, James built his law practice steadily until 1761 when he became involved in the Writs of Assistance case. Although he possessed a penetrating mind, he was prone to moments of insanity. In 1769 he was rendered permanently incapacitated mentally and spent the rest of his life in a facility. He died after being struck by lightning in 1783.

Otis' work in 1761 for the Writs cases gained him by far the most generous portion of his considerable reputation. Writs were letters or orders issued by a court in the name of the monarch commanding a law enforcement official to undertake a certain function. In the instance of the Writs of Assistance which Otis argued against, the writs were geared toward arbitrary search and seizure of colonial establishments or places of business to combat smuggling. The colonists found these writs to be too arbitrary and employed without probable cause. These abuses led eventually to protections being placed in the Constitution (fourth amendment) mandating a warrant for searches in most instances. Otis could only temporarily halt the use of writs and did little more than bring attention to the issue on a larger platform. Otis brought some organization to the long simmering objections to the writs of assistance and developed a notoriety in the process. This awareness among the colonists contributed greatly to the success in 1764 of his *The Rights of the British Colonies Asserted and Proved*.

James Otis' efforts to formulate his pamphlet, one of the first serious attempts by a colonist, was met with a fair amount of skepticism on both sides. Perhaps Otis had difficulty organizing his thoughts, maybe his latent mental issues were plaguing him, or perhaps he was genuinely conflicted; whatever the case, his pamphlet, according to historian Gordon Wood, "left its author vulnerable to criticism from all sides."[1]

Otis' pamphlet was long; indicative of a time when political discourse, or discourse in general, could go on for hours. Otis began with an overview on the origin of government. He clearly though saw one form of government as obsolete: theocracy. Otis felt a government founded among men trying to fathom God's grace was long past its prime:

> [It] is so absurd, and the world has paid so very dear for embracing it, that mankind seem at this day to be in a great measure cured of their madness in this particular; and the notion is pretty generally exploded, and hissed off the stage.[2]

Coming from Massachusetts, Otis can be understood as having grown up hearing about the failed efforts of the Puritan theocracy which settled upon the Bay colony in the seventeenth century. By Otis' time, the reputation of the Bay theocracy was not high among the new leaders emerging in the argument with Britain.

Otis was not, however, an advocate for government without some acknowledgment of God: "The power of God almighty is the only power that can properly and strictly be called supreme and absolute. In the order of a simple *democracy* or the power of the whole over the whole."[3] These two observations highlight the dichotomy of Otis's writing and provide an example as to why he was attacked from all sides.

The natural rights argument, which would fuel the Revolution in the 1770s, was a suspect basis upon which to lay a claim. Natural law, unlike the English common law, was not something that could be pointed to and referenced. Although the English constitution is unwritten, it consists of innumerable written digests that could be consulted. By contrast natural law was far more subjective in interpretation. Therefore, it was a questionable foundation upon which to construct a rational governmental system. Otis knew this, as did nearly every educated colonist of the time. John Dickinson would take a much different approach a few years after Otis with his

Letters from a Farmer in Pennsylvania. The whole concept of natural law versus positive or experiential law would bedevil the colonial leaders until the Constitution was written in 1787, finally removing natural law from the governing equation of America. In the end, for Otis, the purpose of government, any government, was "manifestly the good of *the whole*."[4]

Otis made some of his best arguments in discussing the nature of colonies in general and North America in particular. Otis pointed out that even as late as 1750, learned studies of British North America tended to lump America with the Caribbean holdings. While technically true in the sense that a colony was a colony, the comparison between America and the West Indies ended with their legal standing. The plain fact of the matter was that America had expanded beyond anything imagined a colony could be by 1765. A large, stable, growing population scattered along an immense parcel of land on the eastern seaboard. Socially, politically, economically, and culturally, the North America colonies had matured at a breathtaking pace since 1607. Some of the colonies had progressed through two or three systems of government by the time Otis wrote. America was little understood by British policy makers and even by some Americans themselves—probably even James Otis, who doubled back on many comments and observations made in his pamphlet. One simple fact was that no one, British or American, even knew how big the continent was.

Otis attempted to describe the "average" colonist for his readers, many of whom he anticipated would be Englishmen:

> If I were to define the *modern* colonists, I should say, *they are the noble discoverers and settlers of a new world*; from whence as from an endless source, *wealth* and *plenty*, the means of *power, grandeur,* and *glory*, in a degree unknown to the hungry chiefs of former ages, have been pouring into *Europe* for 300 years past....[5]

Regardless of their origin, "colonists are entitled to as *ample* rights, liberties and privileges as the subjects of the mother country."[6]

One fascinating aspect of Otis' essay is the sheer breath of the time period he covered. He clearly evinced a wide learning and moved between ancient Egypt and Rome as easily as America and Britain. Perhaps too this accounts for the mixed reaction his essay received and has received from historians. While clearly learned, he had trouble organizing or consolidating his thoughts overall to produce a cogent argument.

As he progressed through his narrative, Otis at one point detoured to the topic of slavery. Otis wrote:

> The colonists are by the law of nature free born, as indeed all men are, white or black. No better reasons can be given, for enslaving those of any color than such as Baron Montesquieu has ... given, as the foundation of that cruel slavery ...

which threatens one day to reduce both Europe and America to the ignorance and barbarity of the darkest ages.[7]

Otis was clearly no fan of slavery or of the institutional bias which allowed it to flourish.

Midway through his essay Otis made his simple point:

> Every British subject born on the continent of America, or in any other of the British dominions, is ... by the common law, and by act of parliament ... entitled to all the natural, essential, inherent and inseparable rights of our fellow subjects in Great Britain.[8]

Otis was not alone in his fear that accepting the British taxes would only lead to more onerous taxes in the future. This, among many other reasons, drove most colonists to oppose Britain's attempt at revenue generation. The arguments developed by Otis, Dickinson, and others, were at some level an academic exercise. Few American aristocrats were concerned financially about the taxes they were being asked to pay. Of course, that was not the point. Britain never saw revenue generation as punitive in the early 1760s. The Americans however, reacted as if they were punitive and were convinced more were to come. Otis, Dickinson, and others provided slogans and as we would say, sound bites, to direct against the taxation measures to defeat them.

As he began to conclude his essay, Otis inserted a line few dared to utter but all likely contemplated. He even included one, horrible, terrifying word, "independence."

> The [British] ministry, in all future generations may rely on it, that British America will never prove undutiful, till driven to it, as the last fatal report against ministerial oppression, which will make the wisest mad, and weakest strong.[9]

Otis's conclusion is a condensed overview of not just his essay, but the development of English law and government from distant times to his day. He acknowledged the seventeenth century saw two revolutions in England and some changes resulted from those events. However, according to Otis, England must respect those distant markers of human liberty enshrined in Magna Carta and subsequent legislation. The convulsions of the 1600s could in no way permit England to violate those ancient liberties. This concept would be repeated countless times over the next decade before America and Britain descended into warfare.

Thomas Whately, who introduced the tax bill of 1764, published a pamphlet in 1765 which began with the line, "The immediate defense of our colonies from imminent danger, was the sole occasion of the last war...."[10] Whately was writing from the British perspective and was completely contradicted by Franklin who testified months later. Whately's view is more in line with contemporary learning on the origins of the war rather than Franklin's. While both Whately and Franklin could be partisans to their causes, Whately had less to lose than Franklin. Whately attempted to explain in a rather long pamphlet the intricacies of British colonial policy which he claimed benefited the colonies as much as England itself. Whereas Franklin was trying to frame a concept for the benefit of the colonies in relation to taxation, Franklin only sought to promote the viewpoint of no taxation. Whately saw taxation considering overall British colonial policy. Whately viewed the colonies beyond the Appalachian Mountains purely in terms of defense and settlement. Trade was not an issue, much as Franklin had suggested in his testimony. Whately wrote: "Security both from the incursions of the *Indians*, and from the more regular attacks of other enemies, will greatly promote the settlement of the new colonies...."[11] Whately saw the Ohio Valley and regions south to the Gulf of Mexico as territory for exploitation and ownership. This could only benefit the colonies and Britain as the mother country. Whately delved deep into all colonial holdings in the Americas, not just North America. It is often forgotten that much of the Caribbean was, and still is, part of the British Empire or commonwealth as it is currently styled.

Whately's pamphlet, more of a small book really, was dense with observations on the history, present state, and possible future, of the British empire. His argument throughout was one of conciliation and encouragement to allow the system to work and if not, allow those who manage the system to amend it. Agitation and violence would serve no positive long-term purpose. Whately was a proponent of "virtual representation." This concept ensured every member of the British Empire, whether residing in England or in a colony, was represented theoretically and practically. Naturally, most American leaders balked at this concept. (Interestingly, the United States currently has territories and other designated areas which are not represented by a voting member in Congress. These unique areas have delegates, or observers, in Congress, but they do not vote on policy that affects them.)

Whately went into deep details concerning the fiscal status of Great Britain in 1765. Their national debt at the time stood at over £130,500,000; over half of which was due to the French and Indian War. According to Whately, this alone was evidence enough that taxes were a necessity, however unpleasant. Whately wrote:

> There is no occasion to accompany this account with any observations; only to state it, is to prove the necessity of an additional *American* revenue; they certainly can bear more; they ought to raise more: the subjects and the mode of new impositions are therefore the only considerations....[12]

Whately was correct that America was wealthy and could in theory afford to pay. The problem was what Franklin would point out in his testimony,

America was wealthy with credit, but not hard currency; and both the Sugar and Stamp Acts required payment in hard currency.

Whately pointed out that nearly every monarch since the first English settlement of 1607 had understood the right to tax and had indeed imposed a tax. He admitted they were primarily external taxes on American imports, but he saw the internal/external tax debate as irrelevant. Whately also neglected to point out that the Americans had been avoiding import taxes for years through smuggling. While Britain was partly at fault for not enforcing the law, Americans were just as guilty in their avoidance of the tax. Whately ended on a note of accepting that arguments aside, what is necessary is proper:

> The Parliament of *Great Britain* not only may but must tax the colonies, when the public occasions require a revenue there: the present circumstances of the nation require one now; and a Stamp Act, of which we have had so long an experience in this, and which is not unknown in that country, seems an eligible mode of taxation.[13]

Stephen Hopkins, governor of Rhode Island, and a proponent of the Albany Plan of Union of ten years previous, provided his own essay on the developing situation between America and Great Britain. Hopkins relied on the original charters provided to the early settlers indicating they would "enjoy all the rights and privileges of free-born Englishmen."[14] Like Otis, Hopkins began with a survey of the understanding of the concept of colonies with the ancient Greek and Roman writers who, according to Hopkins, saw colonies and colonists as no different from the mother country. This was especially true regarding political representation and everything that entails. Hopkins pointed to an act from the reign of King George II that declared Americans had all the rights of Great Britain "as if they, and every one of them, had been, or were born within the same."[15] From this Hopkins deduced that colonists "possess their [rights] as an inherent indefeasible right; as they and their ancestors, were free-born subjects, justly and naturally [entitled] to all the rights and advantages of the *British* constitution."[16]

For Hopkins, the argument was colonial representation in Parliament. He was convinced had the colonies been represented the Sugar Act and threatened Stamp Act would never have been passed or even contemplated. Hopkins' biggest statement was also the greatest fear of America's monied class: that should the Sugar Act and Stamp Act be assented to Britain would move to larger targets where the colonists had their true wealth. Hopkins wrote, "For it must be confessed by all men that they who are taxed at pleasure by others, cannot possibly have any property, can have nothing to be called their own; they who have no property, can have no freedom...."[17]

Hopkins ended his essay with a summary of his main points. He would go on to sign the Declaration of Independence but not the Constitution, as Rhode Island did not have a delegation in attendance; and even if they did Hopkins was dead by 1787. Hopkins, not a radical, was one of the more mature colonial leaders who challenged Britain by laying out an argument in a methodical manner.

Franklin and the American Agents

When Franklin and the other American agents met in February 1765 with the prime minister, George Grenville, he sought, along with his colleagues, to find a workable solution to the Stamp Act. The colonial agents agreed the late war had greatly increased the national debt, and they acknowledged that Britain could raise revenue through shipping taxes, but they questioned a direct, internal tax. They recommended to the prime minister that revenue should be raised through constitutional means, "which meant by a request from the king to the various colonial legislatures, who alone had the power to tax their own inhabitants...."[18]

Once the Act passed, Franklin urged Americans to make the best of the unpleasant situation. As we now know, Americans did not make the best of the situation. Instead, they agitated, incited, and inflamed one another to the point of mob violence and sedition.

> At least seven colonies, Massachusetts, Connecticut, Rhode Island, New York, Pennsylvania, Virginia, and South Carolina sent messages to their agents [in London]; Massachusetts, Rhode Island, New York, and Virginia also sent petitions to the king and Parliament.[19]

Franklin badly misjudged the Stamp Act; and he was slow to realize his mistake. Yet, once recognized, he did what he, and others, did so well; he wrote essays against the Stamp Act to assuage anger for his perceived lackluster attempt to prevent the passage of the Act. Indeed, many colonists felt Franklin secretly supported the Stamp Act. Through much of late summer and fall of 1765, Franklin sent his essays home from London for publication and distribution. Franklin's reputation would only fully recover after he appeared before the House of Commons on February 13, 1766, to strongly refute the Stamp Act.

Benjamin Franklin, London agent for the colony of Pennsylvania, and arguably the most famous American in England, took a seat in the House of Commons on February 13, 1766, to answer questions about the Sugar Act and Stamp Act. His testimony was meant to provide an American view of the situation. Had modern news services existed when Franklin took his seat in London, the world press would have fought for the most advantageous positions from which to film and broadcast. Unfortunately, those processes did not exist. Fortunately, Franklin's testimony was widely covered by the means available at the time, traditional print reporting. Franklin was grilled for three hours on questions of taxation and colonial policy. After a period of general questions, the Commons came forward with questions specifically about stamps and the mail service (of which Franklin was quite knowledgeable as Deputy Post-Master General of North America). Several questions proceeded as:

> Q. Are not the colonies, from their circumstances, very able to pay the stamp duty?
> A. In my opinion, there is not gold and silver enough in the colonies to pay the stamp duty for one year.
> Q. Don't you know that the money arising from the stamps was to be laid out in America?
> A. I know it is appropriated by the act to the American service; but it will be spent in the conquered colonies, where the soldiers are, not in the colonies that pay it.[20]

The Commons were not trying to trap Franklin, rather they genuinely wanted the colonial perspective as a way of finding their path to a conclusion of the Stamp Act which had generated so much reaction both in England and in America. The instances of mob violence particularly concerned Parliament and the king. Finding a solution to the problem was initiated in good faith on their behalf. Gathering American reaction in an official setting like the Commons was part of that initiative. The scenes of violence and mob riots were particularly disconcerting to everyone. In his marginalia replies to Alan Ramsay in 1769 (a work to be covered later), Franklin was careful to point out that not all Americans were part of the riots. In fact, he argued, most found them repulsive.

Franklin was quizzed on a variety of topics, especially trade and the evasion of tariffs put in place decades earlier. The Sugar Act of 1764 had its foundation in a 1733 act designed to protect the West Indies rum producers. The molasses left over from producing sugar was the main ingredient of rum. If the colonists were to have easy access to this by-product of sugar producing, they could make their own rum and potentially impact the rum makers in the Caribbean. Therefore in 1733, Britain placed a prohibitive duty on molasses coming into colonial North America. As to be expected, the tax was widely evaded and the Sugar Act of 1764 (also known as the Revenue Act) was imposed to strengthen already existing laws. There was nothing new about the 1764 tax. What was new was a bolder, more confident North America with colonists who saw infringement of rights everywhere they looked, much unlike 1733. Indeed, many of those who were to become famous in the 1760s arguing against taxation were either not yet born in

Chapter 7. The Ink War on the Stamp Act

THE

EXAMINATION

OF

Doctor Benjamin Franklin,

Relative to the

REPEAL

OF THE

AMERICAN STAMP ACT,

In MDCCLXVI.

MDCCLXVII.

[Price One Shilling.]

Transcript of the questioning of Benjamin Franklin by the House of Commons. Morristown NHP. Lloyd W. Smith archival collection MORR 11091.

1733 or were just toddlers. These evasions now amounted to a sizable sum, which Parliament felt justified in collecting. Naturally, Franklin was not of the same opinion. To get at the base of American discontent, Franklin was questioned concerning American attitudes towards Parliament:

> Q. In what light did the people of America use to consider the parliament of Great Britain?
> A. They considered the parliament as the great bulwark and security of their liberties and privileges, and always spoke of it with the utmost respect and veneration. Arbitrary ministers, they thought, might possibly, at times, attempt to oppress them; but they relied on it, that the parliament, on application, would always give redress....[21]

However, Franklin was quick to point out that the colonies' view of Parliament had suffered greatly due to restrictions on trade, the inability to print money, and the inability to import hard currency such as gold and silver. Following the exchange on trade and currency, the Commons asked the most pressing question:

> Q. Don't you think they [the colonists] would submit to the stamp act, if it was modified, the obnoxious parts taken out, and the duty reduced to some particulars, of small moment?
> A. No; they will never submit to it.[22]

Unequivocally, Franklin drew a line concerning the Stamp Act. It had to go; no amendment or alteration, repeal was the only solution. Furthermore, Americans would accept no tax imposed by Parliament. This is where the true issue of revenue came unglued. Franklin went from advising Americans to make the best of the stamp tax originally to testifying that Americans would accept no tax whatsoever. Within less than two years, as manifested by Franklin's viewpoints, America and England found themselves without options. Indeed, the Stamp Act Congress, "produced a set of resolutions and three petitions, to the King, the Lords, and the Commons, all denying the authority of Parliament to tax the colonies."[23]

On the most important issue, Franklin was defiant. The colonists would not submit to a tax no matter what changes were made to the act. Franklin certainly did not speak for everyone in America but he no doubt had a better grasp of feelings than members of Parliament could generate. As agent for the colony of Pennsylvania, Franklin's job was to facilitate trade and economic interests, not to be consulted on tax policy. The Commons had every reason to suspect what Franklin said anyway. A few years prior to his testimony in 1766 he had lost a bitter feud with the Penn family and John Dickinson over whether to alter the governance of the colony from family fiefdom (the process which the Penns and Dickinson supported) to a Royal colony (which Franklin supported). It was a stinging loss

Chapter 7. The Ink War on the Stamp Act

A

SPEECH,

DELIVERED IN

The HOUSE of ASSEMBLY

Of the Province of PENNSYLVANIA,

MAY 24th, 1764.

By JOHN DICKINSON, Esq;

One of the MEMBERS for the County of *Philadelphia.*

On Occasion of a PETITION, drawn up by Order, and then under Consideration, of the *House;* praying his *Majesty* for a Change of the *Government* of this *Province.*

WITH

A PREFACE.

Certe ego libertatem, quæ mihi à Parente meo tradita est, experiar; verum id frustra, an ob rem faciam, in vestra manu situm est. Quirites.
SALL. Bell. Jugurth. in Orat. MEMMII.

As for me, I will assuredly contend for that glorious plan of *Liberty* handed down to us from our ancestors; but whether my Labours shall prove successful, or in vain, depends wholly on you, my dear Countrymen!

PHILADELPHIA Printed:
LONDON,
Re-Printed for J. WHISTON and B. WHITE, in *Fleet-street.*
M.DCC.LXIV.

Pamphlet of John Dickinson's speech to the Pennsylvania House of Assembly against Franklin's plan to change the governance of the colony, 1764. Morristown NHP. Lloyd W. Smith archival collection. MORR 11552.

for Franklin who was not accustomed to losing. Even more damaging was a loss to a young upstart like John Dickinson.

This episode involving Franklin and Dickinson highlights the extent to which Franklin, long holding a cherished position in the American pantheon of Founders, could be so dramatically out of touch with prevailing attitudes. The saga began in the spring of 1764 and Franklin assumed the Speaker's chair of the Pennsylvania Assembly just before the summer break. It seemed at the time that Franklin and his followers were ascendant in their cause. However, over the summer of 1764, news spread throughout the colonies of the Sugar Act (which ultimately included the more infamous Stamp Act) and when the Pennsylvania Assembly reconvened in the fall, Franklin and his followers found themselves with an untenable situation regarding the Royal colony initiative. Dickinson and his supporters had argued the previous spring that switching from a Penn family proprietorship to a Royal colony governing structure was exceptionally risky. Dickinson had argued the potential loss of rights under a Royal colony scenario. Dickinson argued that the Pennsylvania colony had "complete religious freedom; had no oaths or tests to restrict their political rights; and could select the best qualified men for office, whatever the [beliefs] of those men might be."[24]

The move by Parliament over the summer of 1764 seemed to prove him correct—a Royal colony posed a threat to the colony's freedoms. Dickinson was convinced that:

> free government in Pennsylvania, the system of rule by the Assembly according to the Charter of Privileges of 1701, could best be protected against expanding royal power by retaining what he admitted was an iniquitous element, the political role of the Penn family.[25]

Yet, Franklin saw "little relationship between these questions and the dispute with the Penns and directed his fire against the immediate enemy [the Penn family and their supporters]."[26] Franklin still clung to his beliefs that the Penn proprietorship was antithetical to Pennsylvania's future greatness. "Other colonies had made changes in government without losing privileges, he reasoned, and the programs of the present ministry were in some cases beneficial to the colonies."[27] That fall of 1764 Franklin and his followers were turned out of the Assembly in the election and Franklin would move to have himself appointed to the position of Pennsylvania agent in London advocating on the behalf of a system (the Penn family proprietorship) that he had tried to defeat.

Dickinson, triumphant, sought to prevent the appointment of Franklin as agent. On October 26, 1764, he published a short essay entitled *A Protest against the Appointment of Benjamin Franklin as agent for the Colony of*

Pennsylvania. Dickinson and nine other colleagues set out to provide their reasons for opposing Franklin. On the top of the list of reasons—there were seven in all—was the proven fact that Franklin held great animus against the Penn family and their system of government. How, Dickinson argued, could he adjudicate on behalf of the colony? Dickinson wrote, "we believe his fixed enmity to the Proprietors will preclude all accommodation of our disputes with them, even on just and reasonable terms…."[28] Dickinson and his colleagues simply did not trust Franklin to look out for the best interests of Pennsylvania. Further, Dickinson argued that Franklin was "very unfavorably thought of by several of his Majesty's ministers; and we are humbly of opinion, that it will be disrespectful to our most Gracious Sovereign, and disadvantageous to ourselves and our constituents, to employ such a person as our agent."[29] Dickinson also attacked Franklin as a nominee for the agent position because Franklin's views had cost him an election. Why appoint someone whose views are outside the current realm of thinking on a subject? Lastly, Dickinson wrote that as Pennsylvania already had an agent in London, why did it need another? Why did the citizens of Pennsylvania have to pay for a second agent? "[I]n condescension to the members, who think another agent necessary, we will concur with them if they approve of this proposal, in paying such agent at our own expense."[30] Despite Dickinson's opposition, Franklin was appointed.

Whatever the Commons felt about Franklin as a representative of the people's feelings overall in 1766, they could have simply stopped the questioning after his definitive reply that Americans would not accept any taxation. However, the Commons moved ahead with their questions. They clearly felt Franklin was over-generalizing in his responses and he likely knew they doubted him. The questioning continued:

> Q. Have you not heard of the resolutions of this house, and of the house of lords, asserting the right of parliament relating to America, including a power to tax the people there?
> A. Yes, I have heard of such resolutions.
> Q. What will be the opinion of the Americans on those resolutions?
> A. They will think them unconstitutional, and unjust.
> Q. Was it an opinion in America before 1763, that the parliament had no right to lay taxes and duties there?
> A. I never heard any objection to the right of laying duties to regulate commerce; but a right to lay internal taxes was never supposed to be in parliament, as we are not represented there.[31]

Franklin was certainly trying to have it both ways here. You can regulate our commerce (never mentioning of course the blatant disregard of numerous duty acts imposed during the eighteenth century which were ignored by the smugglers in the colonies), but you cannot impose an internal tax such as the Stamp Act. The Sugar Act was in theory an external tax, which Franklin admitted Americans could agree with. Yet we have seen that Americans did not agree with the Sugar Act, even though it was a commerce-based tax. Franklin's testimony showed him at his best and worst. He prevaricated as necessary and used his notoriety to claim he spoke on behalf of all Americans, not just the colony of Pennsylvania. The Commons no doubt knew he was more showman than substance. America by this point was learning the fine art of political and social obfuscation which would become the hallmark of the fight against British aggression both real and imagined.

The best question the Commons could have asked was whether the colonies would consent to self-taxation and self-defense of the western frontier recently acquired in the French and Indian War. The Commons, and Franklin, knew the answer was no. America was nowhere near wealthy or organized enough to act in its own self-interest as a country. This disunity would plague America for the next twenty years before the Constitution finally got all the states literally on the same page.

The Commons were clearly interested in knowing whether the Americas had come upon this idea of constitutional interpretation since the victory and peace treaty of 1763. It is easy to see the Commons' thinking here—were the Americans attempting to have all the benefits of victory (land) without any of the practical aspects of victory (defense)? Franklin again took the middle ground as the Commons clearly anticipated he would. It is difficult to imagine that the Americans would have been as bold prior to 1763 as they now were. The colonies had, as we have seen, become rich and prosperous on the system as it existed, and any alteration would threaten that prosperity. Furthermore, the Ohio Valley and lands beyond the Appalachian Mountains were more accessible than ever before.

On balance, Franklin did a good job in not varying his message—that Americans would not pay a tax they felt was unconstitutional (never mind that most Americans had no knowledge of the English constitution) and that no option existed for the Parliament except repeal. Franklin, for all his genius, did not make the most profound arguments in part because he himself was not acquainted with the English constitution beyond the basics. His explanation of external versus internal taxation was less than commanding. In the end, he essentially warned the Commons that anything short of repeal risked rebellion, period.

However, Franklin, trying to have it both ways, assured the Commons that "the proceedings of the assemblies have been very different from those of the mobs, and should be distinguished, as having no connection with each other."[32] This was a stunning statement given the prevalence for violence in America. Franklin was aware of Patrick Henry's treasonous language in Virginia, and did he not see this as violent? Once again, while threatening rebellion on one hand, Franklin distanced himself from violence with the other hand. Franklin also reminded the Commons that the colonies did indeed raise and outfit nearly as many troops as England sent to America for the French and Indian War--a point which little impressed the Commons.

During an examination on the causes of the French and Indian War, Franklin denied American involvement in the creation of the war. Franklin responded: "As to the Ohio, the contest there began about your [British] right of trading in the Indian country, a right you had by the treaty of Utrecht, which the French infringed...."[33] Franklin was again having it both ways. The British did have trading rights via the Treaty of Utrecht, but Governor Dinwiddie of Virginia was interested in far more than peaceful trade with Indians in the Ohio Valley. Trade was profitable, but Dinwiddie wanted the land. Land speculation was a favorite pastime of America's elite and those aspiring to be elite. This was why young George Washington was sent to the Ohio Valley, and what Franklin conveniently left out of his testimony.

Franklin was a slippery customer in his testimony concerning the origins of the French and Indian War. After re-writing the opening scenes for the Commons, he continued, "they [Americans] were before in perfect peace with both French and Indian, the troops were not therefore sent for their defense...."[34] Franklin here neglected to mention the killing of Jomville by Washington and his men. Finally, Franklin, as he was in the habit of doing, compared Americans to humble farmers, who had little or no interest in the Ohio Valley. "The people of America are chiefly farmers and planters; scarce anything that they raise, or produce is an article of commerce with the Indians."[35] Again, Franklin was prevaricating. While true, colonists were farmers and planters, they were also investors and developers. And although plenty did trade with Indians, even more wanted their land.

The Stamp Act became the first demarcation, with literal battle lines being drawn, of what it meant to be an American. Patriotic groups quickly formed to try and outdo one another in displays of their American attitudes. These groups often adopted a strict interpretation of their mission to oppose the taxes being imposed by Parliament. What they created was a strict for/against paradigm which did not accept deviation or compromise. "[T]he colonial opposition to the Stamp Act centered almost exclusively on ideological and constitutional objections to 'taxation without representation.'"[36] This created a scenario where colonists had little room to maneuver and virtually eliminated all chance at compromise. Those promoting this approach certainly knew Britain would not want to dialog with recalcitrant opposition leaders. This naturally left only one alternative.

It was more than just principled objection to this theory. It was, as some have argued, an attack at the foundation of colonial life. That is, the Stamp Act was to tax title deeds, mortgages, and slaves.[37] "The Stamp Act served as a sin tax on litigation, one whose steep taxes on the legal market would make Americans think twice before taking their grievances to court."[38] Many colonists saw these as the basic building blocks of the colonial, and by extension, the community, and economy. As Claire Priest has written, "to prominent participants in business and government, each of these activities was foundational to the operation and growth of the colonial economy."[39]

Many colonists instinctively saw the Stamp Act as an encroachment on internal, colonial, economic matters. Matters which had taken decades to establish through the work of individual colonial legislatures. "By the early to mid-eighteenth century, colonial legislatures had assumed control over local institutions and the fees they charged."[40] This was one reason why the Stamp Act was so concerning; colonial leaders feared the loss of control over policy and revenue which they had come to rely on. Furthermore, issues of economic growth were a concern of the local leaders too. Excessive taxation threatened growth in ways not fully understood. With imprecise measurements of economic activity, colonial leaders inherently feared a new tax from Britain. "Radical colonists were convinced that confidence in secure property rights was absolutely necessary for investment and productivity."[41] Some of this opposition, and imposition from the British perspective, stemmed from the frontier settlements which would require stamp taxes every time land changed hands. "A central achievement of the American colonial institutions ... was to serve local communities by offering a means of recording land titles, executing land conveyances and mortgages, and resolving debt-related litigation."[42] In the hot property market of eighteenth-century America, this could discourage western land speculation, which is what the British wanted, and colonists feared. Maintaining the frontier lands in America was an expensive undertaking. Britain was aware of this and desired to restrict land settlement to contain defense costs in the aftermath of the French and Indian War. The colonists, however, saw western settlement as an economic engine which could fuel a boom for multiple trades and occupations.

In a similar sense, newspapers were more than the news. "When the struggle over the Stamp Act began in 1765 every colony, except Delaware and New Jersey, had one or more papers to speak for the contending parties and those two colonies were well served by the printers of New York and Philadelphia."[43] Newspapers were "relied upon heavily to market goods and insurance, to announce auctions and foreclosures, and to publish enacted colonial laws."[44]

Newspapers

It has been remarked more than once in this book that the slow pace of communication clearly contributed to the misunderstandings which exacerbated the American and British dispute. One means of the spread of information (and misinformation) which we would recognize was the newspaper. The newspaper would develop into a juggernaut over the next one hundred years; however, in the 1760s, the newspaper was still a relatively low-key proposition which would begin to grow in distribution and influence only in the decades to come. While these early newspapers were more propaganda sheets, rather than actual reporting, they did serve to record and disseminate information which, while of sometimes questionable accuracy, still helped to get points of reference to a wider reading audience. It should not be surprising then, as historian Arthur Schlesinger wrote,

> When the American colonists began to feel the tightening grip of imperial control after 1763, they naturally resorted to the printing-press to disseminate their views and consolidate a favorable public support.[45]

Boston, New York, and Philadelphia, three major colonial cities, were in the forefront with newspapers attempting to impact public opinion over the evolving crisis with Britain.

The distribution of newspapers was equal across the colonies. "If Delaware be considered a part of Pennsylvania, every colony but New Jersey possessed at least one journal...."[46] New Jersey could rely on newssheets from either Philadelphia or New York which fortunately shared similar views of the dispute with Britain which helped the colony from being pulled in opposite directions if the two cities had opposing views. As it was, New Jersey would become one of the most conflicted colonies/states due to its proximity to the gravitational pull of either New York or Philadelphia. While New Jersey is often called the Crossroads or the Cockpit of the American Revolution, the actual loyalties of the population during the Founding Era were much more complicated than those self-applied titles indicate.

Newspapers were particularly susceptible to the Stamp Act as they were a paper-based commodity. As such, they were required to carry the stamp for the payment of revenue. This tax would have fallen along class lines mainly; however, not just class as in financial means, but class in terms of literacy as well. Generally, those who read and had money to purchase newspapers were the better off residents in any town or city. This kept only a portion of the stamp tax from impacting the non-reading public and those without discretionary income. However, other aspects of the stamp tax required stamps on a range of legal documents which impacted virtually every colonist, literate or not, of means or not, at some point in their lives. The colonies of the 1760s were as, if not more so, litigious than currently.

Benjamin Franklin, as a famous printer, was more aware than most concerning the impact of the Stamp Act on newspapers. Writing to David Hall of the Pennsylvania Gazette on February 14, 1765, Franklin stated, "I think it will affect the printers more than anybody, as a sterling half penny stamp on every advertisement, will go near to knock up one half of both."[47] Even though Franklin was a "star witness" before the House of Commons facing questions about the Stamp Act, he was still not inclined to attempt to evade the law. As historian Schlesinger pointed out, "It is clear that Franklin was intent on making the most of a bad business" by ultimately complying with the stamp tax had not Parliament repealed it.[48]

Throughout colonial America, printers and newspaper publishers became, willfully or not, the prime network in opposition to the Stamp Act by default. Nearly every newssheet wrote and published against the tax. This served to spread the word and provided opinion pieces which were printed and reprinted (a common practice of the time). Overall, "at no later stage of the controversy with England did the colonial newspapers display so united a front."[49] As the disagreements with Britain became more confrontational into the 1770s, newspapers began to become much more partisan in their reporting—understanding that reporting in 1770 was not in the exact same sense as today. By the 1780s and 1790s, many newspapers were little better than political party mouthpieces.

During the 1760s, the newspapers were particularly adept at stoking the ill will they wanted to direct towards Britain, the Stamp Act, and stamp tax collectors specifically. Political cartoons had a field day depicting stamp tax collectors as the vermin of society. In concert with organized mobs, "it was the ceaseless propaganda of the press which kept the public mind at fever pitch, and, in large degree, galvanized the populace to action."[50] In this sense, the press was vital to the transmission of attitudes up and down the colonies north and south. "In some instance at least, the printers formed a sort of interlocking directorate with the masters of the mob."[51]

Throughout 1765, many newspapers printed editions with dark borders indicating their imminent demise under the heavy burden of taxation. This proved an effective tool in marshalling and rallying support for newspapers and against the stamp tax. Several newspapers took to altering their names after the tax officially went into use to reflect their precarious situation. Some simply ignored the tax or ceased publishing. The number of ways newspapers devised to either challenge or ignore the tax was a testament to the genuine fear and anger the tax provoked. These efforts on the part of newspapers were critical to the overall colonial movement to oppose the tax and to simultaneously keep the pressure on Britain to repeal the tax. As historian Arthur Schlesinger wrote:

> Colonial opinion must be kept a boil if the ministry were to be convinced of the necessity for repeal. Nor did the editors miss any occasion to heap further contumely on the persons of the late stamp masters.[52]

The treatment of tax collectors by the mobs is the stuff of horror stories. It is truly a depressing example of American violence that was sadly all too prevalent during the period.

The plan of opposition to the Stamp Act worked. By May 1766, when the colonies received word of the repeal of the Stamp Act, "No group in the population, however, could survey the scene with such profound satisfaction as the printing fraternity."[53] Britain deserves a fair bit of recognition in this episode for not seeking retribution against the violent mob members during the stamp tax fiasco. Britain could easily have used its power to smash America before feelings exploded into open revolt a decade later. "Little wonder that the printers emerged from the contest over the Stamp Act with an exhilarated sense of their importance to the community."[54] The colonists found newspapers to be an invaluable tool in spreading information, and misinformation, in an effort to inflame the general public one way or the other. It has been remarked several times already in this book that had communication means been better developed than the late eighteenth century was capable of, events, instead of ending in war in the 1770s, might have been susceptible to mediation and the horrors of war may have been avoided.

The Stamp Act Denied

By all accounts, King George III was caught off guard by the reaction engendered by the Stamp Act. Naturally, George, and his ministers, expected the usual grumblings and verbal opposition to new taxes. Taking the bigger perspective however, George was convinced the new tax was necessary and would be beneficial to Britain, America, and the empire overall. Britain at this point was the supreme power on the globe and it fell to George as monarch to make the most of this moment. As a new king, George clearly felt himself being tested. He was not ignorant, yet he was not an intellectual; not that the moment called for an intellectual. Rather, the moment called for a visionary, and a new king is not always a visionary. Additionally, George was a constitutional monarch, meaning he had seasoned advisors and ministers ready not only to challenge him, but more damagingly, to feed his insecurities. This was precisely what occurred over the debates on the Stamp Act when tensions were rising with America, George's "cabinet meant to make their American policy an issue of confidence" for the king.[55] George's deepest instinct was to follow Prime Minister Rockingham and amend or repeal the Stamp Act in favor of something acceptable to the Americans. The larger picture to George and Rockingham, "the raising a revenue from the colonies with a view to their good government and firm subjection to the mother country," was indisputable.[56] George was not without an awareness of the significance of the crisis the Stamp Act had created, writing to his Lord Chancellor, "this hour is perhaps one of the most critical ever known in the country."[57] The Stamp Act was repealed by Rockingham February 22, 1766. Throughout the Stamp Act ordeal, Dickinson, while clearly viewing them as unconstitutional, nevertheless was content to accept the imposition should it have occurred. He was horrified at the mob violence, especially in Boston, and felt it better to consent than descend into mob rule and treason.

On January 19, 1766, British ministers agreed to repeal the Stamp Act while simultaneously passing the Declaratory Act. The Declaratory Act declared that Parliament could legislate in all cases whatsoever for all colonies, which naturally included America. The Act further "condemned the colonial disorders, proposed punishment of the rioters, demanded compensation for victims, and asserted the full sovereignty of Parliament."[58] While the ministers agreed, they still needed to have the Declaratory Act passed by Parliament. This proved difficult even with George III supporting repeal of the Stamp Act over enforcement.

The repeal of the Stamp Act caused rejoicing and merrymaking in America and finger pointing in Britain. George III was irate over the whole fiasco and felt it was due to the petty snipping of the various parties vying for power in his relatively new reign. George attempted several cabinet level staff changes but had little success. George, for all his preparation to be king, seemingly failed in his first decade as monarch. He could not control the political life of Britain, although clearly some of the developments among the politicians were out of his control. "George's actions during repeal were, at the time and subsequently, a cause of much controversy."[59] George genuinely was conflicted over the Stamp Act and what it represented for Britain, the monarchy, and the empire. Adding to the trouble was the ever-present political situation of Whig versus Tory. The party leaders, as heirs to William Pitt, maneuvered to strengthen the empire without losing it and without antagonizing France, which was still chastened by its defeat in the Seven Years' War.

It was also clear the Parliament had conflicting impressions about America and indeed about the British constitution. So did the English merchants who, as John Dickinson warned, were being negatively impacted financially by the misdirection of Parliament's actions. Overall, what was originally seen as a win-win scenario became a lose-lose scenario. Sadly, both the Americans and British failed to find an equitable way forward.

This was a tragedy from every perspective which was exacerbated by slow communication and combusted by American radicals. Although denounced, these radicals served a purpose for the more mature American leaders. While the leaders could easily disavow something, they could just as easily watch what response the less dignified commentary and actions took. It was not until 1776 that most of these men committed treason by signing the Declaration of Independence that they finally showed their hand.

The various protestations made by individual colonial legislatures were careful to identify the line between Parliament legislating taxation and legislating other areas of governance. This was one-way colonial leaders, while abjuring the right of Parliament taxing colonies, still maintained their fidelity to Parliament. This outlook allowed the colonial leaders to accept the Declaratory Act as almost a victory. While even some British leaders acknowledged a legal difference between legislation (what colonists agreed to) and taxation (what colonists opposed), they could not bring themselves to include the word "tax" in any form in the Declaratory Act, the post–Stamp Act expression of Parliamentary power which said that Parliament could legislate in all cases whatsoever. Colonial leaders saw the lack of the word "tax" as a victory. British leaders saw "whatsoever" to include taxation without saying it.

During the debate which raged prior to the outbreak of hostilities in 1775, Americans firmly founded their argument in the English common law, not elements of some subjective natural law.[60] Thomas Jefferson, through the Declaration of Independence, sought to transfer the argument beyond the confines of common law and into the realm of miasmic natural law. The radical leaders of the 1760s, whose theatrics produced the mob violence that so clearly fanned the flames of revolt, completely discarded "the injunctions of positive law when not in accord with their aims, and resting for their justification, very much as the French did in the Revolution of 1793, on alleged violations of what they were pleased to call the Rights of Man."[61]

Chapter 8

A Farmer Pushes Back

John Dickinson

John Dickinson—The Patriotic American Farmer. The Miriam and Ira D. Wallach Division of Art, Prints and Photographs: New York Public Library Digital Collections.

In 1768, an artist named James Smither created a rendering of John Dickinson. In the image, Dickinson is posed in front of a bookcase. Over his left shoulder is a book leaning on its side on a shelf with the title *Coke on Littleton;* in his right hand is a scroll bearing the title of his *Letters from a Farmer in Pennsylvania*. Tying the print together thematically is his right elbow, which is resting on a volume labeled *Magna Carta*, a symbolic gesture on the part of the artist paying homage, via John Dickinson, to the foundation of American law and the value Dickinson himself placed on the concept of law. The title of the print is "The Patriotic American Farmer." Here, in a nutshell, is the essence of Dickinson's learning and his understanding of law within

Chapter 8. A Farmer Pushes Back

John Dickinson mansion, Dover, Delaware. Historic American Buildings Survey.

the context of the American founding. This understanding of law was especially as it pertained to the debate with Britain over taxation.

For those who venture to his home in Dover, Delaware, they find a fuller picture of course and learn the historical sound bite we have come to love and deem as necessary for understanding the past. In Dickinson's case, we learn he was the "Penman of the Revolution" (a sobriquet hotly debated by scholars as he never advocated revolution). As the Penman, he gained tremendous fame during his life for his *Letters from a Farmer in Pennsylvania*, written in 1767–1768. The letters were written in the immediate aftermath of the Stamp Act crisis, wherein Dickinson tried to show why the Stamp Act, and the associated Acts, were unconstitutional within the English legal system. Although highly educated and from American gentry, Dickinson sought to reach the "average" American (the farmer) through his writings. While Dickinson authored many other pieces as well, the *Letters* were the most famous.

Today, John Dickinson, in America's historical memory, is relegated to the ranks of a forgotten Founder; he earns this title as someone who refused to sign the Declaration of Independence. Yet, he went on to command a Pennsylvania militia with the rank of Brigadier General. Dickinson is however generally remembered, if at all, over his action regarding the Declaration. While factually true, the reasons for his refusal are still debated. Some say his Quaker beliefs kept him from making such a move. Some might say he was a coward; or that he wanted to see what more diplomacy would produce. More likely Dickinson was convinced by the legal consequences of the move toward independence. To attempt to make this picture more complete, it is worth looking at Dickinson's pre–1776 career in terms of Anglo-American relations.

Dickinson was born on November 8, 1732, in Talbot County, Maryland. He was a fourth generation American and was born the same year as George Washington. His father Samuel was already wealthy and well established by the time of John's birth, owning nearly 10,000 acres in Maryland and Delaware. The Dickinsons were owners of enslaved Africans and by 1760 the family counted around sixty at their estates.

John was the son of Samuel's second wife. When he was eight, in 1741, he moved with his family to Dover, Delaware, his father having left the Maryland estates to John's older half-brother. Young John was tutored in Dover by the Irishman William Killen who prepared him well for his future studies. Dickinson spent his late teens reading law with John Moland, a Philadelphia attorney, and showed more than enough ability for his family to invest in a legal education for him in England at the Inns of Court. This step was not taken lightly in the family. Samuel, John's father, had lost three sons in England and sending another would seem to have been almost too much of a risk. Yet, Samuel felt compelled to not just provide John the best education he could afford, he also wanted to cultivate an educated British citizen through his son. The Dickinsons were proud Englishmen. Citizenship evoked and resonated pride. Citizenship was founded, in part, in law and emotional aspects inexplicable to the rational mind. "Liberty and law, they [colonists] were persuaded, were the essential badges through which they could continue to identify themselves as English people, although living far away in climates and places that bore little physical resemblance to the country they had left behind."[1]

Before his English studies commenced, Dickinson already had a well-formed sense of why he wanted to study law. Trevor Colbourn has written that "The intellectual background which Dickinson thus provided for himself affected his political conduct."[2] In this, Colbourn looked at the aggregate of Dickinson's learning and reading. From Dickinson's accounts, it is known he bought liberally at bookstores for years—even before he went to London. Classical history and law were among the most frequent purchases. As Colbourn wrote, "Even the briefest review of his revolutionary writing indicates a wealth of historical allusion, a sincere concern for the past, and an impressive reliance upon history as a vital guide to political thought."[3] Dickinson's tastes were not unique. He shared many of the same interests as most of the best known of the Founders.

The majesty of the law was no mere idle phrase for Dickinson. Law was majestic, law was the apex of power and no individual, or group, could challenge that. Human law for human problems was the greatest antidote to inequity bankrupting the lives of those unfortunate enough to be ensnared in the unseemly black and white world of an unchallenged common law. An unbending or rigid inarticulateness to the varying and shifting arguments of lived law was what Dickinson sought to challenge.

Dickinson arrived in England December 10, 1753, after a two-month, seasick-plagued voyage. Dickinson wrote to his father on December 18, 1753, informing him of his safe arrival. With his letters of introduction, Dickinson, as he informed his father, made his way to the home of John Hanbury, who received him with "humanity and kindness."[4] Hanbury was an important Quaker merchant who moved in the highest circles and who befriended many American Quakers visiting London, or in Dickinson's case, studying in London. He was particularly solicitous of Mr. Hanbury, and he would later write to his mother that "I drop in at dinner, tea, or supper, and pass away two or three hours with the greatest happiness."[5]

Less than two weeks after arriving in England, he was admitted to Middle Temple on December 21, 1753. This was the official start of his career as a student and as he would prove over the next four years, he was devoted to the study of law and in a sense human nature as he observed it in London at the various venues he would frequent over the next several years. He realized, much like today, that an education is as much what the student puts into it as is the instruction, of which there was little at the Inns. The Inns did not provide set instruction in a classroom environment. Rather, students read legal treatises as prescribed by their tutors. Whatever they did or learned was almost entirely up to their efforts. The fact that Dickinson prospered intellectually reflects his character.

In London, he was immediately welcomed into an already existing group of American students studying at the Inns. The Inns of Court were (and are) the ancient seat of legal education for the British empire. It influenced the American legal system immensely. Dickinson's time in England was greatly enhanced by his family connections. By most accounts, Dickinson settled in nicely to the routine of a student in London. He knew several prominent families, including the sister of John Moland, his former law teacher in Philadelphia. It would be six months before he wrote of his voyage in any detail. On March 29, 1754, having previously assured his family of his health, he felt he could tell them of the arduous journey he endured and the ill effects it had on him. Writing to his mother he told her he had convalesced at Clapham, a short distance from London before undertaking anything too strenuous. He was by now in the spring fully improved and gaining weight and exercising.[6]

He wrote his first letter to his mother on January 19, 1754, a month after he arrived. He probably wanted to wait until he could write to her and let her know that he was strengthening his health and that he had accommodations and was getting on with the business at hand. He also probably wanted to form an early opinion of London before he shared it with her:

> At first entering it, I found myself in a social wilderness; as much at a loss, amongst house and men, as in the strangest forest. And in a much more disagreeable situation; for instead of peace and quietness, I was surrounded with noise, dirt, and business, all equally inconvenient; and for which I believe London may vie with any place.[7]

John Hanbury helped Dickinson maintain his accounts, which were meticulously drafted and reflected his analytical way of thinking. He listed purchases of books (in fact, it was the first purchase listed), clothing (1753–1754 was a particularly severe winter), dining, and curiously, multiple attendances at the theater. Dickinson came to thoroughly enjoy theater productions of varying topics—comedy and tragedy. He also seemed to have enjoyed visiting coffeehouses. He purchased a subscription to a library (not all libraries were free). Hanbury attested the accounting for Dickinson to his father, "I have perused this account and do not find in it any charge that tends to extravagance, or that could have been saved, in the usual way of living of such as are the students in the Temple."[8]

On March 8, 1754, in a letter to his mother, he mentioned having seen King George II at a play in London. He found the king short and unremarkable in appearance but possessing every social grace his position required.[9] Writing on February 19, 1755, again to his mother, he emphasized that he was an American above anything else. In the same letter he described the very ornate experience of meeting King George II (through a Penn family friend) and described him as "the greatest and best king upon earth."[10]

Dickinson was a scrupulous student and son. His letters are filled with seemingly outrageous, eye-rolling (by current standards) commentary about the overwhelming love and generosity his parents have heaped upon him. Yet, there is every indication he genuinely meant what he said. In one letter he wrote, "It is impossible for me to think of you without being filled with tenderness, as it is to behold the sun, without being dazzled."[11] Or, again, he sounds more like a Shakespeare sonnet when he stated: "When I reflect on the virtues of my honored parents, I love and admire them, but when I think of their goodness to me, the emotion excited in my breast has no name."[12] No doubt some of this language was due to his need for more money—a never-ending request of college students even today. There is no indication that Dickinson ever wanted for anything while in London.

John Dickinson felt angst over asking for more money while acknowledging not that the money was a burden for his wealthy parents but rather what it would return in terms of his career and future station in life. Dickinson assured his parents that even if they invested money for him to stay in London at the Inns of Court to obtain a barrister degree, the money involved would be less than his classmates spent on a non-barrister track at the Inns. He was proud of his frugality and at times boasted about it. Dickinson proudly included an itemized account list to his father at regular intervals—which was always vouched by John Hanbury.

Dickinson would be one of over two-hundred colonists who studied law at the Inns; many more colonists studied or read law with someone who had attended the Inns. As an example, James Wilson read law with Dickinson in Philadelphia after Dickinson had established himself. Wilson, who would go on to sign both the Declaration and Constitution, was someone who was on an intellectual plane with Dickinson. His appointment as one of the first six Justices to the Supreme Court in 1789 was in part due to the excellent legal education he obtained from Dickinson.

As the most recent biographer of Dickinson has written: "John Dickinson's time at Middle Temple influenced decisively not just his understanding of the manner in which the inclinations become claims, claims become rights, and rights take on a solemnity and power capable of binding a people together."[13]

In many ways, this is the entire biography of John Dickinson. Law was life. Theoretical, and practical, law was for Dickinson the leveling force that made society, government, and indeed civilization, possible. This is important, the weight of John Dickinson's argument on law leading to independence, while certainly looking to maintain "ancient" rights, sought to ensure America the ability to move those rights forward; essentially, an eternal America becoming, not a static, stationary, monolithic society. America would forever be an experiment in programs.

Law was not seen as a remedy for innocence. It was seen from the perspective of rights being vindicated upon those who violated rights of others. Innocence, often associated with weakness, was not a reason for passing laws. That did not mean it could not be employed for such purposes. So, where did John Dickinson acquire these ideals?

The crosscurrents of legal thinking swirling through the academic community when John Dickinson arrived in London were only a decade away from their greatest test in America. This cannot be overstated. The legal atmosphere within which Dickinson moved and lived in was charged with energy during these fateful years. The essence of American opposition to Britain was legal in nature and should have produced a legal solution.

Naturally, this was not to be—can we imagine an independent America that was wrought through an army of legal scholars as opposed to an army of soldiers?

The law that the young John Dickinson came to study at Middle Temple, one of the Inns of Court, was by the early 1750s and amalgam of over a millennium of written law within England. Now, that law was part of vast and growing empire spanning the globe. The secular concepts of law were soon to be put to the test at the bastion of conservative religious learning, Oxford University. There, William Blackstone would ascend the chair of legal studies as the first Vinerian Professor of Common Law. [See Appendix 8.]

Observations of a Student

Writing to his father on March 8, 1754, Dickinson expressed for the first time at length his thoughts about the Inns of Court and the study of law. Contemplating the many scholars who had gone before him at the Inns, his imagination carried him away into thinking he was perhaps occupying the rooms where the great legal scholars of the past such as Francis Bacon or Edward Coke once lived. "I tread the walks frequented by the ancient sages of the law; perhaps I study in the chambers where a Coke or Plowden has meditated. I am struck with veneration, and when I read their works, I almost seem to converse with them."[14] And in a moment of excited profusion he wrote "my breast beats for fame!"[15] He wrote he would rely on the legal greats where law was made a mockery of: In language approaching a threat, Dickinson signaled that he would not allow his conscience to be silenced in the future if bad law were the outcome of a case he was party to:

> as a man may show his learning without success, I shall continue my application that I may be able, when a wrongful judgment is given against me to produce Coke, Plowden, Ventris, Salkeid, etc., and show ... that though they gave judgment for the plaintiff, yet all the learned were of opinion with the defendant.[16]

He could also be quite mundane; writing to his father on August 15, 1754, Dickinson was less introspective about his work. He succinctly said his life was actually quite straightforward: "I rise, eat, read, and sleep, and sleeping, reading, and eating and rising repeated over and over, produce that consumption of time, which is called life."[17]

Dickinson was enamored with Coke's rival, Francis Bacon (both men died in the seventeenth century). Dickinson visited Bacon's grave and wrote movingly about the experience. On August 15, 1754, Dickinson wrote his mother a long letter bringing her up to date with his activities. In one paragraph Dickinson wrote:

> But I was lately at St. Alban's, and in a little church there called St. Michaels, I found the monument of the great Bacon. To see the greatest man that ever lived, whose mind was reckoned a counterpart to nature, whose merit raised him to the highest dignities of his country, and whose discoveries have entailed a debt on all the human race, laid in a little parish church, in a private place, and amongst ploughmen and laborers, had something in it inconceivably affecting; I was struck with grief at entering the repository of such a man.[18]

Sir Francis Bacon. The Miriam and Ira D. Wallach Division of Art, Prints and Photographs: Print Collection, The New York Public Library. New York Public Library Digital Collections.

Dickinson became so inspired by his visit to Bacon's tomb that he re-committed his life not only in service to law, but to law in service to people; in particular those who had become tangled in the intricate web of legal problems through no fault of their own. What concerned Dickinson was the use of law to promote a specific type of law—law utilized in the service of the powerful over the weak. The few over the many. Bacon may seem an unusual inspiration for this. Although a brilliant lawyer, Bacon is remembered primarily as a scientist and philosopher. While Bacon had many faults, he also had big ideas, and among them was the role of the "average" person in society, which was a reason Dickinson probably made the connection of someone of the magnitude of Bacon being laid to rest among the everyday working people. Dickinson elaborated on January 22, 1755, writing to his mother:

> For when I reflect on the end and intent of my profession, and my particular designs in it, I declare…. I find no consideration of equal weight with defending

the innocent and redressing the injured—that seems to me the noblest aim of human abilities and industry.[19]

Francis Bacon was considered the greatest intellect of his age. While he was widely admired "for wide learning, constructive thought, and clear and striking speech," Bacon also possessed an insatiable appetite for royal favor.[20] Under Queen Elizabeth I, he did not receive the posts he felt due him. It was not until King James I ascended the throne in 1603 that his pleas began to be heard. Within twenty years, he had achieved what he set out to accomplish. He also incurred the wrath of a formidable enemy, Edward Coke. Coke, another giant in English legal history (and admired by Dickinson), was far more devious than Bacon.

Aside from Coke, Bacon managed to alienate many politicians by his profuse support of King James I over the Parliament. The House of Commons, angry at the power accruing to the Crown (which would ultimately end in the death of Charles I in 1649), sought ways to limit that power. One effective option was to impeach the king's closest allies. Francis Bacon was the first to experience the power of Parliament to reduce the extended power of James. In 1621, Bacon was removed from office and fined a ruinous amount (remitted by James). Retiring to his estate, he spent the remainder of his life writing some of the most admired studies on an expanded conception of life since Aristotle—the ancient Greek philosopher he is often compared to. It is not hard to see why someone like Dickinson would be attracted by Bacon's comprehensive approach to life.

Sir Edward Coke. The Miriam and Ira D. Wallach Division of Art, Prints and Photographs: Print Collection, The New York Public Library. New York Public Library Digital Collections.

Bacon was to be remembered as a scientist and philosopher, not necessarily the traits routinely attributed to Dickinson. However, Dickinson was clearly a brilliant student and living during a time we often refer to as the Enlightenment. As such, Dickinson was not immune to the common currency of the learned community of which he was a part. This community valued the inquisitive mind which dared to reach beyond the dogma, superstition, and accretion of centuries of retrogression in learning. The materialist Bacon became a sponsor of the positivist Dickinson. Dickinson would always maintain a cherished memory of his time alone with Francis Bacon in that small church in St. Albans, England.

Humbled by this encounter with greatness, Dickinson told his mother he was inspired to do what part he was capable of for the betterment of mankind. Never being able to reach the levels of Bacon, he nevertheless wrote "I am putting in my little oar, and exerting my small strength.... This however I am convinced of, that there cannot be upon earth, a nobler employment than the defense of innocence, the support of justice, and the preservation of peace and harmony amongst men."[21] Dickinson concluded: "these are the offices of my profession, and if my abilities are but equal to my inclination, they will not be undischarged by me."[22]

Bacon and Coke would be hard acts to follow but Dickinson clearly felt inspired by their example and it would be an example that would suit him well. In his exuberance to the legacy of Bacon and Coke and their devotion to study he exclaimed, "every moment is an age, till I am immersed in study."[23] Still reeling from the enthusiasm overflowing he envisioned the majesty of the law: "I had an opportunity of seeing the grandeur and solemnity of the courts of law. The very appearance of justice is awful [awful meant here in the sense of awe inspiring]...."[24] A year later, he expanded on this idea. Writing to his father on February 19, 1755, Dickinson said:

> Laws in themselves, certainly do not make men happy, they derive all their force and worth from a vigorous and just execution of them, and where there is any obstruction to this, from ignorance, villainy, cowardice, people are just in the same condition as if they had no laws.[25]

Dickinson was well known to favor chancery law (or equity) over the common law. He attempted to conceptualize his thinking to his father:

> The laws of England abstracted from the courts of equity are like a body consisting only of bones and muscles and hearty in the greatest degree, but void of that beauty and harmony it has when clothed with flesh.... The most fond admirer of our common law must allow that there are some cases in which the severity of its rules, requires some little softening: in short that the necessities of human nature are greater than our foresight, and that the most excellent institutions

may be extremely just and reasonable in ninety nine instances, and quite defective or improper in the hundredth.[26]

Dickinson packed a great deal into this commentary. Most specifically, he posited the very real circumstances when a black and white legal code drifts into a gray area based on extenuating impacts beyond the field of the accused who is caught up in an unforgiving, and worse, unthinking, legal structure.

As he stated in his notes for the 1759 case of *Paxton v. Vandyke*, "one thing however, their ingenuity can never do [sophistry of common law barristers]—they can't prove black white."[27] The common law, for Dickinson, was incapable of such contradictions; yet the sophistry of barristers garbled the language to such an extent that it literally blurred the line between black and white, day and night. Chancery or equity court was more malleable and responsive to the actual needs of everyday litigants which is why Dickinson held an early affinity for these courts.

For Dickinson, the rule of law was paramount. Especially the one he held most important: the English right to have a say in the elected representatives and the decisions they made; especially as it related to taxation.

Dickinson identified law and government as the foundation of a nation's happiness. He relished the fact that he was able to see and hear some of the finest legal and governmental minds in the world while he attended sessions at Westminster. In addition to his studies, Dickinson often visited the courts at Westminster Hall, to view the law in action. As he wrote, "the bar is a perfect comment upon the written law."[28]

Writing to his father on April 22, 1754, Dickinson observed the quality of legal thought being exhibited in the highest courts of law in England. He wrote, "we see how the courts of justice are crowded by people who know nothing of the law; how much more agreeable then must it be to us who understand everything that is said?"[29] Dickinson experienced too much by way of simple approaches and application of the law. For him, this came close to treason. Law was for people, especially those who were on the lower end of the social divide. He continued in the letter: "I have taken as much pleasure in unraveling an intricate point of law, as a florist receives, when he sees his favorite flower, … at last unfold its glowing colors, and breath its sweet perfumes."[30]

Dickinson acknowledged the difference between reading law and practicing law. Attending the courts was the perfect companion to study: "Here we are not always plodding over books; Westminster Hall is a school of law, where we not only hear what we have read, repeated, but disputed and sifted in the most curious and learned manner…."[31]

Throughout his letters, Dickinson displayed his learning by his multiple quotes from classical writers, Alexander Pope, famous legal thinkers, and of course, Francis Bacon. In fact, some of Dickinson's letters home, when looked at overall, at times approach the design and composition of Bacon's famous essays.

When he was twenty-two years old, Dickinson showed having given great thought to the social complexities of slavery (of which he and his family practiced—in fact, his personal slave Cato was with him in London) and what can be termed the "good master" syndrome. Dickinson seemed to almost be trying to draw a distinction between the brutal and thoughtless slave owner and those like himself who, while they may have ultimately viewed slavery as abhorrent, nonetheless participated in it while trying to view the slave as an equal at least in terms of humanity. In a long passage, he began by denigrating the American popular approach which begins through education: "What a nest of vices shall we find in the education of a gentleman's son in America?"[32] From here Dickinson delved into an overview of the thinking and preparation that goes into raising a son of a slave owner. What is fascinating to witness here is how seemingly Dickinson forgot he was writing a letter to his father. All references to his father suddenly disappear and he was alone in his own world of thought writing to a wider audience. Dickinson continued:

> The little mortal can no sooner talk than he is exercising [his commands] over the black children about him; no sooner walks, but he is beating them for executing his order too slowly or wrong. What passions spring up from hence?[33]

Dickinson particularly attacked the American colonies for their approach to racial slavery, although he acknowledged that the attitude could appear anywhere, even in England. The slave owners in America "acquire a mean groveling way of thinking with the utmost pride and conceit."[34] This was one of Dickinson's first meditations on slavery and although it was not read outside his family, it no doubt proved something of an eye-opener to his relatives. (John Dickinson, unlike some Founding Fathers, would free his slaves by 1788.)

The Making of a Radical

Before his departure from England, Dickinson acknowledged that with war declared between England and France there existed a small chance of his being captured by a privateer on the high seas during his return voyage to America which he was planning for 1757. While acknowledged, he felt completely safe. "I am under no manner of apprehension about being taken."[35] Upon his return to America, Dickinson prospered in Philadelphia after opening a law practice. Further, as was fitting for his station, he entered politics and was elected to the Delaware Assembly in 1759. Early in his political career, he had the support of Quakers in Philadelphia, although he did not observe the Quaker rituals. In 1762 he was elected to the Pennsylvania Assembly and thus began his rise in politics. In the Pennsylvania Assembly Dickinson became known for his oratory and his cautious approach to matters he saw as being considered by colleagues with undue expediency.

The factors leading to the imposition of the Stamp Act in 1765 are varied and complex, as has been covered previously. After achieving victory in the French and Indian War, Britain secured its hold over the American colonies and would not know a moment's peace henceforth in America until 1783. The Sugar Act of 1764, which Dickinson later called the "First Comet" of British aggression, was uniformly opposed by the colonists. It was the first instance of organized resistance to British authority. This proved even more eventful in British colonial relations. From the beginning, the language of taxation was widely employed as were terms such as freedom and liberty— two words that have become synonymous with the American Revolution.

The Stamp Act Congress was the first time the colonial representatives came together to consider their *collective* response to Britain. This was critically important to the idea of the colonies as a unit rather than as separate, individual, units. It is the difference between the United States, and the united states. Dickinson was instrumental in drafting the Declaration of Rights and Grievances. This was his first attempt at writing for someone other than himself or his mentors. He was an instant success. His name became known by the powerful throughout the colonies.

The time that corresponds with John Dickinson's *Letters* was a period when he was out of elective politics in Pennsylvania. He had lost his support and seat by advocating for the continuation of the rule, widely viewed as corrupt, of the Penn family in Pennsylvania. One such example was his debate with Benjamin Franklin over whether to change the governance of Pennsylvania from a family fiefdom of the Penns into a Royal colony (see Chapter 7), as Franklin desired. Franklin's plan was unsuccessful, and Dickinson made a name for himself. While the descendants of William Penn inherited the semi-feudal realm of the colony of Pennsylvania, they did not inherit his idealistic outlook. His descendants over the years grew more covetous of money and status than good government and administration.

By 1765, resentment had percolated to the point where revolt was brewing against the Penn family. Benjamin Franklin was a leader of the faction which sought to have the colony removed from the family and placed under the control of the Crown as a Crown Colony. John Dickinson, although he abhorred the corruption and mismanagement, supported the Penn family with the belief they would reform their governing style.

> The ability and skill shown by Dickinson in arguing that, manifold as were the abuses from which the province suffered under the rule of deputies appointed by the proprietor, it would not be safe to risk a change in the hope that it's condition would be improved under a royal government, made a great impression at the time both on his friends and on his opponents.[36]

While Dickinson won the argument, he lost his seat in the legislature. Although this was disturbing enough, Dickinson soon turned his energy to the matter of government on a much larger scale. If anyone understood the British colonial system, it was John Dickinson. He would direct his attention to the ongoing dispute between Britain and the North American colonies. To begin his task, he developed an alter ego, a representation of an American hero, a disguise which was beyond question; John Dickinson, wealthy lawyer who studied in England at one of the most prestigious institutions in the country, became a humble farmer.

Before the transformation of John Dickinson into a humble farmer, he tested the process of protesting by writing a treatise called *The Late Regulations respecting the British Colonies on the Continent of America considered*. Written in 1765, this pamphlet considered the imposition of the Sugar Act. This first attempt by Dickinson to influence governmental policy was geared toward the English reader. In a methodical, legal approach, Dickinson sought "to prove to his English readers, ... that the metropolis would suffer far more from the enforcement of the new regulations established by the 'Sugar Act' than would the Colonies themselves."[37]

Little over a month later, Dickinson drafted a broadside called "Friends and Countrymen." This was addressed to the common citizen and attempted to distill the issue over the Sugar Act down for everyone to understand. Not just the tax, but the reasons for the colonists to oppose it on legal and historic grounds. The broadside was followed by the first of Dickinson's numerous pamphlets, the writing form that would make him famous. The first, *The Late Regulations Respecting of the British Colonies*, was widely read in America and England. Shortly after his second pamphlet, *Address to the Committee of Correspondence in Barbados*, signaled the role the wider sphere of Britain's empire would have in the global war for American independence ten years later.

Dickinson's career was enhanced greatly after the passage of the Townshend Acts and the Declaratory Act.[38] The Townshend Act of 1767 specifically prohibited the New York Assembly from meeting until they paid their share of the costs for the Quartering Act of 1765. (The Quartering Act response was akin to arguments made a century earlier by Parliament against Charles I, and which would be a complaint against George III in the Declaration and would be part of the Bill of Rights—the third amendment.) It also put duties on commodities. The Declaratory Act, 1766, as the name suggests, stated that Britain, although they had repealed some Acts, could still pass law for the colonies. At the end of 1767, Dickenson began to publish anonymously in the Pennsylvania Chronicle the letters which would make him, and his cause, unquestionably famous. Dickinson's *Letters from a Farmer in Pennsylvania,* twelve in all, captivated the American public with their accessible, yet highly researched, arguments. Dickinson did not name the collected letters the Farmer's letters, but he did refer to himself in the narrative as a farmer, and the name stuck. They were so popular, that they were printed in nineteen out of the twenty-three newspapers in the colonies. Dickinson sought to keep his authorship anonymous, but pressure mounted right from the start. Some recognized Dickinson's distinctive style and immediately asked him for clarification as to whether he was author.

It is good to pause here and reflect on where some of the more "high profile" Founders were at this point. In 1767, Thomas Jefferson was still studying law with George Wythe in Williamsburg; James Madison was still studying at the College of New Jersey; George Washington, famous for his role in the French and Indian War, was in the Virginia House of Burgesses and adjusting to life as one of the wealthiest men in the colonies after his marriage to Martha Dandridge Custis.

Dickinson became the intellectual force behind what would lead to revolt. It was Dickinson who made the revolution about liberty and freedom. These concepts were firmly grounded in British legal thinking and it was Dickinson who was able to bring the two concepts together. By 1770, the British dropped all tax demands on the colonies, except for … tea. We do not need to go into detail about what happened with that in 1773 in Boston. Except to say, what happened in Boston, and several other ports, horrified Dickinson. His opposition to Britain was not about violence. He felt there were plenty of options to deal with the British through existing channels. In fact, the riots caused him to issue another pamphlet entitled "Rusticus" wherein he opposed the Act but condemned the violence.

It was John Dickinson who first wrote about the taxation issue at length and one of the first to publish widely concerning the evolving problems with Great Britain. He made it a legal issue, not a violent issue. The Bostonians accomplished that.

Dickinson and Rights

Before examining the famous *Letters*, it will be useful to continue to delve deeper into the mind of John Dickinson and the issue of legal rights as he based his work on the bedrock of legal right. Dickinson looked at rights that sprang from a global empire whose expansion would test the meaning and limits of the rights that had marinated for over a millennium. Legal rights, moral rights, rights that exist for humans from the simple fact of being born a human being. These rights for Dickinson were pre-existing in much the same way as moral rights.

Natural rights are often associated with the period wherein John Dickinson gained his greatest fame: the Enlightenment. Dickinson is not usually associated with that movement in the same way as Jefferson or Franklin, however, there is a strain or element in his thought that could be attributed to the major philosophical development of the eighteenth century. There was a mission, a duty, ingrained through his religious faith. Rights, through law, become codified in the legal process without, or independently, of having existed outside of some human construct. Regardless of how much the original claim may have been explained through religious belief, it was the evolution of the claim into codified law that created the legal right. This would perhaps work for any number of less theologically minded law students, but Dickinson was at the least an amalgam of positive legal development as well as an adherent to the natural law components relating to the locus of rights. Indeed, Dickinson would state as much during the debates over the Constitution when he said that experience, not reason, must be our guide.

It is hard to delineate the divide between the spiritual and secular aspects of Dickinson's thinking without his own words to guide us. As has been mentioned, he did not write about his religion prior to his fame, and barely mentioned a non-denominational god in his writings from the 1750s. As such, we are left to connect the dots wherever we see a strong connection.

Legal rights can best be viewed as those rights existing "under the rules of legal systems or by virtue of decisions of suitably authoritative bodies within them."[39] Using rights to mean more than duties; rights, existing within the realm of legal requirements may or may not have distant mythical associations with something beyond the secular human realm in the eyes of some.

The concept of seeing rights as a dual construct was more of a nineteenth-century phenomena and was not something Dickinson himself wrote about. Like many of his generation, he saw rights from a duality of sources, synergistically combined to ensure the full force and effect of protection for all citizens, by and to, all citizens.

Scholars recently have tended to push the understanding or use of the modern conception of rights further back, at least to Locke, Hobbes, and Grotius, and to Gerson in the fifteenth century. All thinkers who would have been easy enough for a studious scholar like Dickinson to acquire and study.

Piecing together Dickinson's legal thought development can be compared to a game of connecting the dots. One has available his writings, the writings of those he admired, the general atmosphere of the time, and anything which might spring up. Dickinson never wrote a monologue or narrative study of law and most of what is known or deduced is a compilation of multiple sources. This is particularly the case in terms of his years as a student. Aside from his letters and notebooks, the writing of those he admired must be examined to provide further glimpses of his mind.

A Farmer Speaks

John Dickinson chose not only a pseudonym, he chose an occupation behind which to mask his identity to seriously challenge British fiscal policy. He certainly knew that after a few lines the reader would know the author was more than a humble farmer. Americans, and Europeans, had a habit of masking their identity behind pseudonyms, especially ancient Greek, and Roman figures with whom they wished to identify. Dickinson choose an American symbol (although it had Roman antecedents) for his cover. Gregory Ahern has argued that Dickinson chose the agricultural façade to represent the ancient Roman farmers of the republic who were "industrious, pious, patriotic, and courageous."[40] Thus cloaked in the ancient mantle of Republican Rome, Dickinson cultivated the image of "a gentleman farmer, a man of virtue and contemplative leisure, who understands his country's history and laws and is ready to defend them against the encroachments of arbitrary power."[41] Dickinson's choice of a farmer was well calculated. As one of Dickinson's biographers has written, the use of farmer "called forth an image of sobriety, humility, and a sagacity that touched a common chord."[42] He was aware he needed to reach the "average" American, they were the ones who needed to agree for the concerns of the wealthy to be taken seriously. Dickinson was aware the average American was no constitutional scholar. "Mr. Dickinson always possessed the rare faculty of so stating a legal proposition in ordinary language that his conclusions were as easily understood by one who was ignorant in technical matters as by the professional reader."[43]

Yet, he had to find the language to reach them at their point of processing the information he wanted to relay, which were the intricacies of British law. He knew they would be vital to any debate about the efficacy of taxation. At the beginning though, Dickinson did not foresee a major problem, certainly not one leading to mob violence and ultimately revolt.

"He neither expected nor saw the first colonial outbursts against the British duties."[44] He even recommended a friend as a stamp agent, so sure was he during the Stamp Act crisis that the tax would indeed go into effect in some measure. Dickinson's friend did not last long as a stamp agent.

The first of the *Letters from a Farmer in Pennsylvania* appeared in the *Pennsylvanian Chronicle* on December 2, 1767. The *Letters* show Dickinson fully engaged in the concepts of positive law approaches to English liberty. Dickinson saw the crisis as made in the law and felt a solution could be found in the law. "Dickinson gave form and color to the agitation in this country which brought about the repeal of [the Stamp Act], and ... first convinced the whole body of our countrymen ... that there was a legal remedy."[45] A remedy meant a solution, and Dickinson was offering a way forward without mob violence or violence of any kind. He even at points wrote directly to Englishmen:

> [The] remedy is based upon a cultivation of the spirit of conciliation on both sides, and Mr. Dickinson urges again and again upon his English readers the folly of their policy, by showing them the value of the American colonies to them, and especially how the trade and wealth of the English merchants are bound up in the adoption of a liberal policy toward us.[46]

That type of resolution would have made for a less heroic American founding and left many a modern-day historian with little to write about.

Dickinson's *Letters* differed from much of the rhetoric published during this period. Rather than mere outbursts against Parliament or the king, Dickinson showed "the legal and peaceful methods which they recommended to the Colonists in order that the..." problems facing America could be dealt with legally.[47] That was the key to Dickinson's approach—the law. The law, properly applied, in good faith, was the best antidote ever created by, and for, humanity. While this concept promoted Dickinson's brilliance, it also set the stage for his eventual decline in the eyes of his fellow Americans. As the Revolutionary generation became more and more radicalized, and more and more driven by the rights of man ideology, Dickinson maintained his commitment to law and the legal process. This adherence to established precedent would leave him isolated by 1776.

Dickinson became famous throughout America and Western Europe. Edmund Burke greatly admired the prose styling and graceful argumentation of the *Letters*. Voltaire, one of the most famous men in Europe, was also captivated by the *Letters*. When Dickinson later received a Doctor of Laws degree from the College of New Jersey at Princeton the award specifically identified him as the Pennsylvania Farmer and referenced his work. "Until Thomas Paine's *Common Sense* was published early in 1776, no other document carried such acclaim given the *Farmer's Letters*; none reached a wider public."[48]

Dickinson had struggled to determine the role of Parliament in the affairs of colonial America. The Declaratory Act, and the Townshend Duties, put America on notice that Parliament was not about to abandon its attempt to raise money from taxation. Indeed, the Townshend Duties specifically were designed to adhere to the type of tax, external, which many Americans seemed to indicate they would support. This is exactly the type of tax that Franklin had seemed to approve of in his testimony before the House of Commons. During the summer of 1767 Parliament approved the Townshend Duties to tax America according to their recommendation. While this outwardly was reasonable, the Americans were still stumped by the Declaratory Act of 1766, which as the name implies declared that Parliament could legislate in any manner, they saw fit for the colonies. To the British, who declared themselves sovereign over the colonies, they saw the Townshend Duties, as an external tax, as being lenient. Clearly, the Acts were not lenient, but the type of tax imposed did permit the British to claim to have met the Americans halfway in the increasingly bitter and hostile debate over taxation. The Townshend Duties were a major factor in the creation of Dickinson's *Letters*. "The historical and constitutional approach in challenging the Townshend Acts, backed by the citation of Greeks, Roman, and British authorities, gave peculiar strength to Dickinson's arguments."[49] The Townshend Duties differed from the Stamp Act in that they sought:

> to remove governors and other civil officers from any financial dependence on the colonial legislatures—thereby removing the one lever by which they could enforce their will on the governors and other officers of the crown.[50]

For Dickinson, the period after the Stamp Act Congress only created more questions. He observed the debate and only began to write seriously in 1765, when presumably he had come to some conclusion in his own mind. Dickinson explained his delay in starting his *Letters* series until late 1767 by saying "I waited some time, in expectation of seeing the subject treated by persons much better qualified for the task...."[51] Dickinson felt the exigency of the moment had not been captured by the pamphlets already published. Whether this was an accurate observation by Dickinson is debatable, nonetheless he did attempt to bring a new approach to his argument. Dickinson likely started to formulate the outlines of his *Letters from a Farmer in Pennsylvania* during the summer when the news of the Townshend Duties were front page stories. For nearly three years at this point Dickinson had been waging an internal debate putting his extensive learning to the test to find some solution or response to Britain. Dickinson struggled to distinguish a tax as opposed to a policy developed to regulate trade, which the colonists nearly uniformly felt Parliament had the right to do. For Dickinson though, a tax was a tax, there was no such thing as internal or external. After the

Sugar Act of 1764, the Stamp Act of 1765, the Declaratory Act of 1766, and the Townshend Duties of 1767, Dickinson felt his time had arrived. He was ready to try and explain to his countrymen what was going on in greater detail.

Dickinson wrote a dozen letters addressed to his countrymen as the humble farmer. It was clear from the start that the author behind the veil of a farmer was anything but humble. Many candidates were put forward as the true author as many attempted to discern the identity of the author. Dickinson was identified as a possible source of the letters, but he denied any role in their production. However, the first sentence, by way of geography, narrowed the likely authors down considerably, assuming the author was being truthful: "I am a *farmer*, settled, after a variety of fortunes, near the banks of the river *Delaware*, in the province of *Pennsylvania*."[52] He painted an idyllic scene of complete contentment with his situation in life: "My farm is small; my servants are few.... I have a little money at interest; I wish for no more; my employment in my own affairs is easy ... undisturbed by worldly hopes or fears, relating to myself, I am contemplating the number of days allotted to me by divine goodness."[53] He briefly relayed that he found his most rewarding time to have been spent in his library, studying and learning about history and law. He added to his study observation, which, through experience, confirmed or denied what he had studied. Dickinson, the farmer, and scholar, accepted the lessons of experience.

Dickinson wrote several times in the *Letters* about heeding the example of his ancestors during the seventeenth century in their struggle with the arbitrary power the monarchs (especially the Stuarts) attempted to claim. In fact, Dickinson ended the *Letters* series with a call to remember the English ancestors who struggled to establish their right against predatory monarchs. Dickinson wrote, "For my part, I am resolved to contend for the liberty delivered down to me by my ancestors; but whether I shall do it effectually or not, depends on you, my countrymen."[54] It was most immediately in Dickinson's historical timeline to recall the Glorious Revolution of 1688. Through this Dickinson sought to expand on the notions of power then being questioned. Dickinson was the embodiment of "[t]he notion of sovereignty current in the English-speaking world of the 1760s was hardly more than a century old."[55]

While the parallels between the seventeenth century and the eighteenth were not exact, Dickinson's point was nonetheless clear, liberty required constant surveillance and required a watchful population to ensure it was not lost. Dickinson was comparing the attempts by King James II on the rights of Englishmen to the current crisis, "Parliament's actions in the present crisis were no less arbitrary and no less of a threat to established rights" in Dickinson's mind.[56]

However, as always was the case with Dickinson, there was a proper way to advocate for one's rights. The mob violence seen by 1768 throughout the colonies was repugnant to the purpose for which the mob claimed, namely, redress of grievances over the Stamp Act. As Dickinson noted:

> Prudent judgment, guided by precedent and historical example, is the proper guide for the statesman. To act by any other lights is to risk an excessive zeal which destroys the political and social fabric on which a decent society is based.[57]

For Dickinson, social change was not social unrest. While seventeenth-century England was no one's example of social change without social unrest, Dickinson hoped for the best for the colonies.

Natural rights; ancient liberties; rights of man; these were not some Platonic abstraction seen reflected from the light of a ruler's imagination. Rather, these concepts, while nebulous, nonetheless "were generalizations made from the concrete experience of English law."[58] For Dickinson, these ideas did not exist in some inanimate ether; they were real and based on real concepts that had been established and evolved over centuries of English history. Overall, in the *Letters*, Dickinson served as historian, lawyer, etymologist, and philosopher. His learning was without question easy to discern and was on display on every page. Dickinson was so highly educated it was difficult to hide behind the façade of a farmer, but somehow, he managed to elude being formally identified for several months.

Dickinson's first letter brought forth the overlooked suspension of the New York legislature as part of the Townshend Duties. New York was specifically targeted for not paying its share of the cost of quartering troops in New York City as outlined in the 1765 Quartering Act. This was a rather draconian measure meant to punish the colony by essentially silencing its elective voice. Dickinson saw this as an affront not just to New York, but to all the colonies. Dickinson wrote:

> In my opinion they [New York] acted imprudently, considering all circumstances, in not complying so far as would have given satisfaction, as several colonies did. But my dislike of their conduct in that instance, has not blinded me so much that I cannot plainly perceive, that they have been punished in a manner pernicious to *American* freedom, and justly alarming to all the colonies.[59]

Here Dickinson saw the colonies as one, essentially an attack on one was an attack on all. If the elected voice of one colony could be silenced, then every colony could be silenced. And Dickinson went on to criticize those colonies which did comply with the Quartering Act. They, according to Dickinson, paid a tax. Perhaps it was not labeled a tax, but for Dickinson, "the expense that accrues in complying…" with any resolution is a tax.[60] If a colony had to pay money to fulfill the requirements of a Parliamentary ascent, that was a tax as Dickinson defined it.

Chapter 8. A Farmer Pushes Back

Dickinson made another interesting observation about the Quartering Act. In the language suspending the New York Legislature, the Act specifically stated that New York was being penalized for "disobedience to the authority of the BRITISH LEGISLATURE."[61] Dickinson drew the distinction (as the colonies would do over the next decade) between the Parliament and the Crown. The king could just as easily have prohibited the royal governor from allowing the legislature to gather. However, because Parliament inserted the language concerning itself as the source of the admonishment, this gave "the suspension a consequence vastly more affecting," according to Dickinson.[62] He equated this action of the Parliament to a detachment of soldiers arriving to enforce the order:

> It seems therefore to me as much a violation of the liberties of the people of that province, and consequently of all these colonies, as if the parliament had sent a number of regiments to be quartered upon them till they should comply.[63]

There was certainly some hyperbole at work here. However, in Dickinson's eyes, he made a point that a decree from Parliament could be seen as having the force of military power. In other words, enforcement by the military was inferred by a punitive act from Parliament.

Letter one effectively ended on this less than hopeful or conciliatory tone. The main difference, or one unique point, that Dickinson raised that other writers did not was the issue of Parliament applying a punitive measure as opposed to the Crown. In a way, Dickinson was asserting that Parliament had overstepped its authority or even usurped a power properly exercised by the Crown. What Dickinson did not say was whether or not the Quartering Act would have been avoided if the Crown had imposed the measures against New York and the colony had paid the required amount or if New York would have been under more of a requirement to pay the Crown's request.

In his second letter, Dickinson moved further into the Townshend Duties with the tax on paper, glass, and other items that caught his attention. He began with a now familiar refrain from nearly every pamphlet or appeal from the colonies, "The parliament unquestionably possesses the legal authority to *regulate* the trade of *Great Britain*, and all her colonies."[64] Here Dickinson failed to distinguish between the Parliament and the Crown, unless we are to presume by saying Parliament he meant specifically to exclude the Crown from the power to regulate trade. Likewise, Dickinson failed to explain, as in the first essay, the difference between external and internal and whether trade regulation was just another name for a tax.

Dickinson admitted the colonies were part of a whole, an empire, for, "there must exist a power somewhere, to preside, and preserve the connection in due order."⁶⁵ Here again, Dickinson specifically stated that power resided with the Parliament, not the Crown. This was a traditional view of English politics that Dickinson imbibed while a student at the Inns of Court during the 1750s. This structure of power was a classical Whig definition of the division of authority between the monarchy and the people (admittedly the people, like in America, were a privileged minority, a select group).

In his second letter, Dickinson did something no other essayist had yet done, he:

> looked over *every statute* relating to these colonies, from their first settlement to this time.... *All before* [the Stamp Act], are calculated to regulate trade, and preserve or promote a mutually beneficial intercourse between several constituent parts of the empire....⁶⁶

Dickinson also appended, "for the satisfaction of the reader," significant portions of the original legislation to his essay for those who wanted to see the comparisons he was making.⁶⁷ Dickinson drilled down to find his definition by arguing, "[t]he raising of revenue thereby was never intended," only the promotion of the overall economic health of the empire.⁶⁸ Therefore, if only the overall economic health through regulation of trade was intended without the raising of revenue, these early pieces of legislation were therefore not a tax.

The theme of the second letter clearly was to distinguish between raising revenue versus regulating trade. The king however, according to Dickinson, "has a right to levy money in general upon his subjects."⁶⁹ Again, Dickinson never said whether the colonies would or should pay if King George III would outright tax the colonies. In closing the second letter, Dickinson reiterated, "the single question is, whether the parliament can legally impose duties to be paid *by the people of these colonies...*" for revenue raising specifically.⁷⁰ Stated another way, as Dickinson was quick to point out, can "parliament ... legally take money out of our pockets, without our consent [?]"⁷¹

The third letter commenced with a reflection of the previous two and something of a "pep talk" to further encourage his readers. Surprisingly, Dickinson, who generally abhorred mob violence, seemingly endorsed such activity when he commented "grievances cannot be redressed without such assistance."⁷² Responding to some criticisms of the previous letters, Dickinson stated the purpose of his projected writing exercise to be:

> The meaning of them is, to convince the people of these colonies, that they are at this moment exposed to the most imminent dangers; and to persuade them immediately, vigorously, and unanimously, to exert themselves, in the most firm, but most peaceable manner, for obtaining relief.⁷³

Arguably, Dickinson could have put this in the first letter; clearly, some responses he received to the first two caused him to feel an explanation was necessary. However, could the case have been that Dickinson simply did not state his purpose clearly in the first two essays? Whatever the reasons, Dickinson clearly felt the need to explicitly provide the explanation for his letter writing project. Even while providing his reasons, he strictly enjoined his countrymen to avoid condemning the king. Dickinson's concern was that the king was an easy target for contempt. As such, attacks would mask the real reasons for the feelings the colonists felt over the taxes. And, much like his argument in the first essay supporting the king's prerogative to tax as opposed to Parliament, Dickinson warned his countrymen to be on alert against those:

> Under pretenses of patriotism, to any measures disrespectful to our sovereign and our mother country. Hot, rash, disorderly proceedings, injure the reputation of a people, as to wisdom, valor, and virtue, without procuring them the least benefit.[74]

This was more prescient than it sounded. The Revolutionary period created language that resonates to our own day. That language, then and now, was and is, often used to justify actions which under any other circumstances would be abhorrent. Dickinson understood reckless language could lead to violence, especially when that language was used by leaders to stoke the actions of unstable listeners to commit atrocities while permitting the speaker to often disown their violent actions. Yet, earlier in this same essay Dickinson wrote approvingly of "riots and tumults" as being of assistance in causes such as America faced in the 1760s.

Dickinson concluded his third letter attempting to clarify when and if violent means could be resorted to. He felt that only once all other options were tried and failed, the people at large could then be justified in some type of violent action. Dickinson never threatened violence, and only said that the people could, not should, undertake some type of physical resistance.

In the fourth letter Dickinson again responded to remarks made to an already published letter. The seemingly endless debate over an internal or external tax by Parliament was taken up by Dickinson after some readers reacted to his second letter arguing that there was no difference between internal and external taxation. In fact, Dickinson emphatically stated to those who questioned him about the two types of taxation, "To this I answer, with a total denial of the power of parliament to lay upon these colonies any '*tax*' whatever."[75] Dickinson went on to distinguish his view that any imposition "*for the sole purpose of levying money*" is unconstitutional.[76]

Dickinson had forcefully argued the difference between regulation of trade and revenue raising. He even provided transcripts of earlier pieces of legislation that he claimed proved his point that Americans had never been subject to revenue raising. Dickinson spent the rest of his fourth letter providing a history lesson on the term "tax" and how it was used and defined throughout English history. Dickinson did however take one more swipe at internal versus external taxation:

> There may be *internal* and *external* IMPOSITIONS founded on *different principles*, and having *different tendencies*; every "tax" being an imposition, tho' every imposition is not a "tax." But *all taxes* are founded on the same *principle*; and have the *same tendency*.[77]

The fifth letter showed Dickinson immediately returning to the theme of revenue raising. What could be the reason, Dickinson asked, "That in the long period of more than one hundred and fifty years, no statute was ever passed for the sole purpose of raising a revenue on the colonies?"[78] This was the technical essence of Dickinson's argument—why now? Dickinson acknowledged that Britain faced enormous challenges during the 1750s and 1760s—the Seven Years' War and the French and Indian War; a new monarch; significant personnel turnover in Parliament and with the king's ministers—these events all created havoc in the political fabric of Britain's ruling structure. Even facing such internal turmoil, Dickinson wrote, resulted in a revenue raising plan involving the colonies. "[Y]et none of them [successive governments] ever ventured to touch the *Palladium* of *American* liberty."[79]

The sixth letter saw Dickinson again responding to criticism that regulation of trade is a tax in all but name. Dickinson, who labored to draw a distinction between a revenue raising scheme and trade regulation, entered a more nuanced, or lawyer-like, response in this letter. He argued that trade regulation and taxation are more than simply different terms meaning the same thing. He made his case that regulation is just that, regulating the exports and imports to ensure, as far as possible, an equitable distribution of wealth. This differs measurably, in Dickinson's definition, from a tax designed strictly to raise revenue from the American colonies. By blending the two, and making no distinction, some Americans were falling into the thinking that drove most British politicians:

> All artful rulers, who strive to extend their power beyond its just limits, endeavor to give to their attempts as much semblance of legality as possible. Those who succeed them may venture to go a little further.[80]

Dickinson's argument was to proceed by definitions. By arguing semantics, the Americans would be no different than the British. American leaders needed to distinguish meanings and make their arguments within these meanings.

Chapter 8. A Farmer Pushes Back 149

The seventh letter was another attempt to bypass the chorus of reviewers offering significant challenges to Dickinson. His purpose was to reach the "average" American colonist, not the learned landowner capable of engaging in extended debate. Dickinson made this clear in the opening sentence, "This letter is intended more particularly for such of you, whose employments in life may have prevented your attending to the consideration of some points that are of great and public importance."[81] Following this, Dickinson returned to his overall theme of the farmer. He knew very well that those who commented on his previous letters were not farmers. They were individuals like him. Therefore, he saw it necessary to attempt to avoid those writing to challenge his letters and return to his initial task, convincing those without the leisure to attend to the considerations facing colonial America. For Dickinson, he gathered these people into the overarching category of farmer.

The seventh letter shows Dickinson writing more directly to those who were inclined to not challenge the king or Parliament. He attempted to put the argument about taxation into language which he hoped most would find agreeable. Dickinson wrote, "When any laws injurious to these colonies, are passed, we cannot suppose, that any injury was intended us by his Majesty, or the Lords."[82] As he progressed, Dickinson saw the problem in Parliament to lie not with the British public overall, but rather with a particular political party who sought to influence favor at home at the expense of the colonies. In other words, Dickinson saw the hand of party politicians at work in the passing of the Stamp Act, and the Townshend Duties.

Dickinson, midway through the seventh letter, took up a lesson on taxation from the time of the Roman Emperor Nero. He relayed how the German tribes under Roman rule retreated further into the forests to avoid arbitrary taxation from Nero and how these tribes ultimately brought their avoidance of taxation to England as the Saxons. The history lesson, while it left something to be desired, led to a basic lesson of revenue raising. If a tax is small enough to go almost unnoticed, like Nero taxing the Germans, why fight it? While this was a popular argument among some, Dickinson, found this "most alarming to me."[83] To Dickinson, the greatest threat was to the long term, not short term. A small tax could eventually be much greater than when it began. A small tax, which most would probably not notice, could be increased at intervals so that over a few years, the cumulative effect of the tax could be much greater than when it began. This is what he feared most; allowing for a small tax would only lead to incremental, however small, increases to the point where it would be untenable. This was Dickinson's whole point, once the precedent was set, there would be no turning back. Dickinson ended his seventh letter by reiterating his by now most compelling argument, taxation was taxation; trade regulation was not taxation. It was a superb use of his considerable rhetorical skills.

Letter eight was a continuation of seven. Dickinson wrote, "Regarding the act on this single principle [taxation], I must again repeat and I think it my duty to repeat, that to me it [taxation] appears to be *unconstitutional*."[84] This had been Dickinson's argument from the start. He struck a difference between trade regulation and taxation, and he maintained the difference in opposition to considerable objection that trade regulation was a tax in all but name.

Dickinson questioned the contention that the French and Indian War was for the benefit of the colonies. He agreed that Britain incurred an enormous debt in fighting the War, but that only benefited Britain, not the colonies according to Dickinson. This was a bit of a stretch on Dickinson's part. The American colonies were eager to get into the Ohio Valley and points south to the Gulf of Mexico. Yet, Dickinson still insisted this only benefited Britain, not the colonists. We have seen young George Washington eager to be part of the western land scene. In fact, he became a major investor in western lands (along with countless other Americans) after Britain's victory and his marriage to the wealthy Martha Dandridge Custis. Dickinson must have known he was on thin ice when he wrote:

> What justice is there in making US pay for "defending, protecting, and securing" THESE PLACES? What benefit *can* WE, or *have* WE ever derived *from them*? None of them was conquered *for* US; nor will "be defended, protected or secured" *for* US.[85]

Dickinson was no doubt aware that he was engaging in selective history here. The use of italic and uppercase hints that he was yelling to drown out those he knew would be responding, "hold on Mr. Dickinson," to his accusations.

Letter nine shows Dickinson refashioning earlier arguments and repackaging them with new examples of how once a tax is consented to, a society can never turn back. This was partly why Dickinson was so insistent on stopping the taxation before it ever started. His ending for letter nine summed up his admonition: "Oppose a disease at its beginning."[86]

Letter ten continued in much the same way with refashioning the same themes. Dickinson did drift into the realm of tax policy and the need to ensure it was equitable. However, by letter ten Dickinson did not feel Parliament could not get this aspect properly applied.

Dickinson began letter eleven by reiterating his earlier reiterations on the damages inherent in accepting a tax, however small, for the first time:

> I have several times, in the course of these letters, mentioned the late act of parliament, as being the *foundation* of future measures injurious to these colonies;

and the belief of this truth I wish to prevail, because I think it necessary to our safety.[87]

Near the end of the project Dickinson was obviously restating previous points as he was running out of material. Restatement was also good to ensure they were fully registered with his readers. Yet, he claimed to have good reasons for restating, and restating as many times as necessary. Dickinson felt "there [are] no other people mentioned in history, that I recollect, who have been so constantly watchful of their liberty, and so successful in their struggles for it, as the *English*."[88] He was probably not embellishing too much, and he wanted to make sure this experience was continued in the American colonies.

Again, and again in letter eleven, Dickinson repeated his greatest fear about allowing a tax, even a minor tax, to take hold:

> When an act injurious to freedom has been *once* done, and the people *bear* it, the *repetition* of it is most likely to meet with *submission*. For as the *mischief* of the one was found to be tolerable, they will hope that of the second will prove so too; and they will not regard the *infamy* of the last, because they are stained with that of the first.[89]

As he progressed through letter eleven Dickinson took an extended history tour reaching back to the Roman poet Virgil's *Aeneid*. Dickinson was fond of quoting classical writers throughout his writings when he could; he also found material in the English poet Alexander Pope.

Arrived at letter twelve, the final letter in the series, Dickinson sought his summation. He covered and recovered familiar points and arguments. He sought, in his last piece of correspondence to put the finishing touches on the case he had built in the previous eleven letters. Along the way he quoted more Classical and European literary greats, along with aspects of English law, to further punctuate his points.

This final letter was the result of not just his *Letters from a Farmer in Pennsylvania*, nor were they the result of the previous three or four years of turmoil between Britain and the American colonies over revenue generation and the rights of colonies. Nor was this final letter the result of the period beginning when Dickinson arrived back in the colonies from England. The twelfth letter, and indeed the series, were rooted in 1753 when Dickinson arrived at Middle Temple, and commenced his studies. The *Letters* read so well and were so relatively easy to comprehend because their author was so well prepared by his studies and personal inclinations.

Dickinson's *Letters* were thus far the longest sustained written argument in favor of the American position. In fact, the *Letters* would emerge as one of the longest written works for the entire Revolutionary Era. This effort rightfully made Dickinson famous (it did not take long for those who knew him to figure out he was the author). The influence of the *Letters* was immediate and long lasting. His argument, "subtle but clear," ... "contributed more than any other exposition to convince Americans that they" have the same ability of judging when their rights have been violated.[90] The *Letters* made Dickinson famous but more importantly helped to define the terms of the evolving disagreement with Britain. For many, it was Dickinson who finally put the argument into a language that made sense. "*The Farmer's Letters* thus serve as a guide to understanding the American political mind during the early days of the crises which ultimately led to the American Revolution."[91]

> Less than a month after the newspaper publication of the letters, they appeared in pamphlet form. A second edition came out in June [1768], and William and Thomas Bradford printed a third. Two Boston editions included that town's resolutions to the Farmer and Dickinson's response, and Richard Henry Lee wrote a preface to a printing in Williamsburg....[92]

CHAPTER 9

The Dimensions of Taxation

Montesquieu

Taxes, as has been alluded to earlier, have been around as long as written history. Some of the earliest extant writing deals with taxation. According to the historian Stephen Smith,

> The earliest taxes, in Mesopotamia, ancient Egypt, and elsewhere, take the forms of shares or tithes of crops or other items of production, and also obligations to provide labor services, in the form of military service or work on construction projects.[1]

Throughout history, taxation of one sort or another has been debated and argued about virtually without end. The same holds true for the 1760s. The Americans knew taxation was imperative for a government to function, however, they simply wanted to raise their own rather than having Britain do it for them. The major dispute between Britain and the American colonies was over taxation. Yet, taxation was, however much objected to, vital for affairs of state. We can, and did, and do, argue about taxation, but no one has yet come up with a viable solution for funding a government without them.

Charles-Louis de Secondat, the second baron Montesquieu, was widely acknowledged by the Founding generation as having had a significant impact on their thinking. Much like the Englishman John Locke, who was an equally tremendous influence, the Frenchman Montesquieu left behind many treatises upon his death in 1755. These works were widely disseminated and widely studied among those who undertook formal education. Those fortunate enough (almost exclusively men and those of means) to procure a formal education often went on to positions of civic responsibility. During the Founding generation these positions coincided with the struggle with Britain that began in, for our story, 1765.

Montesquieu (1689–1755) came from the Bordeaux region of France. From a minor aristocratic family, he married well and soon had the leisure to undertake expanded studies on topics he was exposed to at school—principally law, and especially ancient Roman law. Montesquieu quickly made a name for himself as a writer and academic—although he never taught—and was something of a public intellectual. In 1750, after several years work, he published his most important work, *The Spirit of Laws*. Published in two large volumes totaling over 1,000 pages, this study appeared just as many of the young men who would later be what we today call Founding Fathers were beginning or were already into their studies. The work covered an immense amount of material, among which was taxation, the endless topic of conversation in America during the 1760s.

By eighteenth-century standards, Britain was following enlightened tax policy when it implemented the Stamp Act. Montesquieu wrote that a tax on articles was the standard policy for a monarchy as Britain was. Montesquieu wrote:

> The natural tax of moderate governments, is the duty laid on merchants. As this is really paid by the consumer, though advanced by the merchant, it is a loan which the merchant has already made to the consumer. Wherefor the merchant must be considered on the one side, as the general debtor of the state, and on the other as the creditor of every individual.[2]

This was a fascinating observation made by Montesquieu wherein taxes are a community affair. Every citizen plays their role, rather than attempting to loophole their way out of their obligation.

The moderate state for Montesquieu was uniquely a place like Great Britain. By eighteenth-century standards it was an enlightened government. The arguments made by the colonists about tyranny and unconstitutional policy in the bargaining struck the British as nonsense. How could they, as an enlightened nation, be conceived as so unenlightened? This view was truly a difficult question. Leaders in England saw themselves for the most part as enlightened leaders. Arguing whether this was accurate or not, and whether they were indeed following Enlightenment principles, is beside the point. They genuinely were confused over the whole American opposition. As time went on, their view did not change.

The British elite were reading Montesquieu just as the Americans were. The fact that similar people came to such different interpretations was one of the tragedies of the 1760s. Both sides genuinely saw their perspective as the most reasonable application of not just Montesquieu, but many other theorists who produced works during what was and is known as the Age of Enlightenment.

William Blackstone and Taxation

When William Blackstone sat down to begin writing his *Commentaries on the Laws of England* in the early 1760s, he could not have imagined

Chapter 9. The Dimensions of Taxation

the world which volume one of his work, published in 1765, would face. Events moved so rapidly during the writing period of volume one that some parts seemed completely out of date.

Volume one included a chapter on the King's Revenue; essentially, this was taxation, and in 1765 the king as we know was having trouble with the taxation of his realm. Blackstone wrote in relation to taxes, Parliament has "the ancient indisputable privilege and right of the house of commons, that all grants of subsidies or parliamentary aids do begin in their house, and are first bestowed by them...."[3] The reason for this was taxes would be raised upon the people and their representatives should have the initial say in the matter.

Sir William Blackstone. The Miriam and Ira D. Wallach Division of Art, Prints and Photographs: Print Collection, New York Public Library Digital Collections.

Blackstone clearly identified Parliament, as the people's representative, as the originator of tax policy (much like the Constitution would place "all bills for raising revenue" in the House of Representatives). The understanding being that Parliament was the voice of the people assembled; here Blackstone was delineating between king and Parliament as the seat of taxation policy. This would be a topic which colonial leaders would blur the line on in their arguments against taxation during the 1760s. Historian John Jezierski wrote:

> The problem of how to qualify, undermine, or reinvent this tenet [the power of Parliament] of English political theory so solidly established by Blackstone in his *Commentaries* became the major task confronting the leaders of the American cause before the actual outbreak of the Revolution.[4]

To more fully understand the thinking which animated the colonists it is worthwhile to review Blackstone's understanding of taxation as his work was, and still is, influential in Anglo-American legal thinking. Blackstone's writing at the same time as the taxation issue was boiling over in America provides a contemporary observation of British thought of the taxation or revenue system at the highest levels of the government.

Blackstone, in chapter eight of book one of the *Commentaries*, introduced his topic as an examination of "the king's fiscal prerogatives, or such as regard his revenue … in order to support his dignity and maintain his power."[5] This money, "a portion which each subject contributes of his property," can be seen as what was necessary to run the government of the United Kingdom.[6] While the monarch had a vast amount of power, they did not acquire every portion of the revenue for their use, at least not the English monarchs. When King George III ascended the throne, he "spontaneously signified his content, that his own hereditary revenues might be so disposed of as might best conduce to the utility and satisfaction of the public…."[7] George signaled he was willing to reduce his annual income by nearly £200,000. However, as Blackstone quickly pointed out, the entire wealth of the kingdom, while kept by individuals primarily, was theoretically the property of the monarch from as far back as anyone could trace. As Blackstone wrote:

> The king is [not] at present in the actual possession of the whole of the [wealth]. Much (nay, the greatest part) of it is at this day in the hands of subjects; … which has rendered the crown in some measure dependent on the people for its ordinary support and subsistence.[8]

England by the 1760s had a complex, multi-layered approach to financing not just the life of the monarch, but the English government as well. In all, Blackstone counted eighteen separate branches that constituted the monarch's revenue by right or the ordinary revenue. Confusingly, many of these multi-layered sources of revenue also had multi-layered, hierarchical roots that ran the entire length and breadth of England which bound the country together in a web of money and entitlements. These were not considered taxes, although many American leaders during the 1760s considered them as taxes by another name. This was one of the reasons the colonists were so averse to such a blatant tax. England tried to claim some sort of ancient right of revenue on the colonies (as England had no ancient colonies). The Sugar and Stamp Acts were taxes, straightforward. For centuries England had raised revenue through entitlements. Those entitlements came from the Church, the aristocracy, the peasants, and customs duties, among others. Although traditional taxes existed in England throughout its history, they were, overall, not burdensome.

Ordinary revenue was the "proper patrimony of the crown."[9] By this mechanism, the reigning monarch had a steady, reliable income stream that would occasionally fluctuate. During these periods of fluctuation, the monarch had to resort to what Blackstone termed an extraordinary revenue;

this meant taxation. According to Blackstone, the ordinary revenue was "unknown to our early ancestors."[10] This meant that taxation, when Blackstone wrote in the 1760s, was a relatively recent formal English phenomenon. Taxation as a concept though was not an issue for Blackstone; he wrote, "the public patrimony being got into the hands of private subjects, it is but reasonable that private contributions should supply the public service."[11] By this theory, all the wealth of the kingdom belonged to the crown who allowed their subjects to utilize the money until it might be needed and a portion recalled through taxation. Naturally, this theory was not universally accepted. Blackstone reinforced his acceptance of taxation when he wrote:

> The thing therefore to be wished and aimed at in a land of liberty, is by no means the total abolition of taxes, which would draw after it very pernicious consequences, and the very supposition of which is the height of political absurdity.[12]

Everyone benefited from this system according to Blackstone, who wrote the average subject or citizen, "when properly taxed, contributes only, ... some part of his property, in order to enjoy the rest."[13]

Blackstone provided a thorough interpretation of taxation policy in a few sentences when he wrote:

> These extraordinary grants [taxes] are usually called by the synonymous names of aids, subsidies, and supplies; and are granted, we have formally seen, by the commons of Great Britain, in parliament assembled....[14]

Blackstone devoted a separate section to stamp duties. Whether he wrote this before or after the Stamp Act is unknown, but he did attempt to explain the concept.

> A fifth branch of the perpetual revenue consists in the stamp duties, which are imposed upon all parchment and paper whereon any legal proceedings, or private instruments of almost any nature are written....[15]

Blackstone highlighted what has already been pointed out; the Stamp Act targeted items utilized by nearly everyone, while greatly impacting a specific class—lawyers. Of all professions, lawyers would have been the best prepared to protect themselves against the tax and this approach was clearly what occurred in America. Blackstone's writing about stamp taxes showed they were certainly not a new concept when the Stamp Act was introduced in 1764.

Edmund Burke

Born in 1729 in Dublin, Ireland, Edmund Burke did not have the pedigree of someone destined to fill the role of philosophical patron of British colonial policy. When he came upon the scene in 1757 with his first extended philosophical study, Burke became an instant force of thought and when he entered politics in 1765, he had an immediate air of authority. His career would run over three decades during which time he encountered and analyzed every concept of British colonial policy. His period of activity ensured he had a firsthand observation of truly world-shaping events.

Burke's first foray into the world of North American settlement was during the pivotal period of the late 1750s and early 1760s. During this period, when Britain became the largest and most powerful empire on earth, Burke labored to write a history of British colonization in America and the Caribbean. The work, *An Account of the European Settlements in America*, was a well-regarded overview of British policy toward the "new world." These observations of Burke represent a contemporary line of thought relating to the American scene.

Edmund Burke. The Miriam and Ira D. Wallach Division of Art, Prints and Photographs: Art & Architecture Collection, The New York Public Library. New York Public Library Digital Collections.

Politically, Burke traced the involvement of the Crown in British North America to the reign of Charles I, who oversaw a vast insertion of the British government in the affairs of what had primarily been business concerns in North America. Part of the impetus for British involvement was the greater interest the governments of France and Spain were devoting to North America and this caught the attention of Charles I. The long history of colonial agitation between England, France, Spain, and Sweden, began in earnest in the early mid-seventeenth century.

In writing about the religious settlements that ripened into Massachusetts Bay Colony, Burke touched on a legacy of colonial government which the American leaders would refer to frequently, the right to make law. As Burke observed, "By their charter, they [New England] were empowered to establish such an order and to make such laws, as they pleased, provided they were not contrary to the laws of England."[16] This overture of independence would guide the New England colonies, unlike the southern colonies. New England would experience more agitation over the decades leading to the 1760s then their southern counterparts primarily due to the degree of self-rule afforded them early in the colonial process.

Burke was no friend of the Puritan fathers who settled New England. In fact, Burke poignantly identified their hypocrisy, writing:

> In short, this people, who in England could not bear being chastised with rods, had no sooner got free from their fetters than they scourged their fellow refugees with scorpions; though the absurdity, as well as the injustice of such a proceeding in them might stare them in the face![17]

Burke was popular in America as he tended to blame the British government for the problems which arose in the 1760s. Burke saw the root of the problem to lie with the Stamp Act of 1765. For Burke, the government had indeed altered long held policies on taxation and indeed on several initiatives. What should have been Britain's hour of glory became instead a search for meaning. "[T]here was a great deficiency of temper and judgment and ... comprehension of the public interest."[18] The government was aware of the disaffected feeling among the population. One measure Parliament thought would help re-focus the British mind at home was a greater share in the burden of taxation by inclusion of the colonies. These efforts by the authorities included enforcing any number of trade regulations that had been ignored for decades. According to Burke, this caused "some of the most valuable branches of trade [to be] driven violently from our ports."[19] Rather than relaxing the national anxiety, it only magnified it. Burke argued that taxation, and the reasoning behind it were terribly ill considered by Parliament. "Never could any argument be more insulting and mortifying to a people...."[20]

Burke felt the imposition of taxes from Parliament on the colonies to be a violation of their long-held rights to legislate for themselves. These new laws were inimical to a government which had been responsible for "all the purposes necessary to the internal economy of a free people, and provided for all the exigencies of government which arose amongst themselves."[21] Burke saw the crisis as the making of Parliament who responded recklessly to American concerns.

The Americans focused their resentment on Parliament not just because they passed the taxation legislation; Parliament was also, as every educated American leader knew, the legal seat of power. After the Glorious Revolution of 1688, the Settlement of 1689 (Bill of Rights), agreed to by all parties, "determined that in future supreme power should lie in the hands, not of the crown, but of the two houses of Parliament."²² This aspect of the 1688 Revolution, a period in English history the Americans admired, provided the polemicists of the 1760s a convenient target for their scorn and outrage. The English acts surrounding the deposition of James II and the accession of William and Mary constituted the main boundaries erected around the monarchy, Parliament, and the people. It is signified to this day whenever the British monarchy is referred to as a constitutional monarchy. While Parliament in 1689 felt secure in this recognition of their power, it was not challenged for nearly a hundred years, until the Americans questioned the Parliaments right to tax them. Certainly not every aspect of the 1689 English Bill of Rights and the ancillary legislation appealed to the colonists of the 1760s. They took only what they felt pertained to their fight against Britain and the Parliament. The Americans did a marvelous job of combining aspects of British legislation and history to produce their cobbled-together arguments to justify their opposition to British rule. The idea that the colonists had some organic, once-in-an-epoch epiphany concerning government was, while providing simple to understand history today, completely inaccurate.

Even with this new challenge, Parliament felt it had the authority it needed to challenge the Americans. "The underlying unanimity shown by the major political factions on the American question is indicative of the extent to which the principle of Parliamentary sovereignty was now accepted in England...."²³ Edmund Burke, who granted the Americans significant leeway, understood Parliament to have the authority to pass legislation, including revenue, on the colonies. What Burke and others felt was that there were more effective means to exercise that authority. Americans differed with this only in terms of revenue bills. There were few if any Americans who thought Parliament had no right whatsoever to legislate for them.

The issue however that carried the most weight with Englishmen was the issue of representation of the colonies. "[T]he majority of Englishmen who sympathized with the colonists did so on grounds of representation..." as many members of Parliament saw it as "closely linked with their efforts at home to reform parliament and make it more representative of the people."²⁴ These views were not convincing enough in America or Britain to change enough minds on the taxation issue. The two competing theories in Parliament over reform versus the 1689 statement of power in favor of Parliament were carried out with the Americans stuck in the middle. In the end, neither side gave the Americans enough attention. Historian Anne Pallister wrote, "Yet despite their differences, the colonists and their English supporters agreed in denying the unlimited sovereign authority of parliament, and they did so on grounds of both common and natural law."²⁵

Aside from the taxation debate, Burke struck the Achilles' heel of colonial American existence: racial slavery. Burke wrote the "[t]he negroes in our colonies endure a slavery more complete, and attended with far worse circumstance, then what any people in their condition suffer in any other part of the world or have suffered in any other period of time."[26] Burke identified this as a topic which not only set America out for the way it practiced slavery, but also because he felt it to be the true weak aspect of American existence. He did not prophesize a civil war, but he certainly expressed concern that without a settlement America would have a troubling future.

A Debate

After his much-publicized questioning before the House of Commons over the Stamp Act, Benjamin Franklin engaged in another type of debate over the topic of taxes, the relationship between England and the American colonies, and the nature of government. Alan Ramsay was a portrait painter and son of the Scottish poet Allan Ramsay. While the younger Ramsay became the official painter to George III and his family, he also engaged in political matters and expressed his feelings through essays which were published as pamphlets. He wrote two essays for publication on the topic of the American crisis which were bound as a large pamphlet or small book. Both essays strongly advocated the British perspective although he was accommodating of the American colonists. Benjamin Franklin, living in London, acquired a copy of the small book with the two essays and sat down in the winter of 1768 to read Mr. Ramsay's work. What resulted was a silent debate between Ramsay and Franklin wherein Franklin wrote responses to Ramsay's assertions in the margins of the book. Franklin's small book itself is an American treasure, having ended up in the library of Thomas Jefferson before being acquired by the Library of Congress where it resides to this day.

Franklin and Ramsay

Alan Ramsay's two essays combined into one small book were *Reflections Moral and Political on Great Britain and Her Colonies* and *Thoughts on the Origin and Nature of Government*. Alan Ramsay, as mentioned, was an artist who secured significant commissions including several from George III and his family. In 1767, Ramsay was appointed Principal Painter in Ordinary to the king. His writing took a traditional Tory approach to relations between Britain and the colonies, meaning a conservative alignment wherein Britain passed appropriate legislation and controlled the machinery of government with only the base minimum of autonomy for the colonies.

Ramsay put the purpose of his essay immediately in the preface in the second paragraph. Writing of himself as author in the third person, Ramsay stated, "The good of the whole British empire is what he aims at: the colonies of course must come into consideration; which has obliged him to hasten his work, that it may be printed before the Parliament decides what shall be done in regard to them."[27] This sentence by Ramsay elicited from Franklin the reply in the margins, "This is the true political idea, that every writer of these subjects should have in view. Most of them think only of the good of a Part, Britain."[28]

As an artist born in Scotland, being the son of a famous poet, the younger Ramsay felt he was qualified for political writing by the fact that "[h]aving lived many years in America, he believes he is well acquainted with the manners prevalent in most of our colonies, as well as those which are in use at home."[29] The younger Ramsay also acquired a not so subtle Tory approach to politics from his father, who was deeply immersed in Scottish political thought.

Benjamin Franklin. The Miriam and Ira D. Wallach Division of Art, Prints and Photographs: Print Collection, The New York Public Library. New York Public Library Digital Collections.

The concept of liberty to the world of the 1760s has been an overarching theme of this book. There was no one settled definition that was agreed upon at that time or indeed now. Historians and scholars of the period will provide just as many interpretations as the colonists would have. In his first essay, Ramsay was just as interested in trying to determine what liberty meant. He wrote:

> In the present disputes then on *liberty*, it seems highly necessary to understand, what should be meant by the word. Mankind is certainly formed for society, and could hardly exist long without it. We must therefore consider that degree of liberty, which men may enjoy in society.[30]

REFLECTIONS

MORAL and POLITICAL

ON

GREAT BRITAIN

AND HER

COLONIES.

LONDON:
Printed for T. BECKET and Co. in the Strand.

M.DCC.LXX.

[Price One Shilling.]

Title page of pamphlet by Alan Ramsay. Facsimile of original edition.

Ramsay was clearly laying the foundation for proposing that civil government was an absolute necessity, anything else being near anarchy. Society provided man protection for his family, unlike the case of the Native American (whom Ramsay referred to as "savages"). Ramsay argued that societies pulled together to assist one another in times of hardship and therefore were a sure benefit to humanity and worthy of regulations as government. Franklin, in marginalia notes, took Ramsay to task, pointing out his belief that the Native Americans are happier in a "state of nature" without the human constructs of government. Franklin wrote "no European who has ever tasted savage life, can afterwards bear to live in our societies."[31]

Ramsay sought to strike a chord for the betterment of society overall, and squarely came down on the side of society over the individual. This was a classic Enlightenment debate that many felt the American colonists eventually won when they achieved their independence. The Enlightenment was, if anything, the rise of the individual over the state as composed through society. Therefore, the Americans are sometimes referred to as the "children of the Enlightenment." Setting aside the efficacy of such a statement, Ramsay was not an advocate of the Enlightenment. Ramsay was much more in line with the English political writer Thomas Hobbs. Ramsay, via Hobbes, argued for a collective, a society, of mankind very reminiscent of the conceptual construction of organized religion. Ramsay summed up his thinking as:

> If then a man owes his life to the good of the society, he certainly owes affection and obedience; and the society owes him protection, with the allowance of every liberty that may be consistent with the good of *the whole*.[32]

It seems the American leaders of the 1760s truly struggled with this concept. Looking ahead to the Revolution and ultimately the Constitution, the dichotomy is clear in the two foundational documents representing those two periods. The Declaration is much more individualist, while the Constitution is much more social. It is a struggle we live with to this day.

Ramsay acknowledged that in a system of law such as existed during his lifetime, the individual, as part of a whole (society) would act in concert with the law as duly promulgated. Ramsay realized this assumption on the part of the law could be easily transgressed, thereby harming society. To prevent this, Ramsay felt political bodies like Parliament had a duty beyond duty to see to it that safeguards were established, such as courts, to deal with recalcitrant members of society. Again, Franklin left no notes to indicate his thinking, so it is difficult to gauge his response to these passages in Ramsay.

Ramsay went so far as to indicate a specific date when in his estimation England, through Parliament, moved society away from the pure concept

Chapter 9. The Dimensions of Taxation 165

of social political discourse (such as it existed in the early eighteenth century). He identified the year 1709,

> when an act was made to shut every one out of the House of Commons, who had not £300 per annum in land…. This was in effect giving honor to wealth, and had the appearance of computing the abilities and integrity of the English by their possessions.[33]

This move by Parliament shut out of the political process hundreds, if not thousands, of potential members of Parliament with the effect of lessening the overall voice of the people in English political society. As in the previous pages, Franklin made no comment on this observation by Ramsay.

Franklin seemed to revive shortly when Ramsay began to discuss revenue. Ramsay wrote:

> This Parliament and ministry have been vilified by all means possible, because they have supported pre-eminency of Great Britain over her colonies, and would oblige them to contribute to the public expense, which lies at present on Great Britain.[34]

This observation was too much for Franklin to let go without comment. In marginalia notes, he wrote, "Why should you oblige those that never were unwilling?" Franklin protested.[35] For Franklin, it was not the willingness of American colonists to pay their fair share but rather the method employed by Britain to acquire the money, direct taxation. Franklin continued, "only adhere to the ancient method of requisition, and you would have their contributions as usual."[36] Franklin accused Ramsay of rushing to judgment against the colonies, "this author decides before he examines."[37] Ramsay stated his case against the colonists claiming ancient privileges, arguing,

> The colonists, by their emissaries, keep this apprehension alive, and by applying the words of ancient laws to their case (which is totally different from the objects which those laws had in view) have made many believe that they (the Americans) have been unjustly treated.[38]

Franklin replied in his marginalia, "What ancient laws? Probably Magna Carta, the Bill of Rights [1689 English Charter of Freedom], Petition of Rights, etc."[39] Franklin was unable to identify which laws were specifically referenced by Ramsay and by extension the colonists. The amorphous "ancient laws and liberties" existed nowhere in written format. Ramsay's point however was present "ancient laws" rarely bear any resemblance to a contemporary situation, especially after hundreds of years. It is like the contemporary concept of originalism in legal thinking which seeks to impose centuries-old concepts on a modern world regardless of the absurdity involved.

Ramsay asserted that the Americans wanted to dissolve Parliament and have a new election to ensure members who were friendly to America would be more in the majority. Franklin responded this was nonsense; he argued the taxes imposed on sugar and paper would promote American industry.[40] If Americans boycotted British goods because of the tax, in theory this would boost Americans to undertake the manufacture of those boycotted goods. By ignoring the taxes, Americans would look to substitutions which would effectively bypass the taxes. These substitutions would necessarily be made or manufactured by Americans thus enhancing American manufacturing and economic independence. The promotion of American paper manufacturing would directly enrich Franklin, who was heavily invested in the nascent American papermaking industry.

Ramsay took great care to differentiate those elements in the colonies he saw as the problem. Ramsay stressed he was not combining all the colonists into some prototype colonist. Rather, he specifically singled out the mobs, the violence prone men who, goaded on by a small group of disaffected colonial leaders, destabilized the political social fabric Ramsay so valued. It was again compelling that Franklin made no response to these observations of Ramsay concerning mob violence and the prevalence of the moneyed members of society agitating for violence, or at least not trying to stop it. Ramsay knew the violence was not spontaneous. It was created from an event by loose organizers who found it an effective way of engaging those members of society who might not have had an opinion one way or the other. For all his contemporary reputation as a Founding Father, Franklin, during his life prior to the Revolution, lived a complicated existence in terms of his loyalties and especially his understanding of the American colonial psyche while he was in Europe. Franklin was in many respects more European than American.

At the beginning of part II of *Reflections Moral and Political*, Ramsay again accused the Americans of blurring the lines of law, whether ancient or modern. "The colonists found their arguments, not on the letter of the law, but (as they say) on the spirit of our constitution."[41] This was a convenient argument for the colonists. The spirit of law provided anyone arguing that premise with an immense canvas. Furthering this complication, the British law existed as a spirit. This meant the Americans could twist, tumble, and turn virtually any legal concept to their advantage. However, the Americans did have charters; written, defensible, charters from the various kings and queens over the century and a half of English settlement in North America. Ramsay pointed this out: "They allege, that having particular charters to hold assemblies, they owe no obedience to the British Parliament in point of taxes, because they are not represented there."[42] Franklin protested in the margins. Rather than go after Ramsay on legal grounds, Franklin argued that Britain had as much at stake in North America as the colonists did. Britain needed an outlet for the small manufacturer and the products produced; whether this was buttons or clothing.[43]

Ramsay turned to land ownership, the main constant of wealth and citizenship since Saxon times. Ramsay argued that the monarch, as sovereign, owned all land with subjects "owning" parcels over which they had the responsibility to defend and enhance it. By this approach, everyone, citizen, or subject, had a direct say in the prosperity of society, the body politic. Ramsay pointed to Hengist, the semi-mythical Saxon leader who ruled c. 480 CE. Hengist, the first Saxon to subdue England after the departure of the Romans, established the outlines of property ownership in place during Ramsay's time:

> Was Hengist then proprietor [after his victory] of all the lands he governed in England? No, but they were put into his hands to be divided among his people in such manner, as should best suit their manners, customs, situation, and interest.[44]

Through this, all worked towards the common good of the whole. Here too, Franklin was silent. This arrangement was predicated by Ramsay on one simple premise: "the condition of all land-tenures was fidelity and obedience to the state."[45]

Franklin took umbrage with Ramsay's reason why Britain originally wanted to colonize North America: trade with Native Americans. Franklin countered that "Great Britain as a nation had no such views. The Parliament was not at any expense [and] gave no directions and not so much as consulted about the settlement of colonies before George II's time."[46] Both Ramsay and Franklin overstated their points on this issue. However, it was the case the Britons often neglected the colonies at crucial moments, which to their feeling of independence they eventually saw as under threat during the 1760s.

One argument made by many Americans at this point was if Parliament could lay the stamp tax. However small it might be, it was, the argument ran, just the first of a long line of future increases. Ramsay addressed this by stating the colonists should take security in the fact that Parliament would not act unjustly towards the colonists with its power of taxation. "A very poor security indeed," Franklin responded in a margin notation.[47] Franklin based his responses partly on the distance between America and England, "How can we trust you, we who live at such a distance from you…?"[48] It was Franklin's contention that by taxing America, Britain was enriching itself beyond her island territory; "she is not to apply to her own advantage unjustly foreign settlements made by others."[49] This was one reason Britain specifically indicated that any revenue generated would be spent for the maintenance of the North American colonies.

Ramsay argued the transient nature of British law, stating that where Britain went its law followed. Franklin countered by writing there was "no British law in force in the colonies but what they voluntarily adopt."[50] This was a topic where neither Ramsay nor Franklin could claim certainty. Whether British law followed British conquest, much like the ancient Roman concept, was something which had been debated for centuries.

Midway through his essay, Ramsay sought to provide an overview of the colonies as he felt many English readers would not be familiar with them enough to understand the issues involved, to which Franklin agreed. He wrote, "the ignorance of Parliament in these and many other parts, shows how improperly they would undertake to tax us."[51] Franklin hit on another favorite theme of American polemicists—the fact that England, much less Parliament, had no idea what the colonies were like from either a social, economic, or political perspective.

As part of his overview, Ramsay drew distinct portraits of northern and southern colonies. Generally, southern colonies he graded lower on most categories given the presence of enslaved Africans who did most of the work, causing their owners to be less robust and healthy. Ramsay felt the power to command the enslaved in the South led the colonists to lose perspective of their place as British subjects. The prevalence of farms in the northern colonies meant that families often took children out of school early meaning few got a thorough education, according to Ramsay. To this, Franklin exclaimed, "How ignorant this writer is!"[52] Franklin identified the various universities in the colonies both north and south. Ramsay addressed the violence endemic in the colonies, leading "at present a real gentleman (in which title that of a good British citizen is included) must either hold his tongue, or speak his sentiments at risk of being insulted."[53] Franklin retorted, "A British citizen in his idea is a colonial that thinks the Parliament has a right to tax him. There is no such man."[54]

Without question a major point of debate was the role manufacturing and trade played in the overall economics of taxation. Ramsay took the British viewpoint that if revenue customs lessened in Britain, they would be forced to raise taxes in England. If the colonies had an independent trade plan, "The revenue of the customs at home would lessen, which deficiency must be made up by taxes; this would raise the price of our manufactures too high for the markets...."[55] Franklin again lamented Ramsay's lack of financial understanding, "Ignorant of the effect of taxes, they will not make manufacturing too high for foreign markets."[56]

Ramsay made a strong point concerning the interaction between the colonies themselves. The lack of coordination and willingness to work together would plague the colonies for decades to come. Ramsay noted, "the only reasonable hope the North Americans can have of preserving the

British constitution with peace and safety, is their dependence on Great Britain, which is the natural umpire when any differences arise between the colonies...."[57] Franklin agreed to some extent here. Having been a major supporter of the 1754 Albany Congress, he was aware of the inability of the colonies to work together toward a common goal. Franklin clarified Ramsay's remark by inserting that "there is only a connection, of which the king is the common link."[58] In frustration with the lack of coordination among the colonies, in response to Ramsay asserting "their division into provinces at present makes every colony a little state of itself."[59] To which Franklin replied, "There you hit it. And they will always (probably) continue so."[60] Ramsay acknowledged that given enough time and the right circumstance, "Europeans and American Britons [may] be no longer of service to each other, but as friends and allies."[61] Ramsay was essentially forecasting an independent America. To this Franklin can only concur and advise "then don't make enemies of them [the Americans] if you are wise."[62]

Ramsay made another point difficult to counter concerning Englishmen abroad, "If a British subject, by going to America has not lost any right that he possessed in Britain before he went to America, I say, if his right remains that he may exercise when he pleases, there is no injury done him."[63] Franklin here only replied that King George III was the American sovereign, and to once again ask, and distinguished between king and Parliament, why did England take "away our rights in order to subject us to Parliamentary taxation?"[64] Once again, a major American figure drew a distinction between the king and Parliament, putting the Parliament in the position of having wronged the colonies. Numerous times throughout the essay Franklin wrote in the margin to clarify Ramsay over the issue of king versus Parliament. Franklin consistently emphasized that the colonies were subordinate to the king, not Parliament; and furthermore, it was Parliament, not the king, who was attempting to tax the colonies. As an example, when Ramsay ventured to suggest the Royal Charters were being misrepresented by the colonists, or that they were out of date, Franklin concluded, "it seems high time to annul or amend them."[65]

The thought of altering existing charters to account for current conditions has a reasonable component to it. It was, and is, silly to expect a document for governing to remain unchanged over decades, much less centuries. Yet, this observation of Ramsay caused Franklin to issue a warning: "Meddle with them at your peril. No alteration can be made in those but by consent of both parties, the king and the colonists."[66] Here again, Franklin emphasized the king, not Parliament. In fact, Franklin argued that the emigrants left England specifically to remove themselves from Parliamentary control. This was an intriguing observation from Franklin. The idea that a member of a political body (England) could self-separate without some notice or purposeful legal action is hard to accept. England itself, whether the king or Parliament, never mass promoted the colonies as a place to go to leave unfavorable legislation behind. No doubt this motivated some emigrants, but the purpose for establishing colonies in North America was not to provide a neutral space for recalcitrant subjects.

Ramsay's first essay, *Reflections Moral and Political*, was not specifically geared toward the rising dispute between Great Britain and colonial North America. His second essay, however, was another matter. This essay directly approached the dispute beginning with the title, *Thoughts on the Origin and Nature of Government Occasioned by the late disputes between Great Britain and her American Colonies*.

As with the essay *Reflections*, Franklin took great care in reading and offering his response through a series of marginal notes, some nearly covering every open space on the page. Ramsay wasted no time getting to the purpose of his essay:

> The question which has been for some time agitated, *whether the legislative power of Great Britain has a right to tax its American colonies*? is of all questions the most important that was ever debated in this country.[67]

For Ramsay, this question went beyond the simple mechanics of who will pay for what, it struck at the very foundation of what to him was constituting civil government. "[F]or it is not concerning the forms of our constitution, or the share which this or that man, or this or that family, should have in the supreme government; but whether there should be any supreme government at all...."[68] For Ramsay then, the issue boiled down to governed and governor. No society can exist in anarchy—even the Americans would agree to that. Furthermore, the Americans undertook to create a supreme government through the new Constitution of 1787. After their surprise victory in the 1775–1783 Revolution, Americans had no idea what to do with victory. Many American leaders felt betrayed by the Constitution with its powerful federal government. That betrayal had its roots in the arguments brought forth in the 1760s. These men in the 1780s, who felt betrayed, were the ones telling Ramsay in the 1760s that a supreme government was a bad thing, not a good thing.

Ramsay addressed an issue that has been alluded to before, Americans never seemed to get behind one main point of contention. Or, if they came close, it would only be a temporary condition of agreement which would soon be overthrown by another objection. This was symptomatic of the larger illness of the fragmentary nature of the colonies. They were unable to speak with one voice. As mentioned, this would plague the colonies for at minimum twenty more years. Ramsay wrote this inability to coalesce around a central message was going to damn the Americans, "The great difficulty attending this American controversy is, that the question changes upon us from day to day; and what would be a complete answer one week, by the next is nothing at all to the purpose."[69] With over two dozen writers providing published arguments against Britain it was hard to know just which one spoke for America as America. This was partly the legacy of the British colonial system which, although they tended to view the colonies as one, kept them separate in practice.

It was some pages into the second essay before Ramsay even mentioned America, except for the title. The previous pages being given over to theoretical disputes on government. However, when the discussion returned to America, Ramsay immediately started with a review of the idea that Americans could not settle on the source of their opposition to British taxation. Ramsay wrote, "It is, at one time, by the law of nature. When you ask them to quote the page; or show them some law of nature which speaks the very reverse, it is then by the constitution of Britain."[70] The American leaders no doubt had difficulty trying to place their arguments within the canon of English law.

Ramsay pointed out that there were thousands of people in Britain who are not allowed to vote but still were represented in Parliament by virtual representation. To this, Franklin argued that most who do not vote are not impacted by the taxes Parliament imposed. While Franklin had a point, he was also no doubt aware that a stamp tax had been in place in England since the late seventeenth century. That tax had the same implications as in America. The only difference being those men of property in America, who would qualify to vote in Britain, could not vote in America. Those who could not vote in America due to lack of property would not have been able to vote in Britain either. Ramsay doubled down on the concept of virtual representation by tracing it back to Magna Carta in 1215.

In frustration over what he perceived as American inability to accurately make their arguments, Ramsay wrote, "one moment they desire no more than what belongs to every British subject; the next they refuse to be taxed like other British subjects...."[71] To be expected, Franklin, pen at the ready, responded, "A falsity! They were always taxed like British subjects by their own representatives, and are willing to be taxed."[72] Ramsay continued to roll his attack against American indecisiveness (he termed it "contradictory pretensions") and Franklin responded in kind.[73]

For Ramsay, there was no greater system existing in 1768 than the British legal and political system that had evolved over a millennium within the British Isles. He wrote, "Since the creation of the world there never was a more voluntary, more deliberate, more legal, and more solemn paction than that which was made by the union of the two ancient and independent kingdoms of England and Scotland...."[74] Ramsay was on solid ground here and he knew it. Franklin made no response to this assertion and frankly there was not much to say. England had the longest running constitutional government in Europe. It had one of the longest-running legal systems in the world; indeed, it was a system, however imperfect, which was admired throughout much of the world.

Ramsay concluded the *Thoughts on the Origins and Nature of Government* by stating: "that the separation of Great Britain from her American appertinencies would be destructive of the prosperity and liberty of both."[75] Franklin did not respond to this as he probably at the time agreed. Franklin did however offer his assessment of Ramsay by writing:

> This writer [Ramsay] is concise, lively, and elegant in his language, but his reasonings are too refined and paradoxical to make [an] impression on the understanding or convince the minds of his readers. And his main fact on which they are founded is a mistake.[76]

Chapter 10

Ancient Liberties

When American colonial leaders spoke of the ancient constitution or ancient liberties, they had a specific reference in mind. Primarily they, as well as Englishmen in general, saw the constitution as being something which pre-dated the Norman Conquest in 1066, yet not so ancient as to harken back to memories of the Romans in England. For the educated Englishman, the ancient constitution was to be in time around the appearance of the Saxons in approximately the fifth century CE. While there may have been some slight overlap with the Romans, the Britons were more prepared for the arrival of the German Saxons than they ever were for the Romans. Even though eighteenth-century Englishmen revered the Anglo-Saxon period as the beginning of the English constitution, it was not a constitution that was written to any great extent and it did not have a firm fixed date that it was created. Consequently, "Whether the constitution had evolved first among German tribes or later with the Anglo-Saxons after they had conquered the Britons was irrelevant to eighteenth-century constitutional thought."[1] American colonial leaders knew there was no physical constitution which Britain could produce to argue their points. This allowed the Americans the flexibility to enhance their arguments in ways that would be difficult to counter.

The 1688 Glorious Revolution and Governor Edmund Andros

The concept or idea of an ancient liberty is hard to define. Yet, when enough people can come together and fashion a liberty, of ancient lineage, and all agree to the definition, history-making events can happen. One episode impacting ancient liberties sprang into existence during the late 1680s in Boston and was frequently pointed out by colonists in the 1760s as an inspiration for their nascent movement against what they saw as the unconstitutional Sugar and Stamp Acts. While this episode was less than

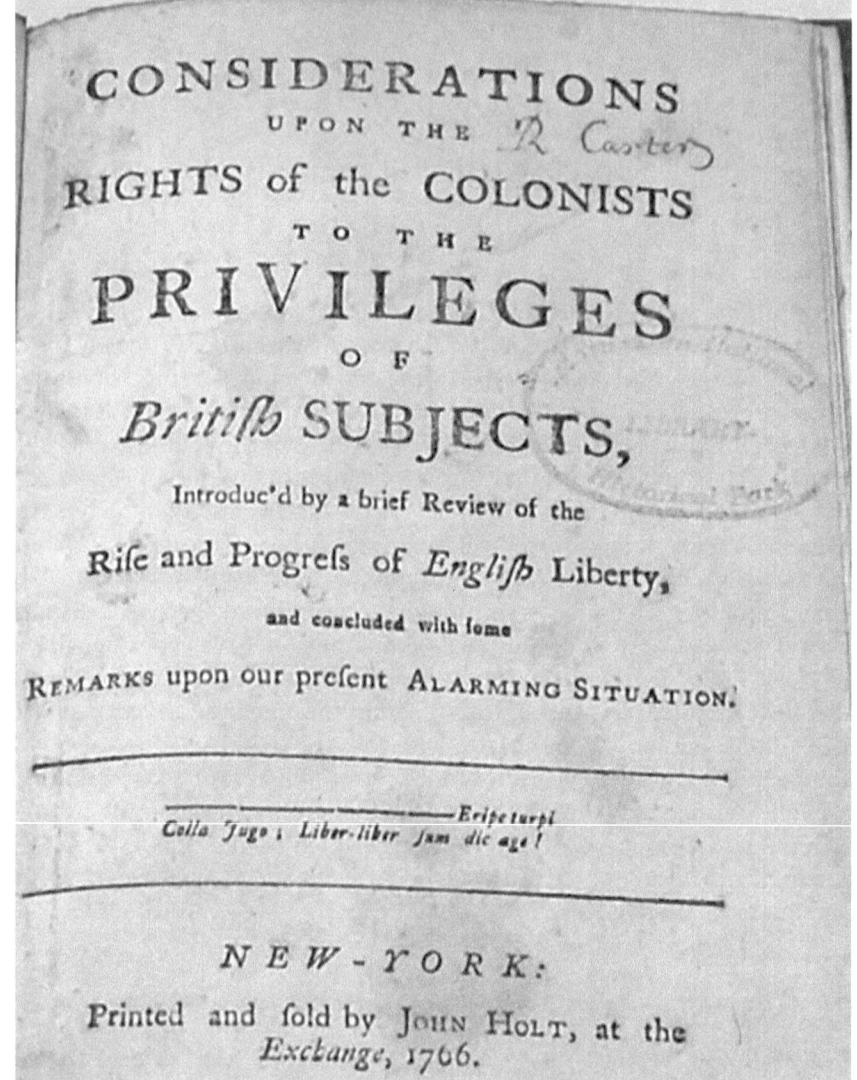

Pamphlet examining the "Rise and Progress of English Liberty" along with "Remarks upon our present alarming situation." Morristown NHP. Lloyd W. Smith archival collection MORR 11087.

one hundred years old by the time of the Stamp Act, it nonetheless fired the imagination of the colonists. "The shift of constitutional power in England from the Crown to Parliament would take time to be felt and never be fully comprehended by the colonists."[2] This observation is borne out by the conflicted nature the revolutionary generation, including John Dickinson, exhibited in their writings wherein one moment they blamed Parliament and the next moment the king. It was a confusion borne of confusion.

Throughout its history, England was no stranger to internal upheaval, revolt, and civil war. The revolt most closely related in time and consequence with the American Revolution of the 1770s was the so-called Glorious Revolution of 1688. The revolt was determined to have been glorious because it restored a Protestant monarch on the throne of England, and secondly because it saw no major military battles.

This revolution, and its American counterpart concerning the Dominion of New England, held a special place in the mythology of the American Founders. Much of the philosophy that came to represent the American Revolution had its foundation in 1688. Many of the reasons for revolt in 1775 were justified by the revolution of 1688. The romantic visions of the popular overthrow of a monarch provided sustenance to the Founders during the years of war and the years leading up to the actual conflict. While it should not be overlooked that the 1688 revolution was precipitated by religion, and the 1776 revolution had religion only as a component, it has not lost the power that a stylized mythology can have on a group of alpha white males who see in themselves elements of a bygone era. If there was any doubt of the impact of the events of 1688–1689 on Revolutionary America, it need no further explanation than to say that the 1688 revolution "greatly strengthened the established church in England, and the effect would be felt in America through the eighteenth century."[3] The establishment of a government-sanctioned church would be one of the principal rallying points in opposition to Britain. It is a bedrock feature of American identity that is with us to this day.

King James II (r. 1685–1688) struggled greatly to reimpose the Catholic faith in England after he had ascended the throne. This move was too much for the aristocracy and many of the vote-less populace to accept. "The national fears and hatred of Catholicism were inflamed by the daily landing on the British shores of miserable victims of Catholic 'toleration' as practiced in France by the most powerful sovereign in the world [King Louis XIV—a Catholic]."[4] James was deposed and William of Orange (from Holland) and his wife Mary (daughter of James II and a Protestant) were offered the throne. William and Mary were completely Protestant and for the second time in the seventeenth century a Stuart monarch was removed from the throne (James' father Charles I was the first Catholic Stuart removed). In other words, France was purging Protestant believers from the country to purify not only its religious adherents, but also its political strength. The admixture of religion to politics was a potent ingredient which the Founders eventually found no use for.

Eighty years prior to the issues of taxation in the 1760s occurred an event which many of those opposed to Britain in the 1760s would find common ground with. In 1688, English King James II was forced from his throne by William of Orange in what would become known as the Glorious Revolution. James, the last Catholic Stuart to be monarch, was deposed for not only his religion, but also his increasingly tyrannical methods. When news reached the colonies of the revolt, they quickly decided, emboldened by their fellow Englishmen, to challenge the increasingly dictatorial governor of the Dominion of New England, Edmund Andros. The Dominion, a never fully formed entity, operated internally under Andros' increasingly dictatorial methods. Many felt Andros was little better than James II as he gained more power over the Dominion. Inspired by the revolt which overthrew James, the Bostonians embarked on a mission to unseat Andros and liquidate the Dominion of New England.

The Dominion had its origins in the drafting of a royal charter for Massachusetts which came to include New Hampshire, Massachusetts, Connecticut, Rhode Island, and New Jersey. This was a period of much transition where many residents were becoming uncomfortable with the dour Puritan days of old and yearned for some freedom from the religious straightjacket many felt they walked in. To traditionalists, these were heathen days which could only bring tumult on the communities. It will be remembered that the infamous Salem Witch Trials occurred just a few years later.

Under the new organization created by the imposition of a new royal charter, the new governor-general, Sir Edmund Andros, arrived in Boston on December 16, 1686. Andros arrived at a city and colony struggling with social change and significant apprehension of the new governing arrangement. A royal charter was to replace the governing private charter Massachusetts had operated under for several decades. Andros was not unfamiliar with the American colonies. He had worked in New York and was also aware of the governing protocols from his various posts held in England. He was familiar with the working policies "of the Lords of Trade which attempted to consolidate the northern colonies into a single government for the execution of the acts of trade and defense against the encroachments of the French and Indians."[5] Andros had little discretion in his orders, "He and his advisory council were to make the laws, levy taxes, exercise justice, and command the militia."[6] These instructions were nearly perfectly designed to ensure Andros would run headlong into the relatively self-governing New Englanders. Whether consciously or not, Andros' superiors in London set him up for certain failure.

Surprisingly, the English military had never "set foot on the streets of Boston" prior to the arrival of Andros in an official manner.[7] This was clearly a surprise for the Bostonians who probably had no knowledge of what the military looked like, with the exception of the local militia. Not only were the residents dealing with elements of social change, they now had to contend with what to them seemed like an invasion. From Andros' perspective, perhaps it was an invasion. He clearly understood his mission in part was to counter the French and Indians in the very same regions which would ignite once again in the 1750s and 1760s.

Andros quickly established himself and the Dominion, and it was not long before people came to realize that "Andros was self-willed, imperious, and impatient of discussion."[8] Andros was a man of action. Boston was not a city of action. Of all the colonies in 1686, Massachusetts was known as a place of deliberation and meeting. New Englanders talked through an issue. They did not run through an issue. Like England seventy-five years later, one aspect that Andros ran afoul of with the Boston fathers was taxation. The Bostonians greatly resented "the absence of a representative assembly and the levying of taxes by the fiat of the council" headed by Andros.[9] "As Englishmen, the people preferred to levy their own taxes and considered any other method of imposition as contrary to their just rights."[10] For "just rights" it would be easy enough to replace "ancient liberties" and we would have a nearly verbatim argument and language used by the Bostonians of 1765. "The English heritage, ... and the American experience of self-government had combined to provide the rebels of 1689 with the rationale for overthrowing the Andros government."[11]

The remarkable aspect of the 1688 English revolt was the simple fact very few were injured, let alone killed. "By one spontaneous, tremendous convulsion the English nation repudiated James."[12] Yet even James II was convinced a military component would accompany the revolt against him, much as his father Charles I faced during the English Civil War of the 1640s. The extent that overwhelmingly Protestant England impacted the actions of Catholic James II cannot be underestimated. Emboldened by the mass support of Englishmen to replace James, the aristocracy worked with haste during the summer of 1688 to persuade William of Orange, husband of Mary, daughter of James, that now was the time to act. The dizzying pace of events left the military wondering exactly what was occurring.

Rumors raged wildly concerning Governor Andros especially in the grim and chaotic aftermath of Indian raids that left many New England communities terrified and transfixed on any number of conspiracy theories. As many of these theories involved Andros, it was clear his term as governor was nearing its end one way or another. "When news of William and Mary's accession arrived, it required little to persuade the people that Andros must be imprisoned if his plans were to be thwarted."[13] The conspiracies that, rightly or wrongly, swirled around Andros were impossible to overcome. It will be recalled that 1689, when Andros was deposed, was just three years before the Salem Witch Trials, one of the most tragic conspiracy theories ever to stalk America. To say the region was awash with dark conspiracies is an understatement.

As events progressed, and Bostonians became more agitated by the undertakings of their new governor, influential minister Increase Mather went to England to plead with James II to have Andros recalled. Unfortunately, James II was facing his own issues and relinquished the throne in November 1688, before any real decision could be provided on Andros. It was uncertain whether James II even was concerned about the complaints of the New Englanders. However, Mather was not unsuccessful in his efforts. "After three years of negotiations with James II, the Parliament, and finally William III, Increase Mather was able to obtain a new charter for Massachusetts."[14] Mather's new charter reflected the change in Massachusetts to a Royal colony, which did not please everyone in the colony. However, the new charter was a vast improvement on Andros. Mather had scored a win in his eyes. "According to Mather, the Revolution of 1689 had succeeded beyond all expectations. The new charter was better than the old and would protect the residents of the Bay colony from any repetition of the Dominion tyranny."[15] Mather's account of his journey to England and his interpretation of the new charter held sway over Massachusetts till 1765 when the political leaders, raised on stories of the 1689 Revolution and the new charter, set out to oppose what they saw as a new challenge to their liberties as embodied in the 1691 charter. "The influence of the first American Revolution on the second cannot be measured, but it is clear that it existed."[16]

Once the news of James' overthrow was received in Boston, there was great rejoicing and much excitement. "[T]he arbitrary quality of royal administration faded; never again was there an attempt to rule without a colonial legislature...."[17] On April 18, 1689, not quite two and a half years after his arrival, Andros was deposed. "The immediate result of the uprising of April 18, 1689 was a statement of what the rebels regarded as their rights as English subjects."[18]

As historian Charles Andrews has written:

> [T]he leaders in the city, including many members of Andros's council, supported by the people of Boston and its neighborhood, rose in revolt, overthrew the government of Andros, and brought tumbling down the whole structure of the Dominion of New England, which had never from the beginning had any real or stable foundation.[19]

The other colonies in the Dominion "followed the example of Massachusetts, and miniature revolutions took place..." in a successful effort to remove the Andros regime.[20] The new king, William III, ruling jointly with his wife Mary, made no objection to the overthrow of Andros and the colonies of the Dominion resumed their established means of government almost as if Andros had never appeared.

The Dominion of New England was completely out of character with America in 1687 and virtually doomed from the start. The colonies were not even a century old at this point. They were still growing and learning to maneuver in a new and still extremely dangerous world. The idea that a half-dozen colonies could be lumped together was absurd. Each colony was too individual to be ruled as part of a group. Their needs, aspirations, and political, social, and economic makeup were too dissimilar. The arguments the rebels of 1689 made were reflected by the rebels of 1765 and 1776. The long-troubled history of English liberty propelled the thinkers in America over nearly a century of disputation with Britain.

The value of the 1688 English Glorious Revolution, aside from the Andros episode, was primarily psychological. "The Liberties John Dickinson would write about in 1766 in *Letters from a Farmer in Pennsylvania* were those he saw emerging out of this era."[21] It unleashed a feeling of mind that, coupled with the removal of Andros, change, even at the highest level, was possible. "The colonists retrieved only a single immediate benefit from the Glorious Revolution: they used it as an excuse to stake revolts of their own."[22] Symbolically, the Glorious Revolution of 1688 provided an unmistakable link to the 1760s when John Dickinson chose to premiere his *Letters from a Farmer in Pennsylvania* on November 5, 1767, seventy-nine years to the day that William of Orange arrived in England to replace the deposed James II.

The Anglo-Saxons

Like many of the American colonial leaders in the 1760s, twentieth-century historian John Phillip Reid asked the question, "But what was the ancient constitution in the eighteenth century?"[23] American colonial leaders wondered this for years. Where, and when, did the English liberties they so jealously felt they were guarding come from? Many felt from at least the Anglo-Saxon period, approximately c. 480–1066. This was a long period with few written records surviving for the colonists to point to. Historian Reid, in his essay *The Jurisprudence of Liberty*, looked to a 1735 newspaper which offered this answer:

> Though it must be confessed that our old Saxon constitution hath undergone many violent convulsions, since the conquest [1066], I think the whole series of our history, as far as we can discover it through the gloom of antiquity, is one continued proof that the foundations of it were never entirely overturned; … and though various alterations have been made in the form of our Parliaments,

the essentials have been preserved, and the people were never totally deprived of their share in those assemblies.[24]

The colonial leaders argued intensely that they had no representation in Parliament (they did not agree with the theory of virtual representation) and that they were losing control of their assemblies. Local, or colony-wide representation was a cornerstone of the colonial government and colonial leaders saw any attempt by Britain to reduce the power of these assemblies as a clear threat to their ancient constitutional rights. As with the quote above, the colonial leaders struggled to look through the gloom of antiquity to find not only the beginnings of English law but attempted to understand the rights it granted to the subjects of England. The colonial leaders were sure the ancient Saxons had developed the outlines of representative government which they felt were being threatened in the 1760s.

Two major factors render understanding ancient English law nearly impossible: (1) the lack of written evidence, (2) the various invasions suffered by the Britons over the course of two millennia. Naturally, English history goes much further back than two thousand years, but those pre-Roman days are too far back for our purposes. Historians of English legal development found at the base of the English constitution the Saxon hand and thought. One of the great English legal minds of the early eighteenth century, John Fortescue-Aland, wrote in his 1714 work *De Laudibus*:

> …we find the stream of the laws of Edward the Confessor, flowing from a Saxon fountain, and containing the substance of our present laws and liberties …; … both mixed and incorporated itself, with the great charter [Magna Carta] of our English liberties, whose true source the Saxon laws are, and are still in being, and still the fountain of the common law.[25]

Fortescue was someone who would have been studied by many of the colonial leaders of the 1760s and many of the British leaders of the time as well. The Saxons in the eighteenth century were as much myth as reality. Study of the Anglo-Saxon period was always popular, but it gained a greater interest in Britain after England and Scotland formed into Great Britain. One of the most enthusiastic historians of the Anglo-Saxon period was Thomas Jefferson, who will be the subject of a later chapter.

Part of Jefferson's, and other Founders' interest in the Saxon concept of liberty can be summed up as:

> The common law was the "best" of Saxon laws. Not all Saxon laws were incorporated in the current constitution, only those laws that were the "best" had survived. The best laws of the Saxons surviving in the immemorial ancient constitution were laws that in the eighteenth century were identified with "liberty."[26]

Virtually every colonial knew what liberty was, but none could explain much less articulate how it impacted America. The number of definitions was breathtaking: "Give me liberty or give me death"; "ancient liberties"; "the liberty tree"; "the liberty bell"; "the sons of liberty," etc. The list could go on, but the question remains the same, what was liberty? Even the Britons, whose Saxon ancestors had developed the concept, could not put one definition on it. John Reid referenced English jurist John Reeves as seeing liberty, while elusive, as the common ingredient binding the unwritten constitution together through the centuries. Reid wrote "Reeves's measure of continuity was liberty."[27] By this definition, liberty was forever keeping pace with contemporary developments—it was not static. No one in the eighteenth century would want to live with precise Anglo-Saxon definitions any more than no one today would want to live with eighteenth-century definitions. Again, the thread being liberty; as Reid wrote, "the liberty of the Saxons was the liberty of eighteenth-century Great Britain" and by extension the American colonies.[28]

"The most celebrated practioners of ancient history during the eighteenth century were the American founding fathers."[29] Perhaps the two greatest historians among the Founders were John Dickinson and Thomas Jefferson. While we have yet to look at Jefferson, Dickinson seemed to lose himself in the arguments presented in the *Letters*, which have already been reviewed. History can no doubt be a valid weapon but anyone who uses it runs the distinct risk, nearly unavoidable, of politicizing historical data to the point it becomes meaningless.

"The past was used for liberty in two ways: to define not the historical but the current meaning of liberty and to defend the contemporary constitutional right to liberty."[30] It was on the back of historical interpretations of history that Americans saw their future. What irritated American colonists was the fact that their learned British counterparts knew their history just as well. The British were as aware, if not more so, than their American counterparts concerning the history of English liberty leading back to the Saxons in their German forests. These early lovers of liberty who emigrated to England following the departure of the Romans were chronicled by the Roman historian Tacitus, who spent many years fighting them in their home territory in Germany.

As much as the Founders admired Classical civilization, especially Roman, they admired almost more the civilizations that the Roman's respected and wrote about. One of those civilizations, the ancient Germans, was the topic of a work by the historian Tacitus. Tacitus (c. 56–120 CE) was a senator from an old semi-noble family. His career in politics was not as memorable as his career as a writer. It was through his histories that the Founders became so enamored with the Germans who became the Anglo-Saxons seemingly providing the liberties the Americans of the 1760s felt was their birthright. However much this may have been the case, colonial Americans would likely have never changed places with Tacitus' Germans.

What Tacitus produced has long been highly regarded as one of "the best of its kind in antiquity, perhaps in any age."[31] Written in the year 98 CE, it promoted itself as "a study of the character, customs, and geography of a people."[32] Like the Romans, the Saxons enjoyed a reputation as freedom loving—a less than precise term. In fact, Tacitus saw their love of freedom as their most potent weapon.[33] Tacitus wrote the Germans had "a strong love of freedom, a keen sense of honor, and a regard for the sanctity of home-life."[34] These qualities would have been second nature to colonial Americans. Jefferson even placed honor (our lives, our fortune, and our sacred honor) as one of the personal attributes underpinning the Declaration of Independence.

The study of the ancient past, especially for Americans like Dickinson and Jefferson, enabled them to pursue two of their passions, history and law combined into political theory relating to liberty. As Trevor Colbourn has pointed out, "As a lawyer, Dickinson frequently turned to Tacitus for details of the Germanic customs that constituted precedents for English habits of government...."[35] This history became the narrative that Dickinson based so much of his argument on:

> This concept of ancient Saxon England was the foundation for the whig historical perspective offered Dickinson in his reading. Its charms were not hidden, for it presented with a blatant pride a sort of historical utopia, replete with liberty, representative government with an annually elected House of Commons or its equivalent in the Saxon *witenagemote,* kings who were often elected, and all defended by a popular armed militia.[36]

The English common law was common to all of England because it had stood the test of time. It had the mark of antiquity itself and carried the very essence of the past in the continual reliance on it in court cases. The more it was referred to, the more it lived, and the more it lived the more it gathered reverence in the eyes of citizens.

"The law, which was the seventeenth and eighteenth centuries' custodian of civil rights, had to be independent of sovereign command or liberty would have been no more secure than any ordinary revocable grant."[37] Therefore, Parliament, and certainly the king, were prohibited from passing laws, or declaring laws, which violated the ancient constitution. This could prove difficult at times to enforce as Britain, with an unwritten constitution, had nothing tangible to point to.

The English constitution was a battlefield long before John Dickinson or Thomas Jefferson began writing and the colonies began to agitate for independence. Having an unwritten constitution only added to the misery of interpreting the concepts held within it. On one level this may have inspired the Americans to commit their constitution to paper in 1787.

Anglo-Saxon Law

Historian Henry Adams was able to write more than one hundred years after the Revolution:

> The student of history who now attempts to trace, through two thousand years of vicissitudes and dangers, the slender thread of political and legal thought, no longer loses it from sight…, but follows it safely and firmly back until it leads him out upon the wide plains of northern Germany.[38]

Many of the leaders of the Founding generation acknowledged in varying degrees the relationship of the colonial complaints against Britain as having an Anglo-Saxon pedigree. The Anglo-Saxons, wedged in time between the Roman and Norman conquests, did indeed leave their mark on English customs: language, dress, economic and political developments; essentially English society can be placed at the feet of the Anglo-Saxons. Our concern however are the law traditions created by the Anglo-Saxons and the descent of that legal heritage across nearly a millennium to the colonies of North America. The trouble was, and is, the Anglo-Saxons wrote extraordinarily little. As historian Frederick Pollock has written, "Our Germanic ancestors were no great penmen…."[39] As such, "We cannot expect, then, that the extant collections of Anglo-Saxon laws should give us anything like a complete view of the legal or judicial institutions of the time."[40] How then, did the American leaders come to point to the Anglo-Saxons as their inspiration? There was no one answer. Anglo-Saxon studies at that time were virtually non-existent as a discipline. Yet that did not stop Americans from claiming a lineal descent from the Anglo-Saxon legal tradition of liberty.

English legal historian Sir Matthew Hale (1609–1676), writing in his *The History of the Common Law of England*, published in 1713 after his death, pointed to the major problem with understanding the English constitution before 1215, the year of Magna Carta, Hale wrote:

> The kingdom of England being a very ancient kingdom, has had many vicissitudes and changes (especially before the coming of King William [1066]) under several either conquests or accessions of foreign nations. …and hence arises the difficulty, and indeed the moral impossibility, of giving any satisfactory or so much as probable conjecture, touching the origins of our laws.[41]

Based on Hale's observation, and other similar commentary, could the American colonists have accurately grounded their arguments in ancient legal thinking and practice?

Indeed, by all accounts ancient Anglo-Saxon law had no concept for liberty in the sense Americans were appealing to it in the 1760s. In fact, Frederick Pollock had found "differences of rank and degrees of independence among free men."[42] Anglo-Saxon men were not created equal. The danger of invoking millennium aged doctrines, as the Americans did, is that those doctrines rarely age well. Nuances in meaning and language shift and alter over centuries. While the goal was noble, basing their claims on some ancient patterns of life which had little meaning to contemporary problems in 1760s America was foolhardy. Ancient Anglo-Saxon legal systems were all about hierarchy and would seem to be the exact antitheses of what we associate with the desires of colonial America.

Hale advocated what seemed axiomatic. That the law or tradition of ancient times was not necessarily the law or tradition of the contemporary period, which would be a positive development. Hale wrote:

> From the nature of Laws themselves in general, which being to be accommodated to the conditions, exigencies and conveniences of the people, for or by whom they are appointed, as those exigencies and conveniences do insensibly grow upon the people, so many times there grows insensibly a variation of laws, especially in a long tract of time....[43]

Hale further pointed out that not only do laws change over time of necessity, but people change. The England of 1765 was not the England of 765. A certain law may work fine when imposed by and for people of a certain disposition and heredity. Once new people, "others," begin to mix with one group or another, their "pure" law will eventually need to accommodate and keep pace. In England, the eldest identifiable law would be Roman, but then came the Saxon, and then the French. English law, like its population by 1765, was anything but pure.

Given the mixture of peoples and ideas in England over the centuries, Hale concluded, "it is almost an impossible piece of chemistry to reduce every [law] to its true original, as to say, this is a piece of the Danish, this of the Normans, or this of the Saxon...."[44] Hale wrote roughly a century before the American colonists began to invoke what they believed to be their ancient traditions. Those traditions, they argued, were being violated by Parliament through the imposition of new taxation. The colonists were aware their arguments on ancient rights were on less than steady ground. Yet, Jefferson, Dickinson, and others, sought that ground for their assault on Parliaments actions in law whose origins were lost to the mists of time.

One of the earliest existing Anglo-Saxon legal manuscripts dates to the late fifth century. Named after the reigning monarch of Kent, Wihtred, the Laws of Wihtred were not extensive (at least what has survived) and were certainly not something the Founding Fathers would have found of much use; yet, they would have recognized incipient elements of eighteenth-century common law. Of the two concepts of ancient legal standing that the colonists traced back to the Anglo-Saxons, taxation and representation, only taxation is referenced in the Laws of Wihtred. It reads

"The Church [is to be] free from taxation."[45] Naturally, the Laws of Wihtred were far too ancient to have any specific application to the 1760s.

The Roman law never took hold in Britain. Even after nearly four centuries of occupation, the Britons had not embraced the Roman jurisprudence. With the departure of the Romans in the early fifth century, the Britons quickly reverted to their pre–Roman conceptions of civil society.

Over the next roughly two hundred years, before the arrival of the Saxons in large numbers, "the British mainland was subject to repeated waves of immigration from across the North Sea."[46] This meant peoples from the present-day regions of Holland, Germany, the Scandinavian countries, and perhaps even Russia. Without the Roman presence in England the borders were much more porous. Why exactly people were going to England may not be fully understood but go they did. Their mixture with the native tribes helped to shape the post–Roman development of the island before and during the more specific influx of north German Saxons. This continuous churning impeded the attempts of native Britons to fully re-establish their ancient, pre–Roman approach to governing and social interaction. What further upended the reversion of Britons to their pre–Roman ways was the introduction of Christianity by the close of the sixth century, shortly after the arrival of the Saxons. This period, often referred to as the Dark Ages in England, was a bubbling cauldron of peoples and ideas trying to coalesce around a unifying culture. England was a hugely complex place, not to mention Scotland and Ireland. Their unique positions at the end of the known world made them attractive outposts for the people like the Vikings who pushed the known edges of the Western world by going farther west than anyone up to that time. Their raids in England, however savage and brutal, helped to bring together a people who found it difficult to come together around a central cause. It also produced some of the most beautiful and fanciful literature known.

The native Britons, already weakened by centuries of Roman occupation, suffered, at times, grievously. They would never truly re-establish their pre–Roman life after the Romans left. The constant onslaught of invaders from Europe kept the island from ever being homogenous again.

"The Anglo-Saxons were the first native inhabitants of England of whose legal usages anything much is known because they were the first to introduce written laws."[47] What was it about the Anglo-Saxon laws and life that so appealed to the American colonists of the 1760s? The Anglo-Saxons after all were immigrants. The native Britons should have been the ones looked to by the American colonists of the 1760s, it would seem. Yet, this was not the case. Why? Americans had multiple reasons for finding inspiration wherever they could. One reason the Saxons were so interesting to our Founders was the way the ancient Roman historians wrote about them.

The Saxons were well known to the Romans as the "savage" inhabitants of the German woods who could not be conquered by the might of Rome. They had cunning, drive, and inspiration to fight the greatest empire on earth and they won. Certainly, this was not the only aspect marking them for admiration by the Americans, yet it was what they knew given their admiration of ancient writers. Their people were the direct ancestors of the Americans and formed part of the shared ancient past with England.

While the Anglo-Saxon period, that age between Rome and the arrival of the Normans in 1066, was generally a time of discontent with attempts to establish the pre–Roman ways, there were times when great advances were made. Through the combined efforts of kings such as Alfred, and teams of learned courtiers, advances were indeed made in the creation of law. These creations often involved a combination of pre–Roman, Roman, post–Roman, and European conceptions that were for the first time written down. These provide the earliest law that the American colonists could point to justify the infringement of their ancient liberties as they claimed. The trouble of course was that it was impossible to pinpoint any ancient English law, Saxon, Roman, or other, which spoke to the conditions that the colonists were agitating about. Yet, their efforts bore some success as some of the more articulate Founders, such as Thomas Jefferson, looked to the Saxons to frame the outlines of their pamphlets. These attempts, while representing questionable historical research methods, nonetheless rose to the level of inspiration desired. Jefferson, Dickinson, or nearly any one of the Founders who looked to the Saxons, Normans, Romans, or even the Britons themselves, came up with disappointing results although they did not let that deter them. Much to their credit, they persevered.

CHAPTER 11

James Wilson, Thomas Jefferson, and the Final Arguments for America

Thomas Jefferson

Of all the Founding Fathers, Thomas Jefferson holds a unique place in the American imagination. A man of intense contradictions, Jefferson is someone who nearly everyone can simultaneously either admire or revile, or both. These unique qualities brought together in someone who died nearly two centuries ago ensures that Jefferson will continue to be a topic of conversation for decades, if not centuries, to come. The slave owner who also has two of his architectural creations (built with enslaved labor) as UNESCO world heritage sites, Jefferson is indeed the embodiment of the fragile nature of fame left to us by history.

This unique quality elicited by Jefferson's memory affords us many ways to approach the story, or stories, of the Founding generation. In the case of Jefferson, for our purposes, we will look at a small essay he wrote in 1773–1774 as a follow-up to the many and varied pamphlets that were created during the 1760s and 1770s in the period just before the outbreak of armed conflict with Britain in 1775. This period, before Lexington and Concord, was a moment when the American cause hung in the balance. Most of the Founders knew the inevitable outcome of their opposition to Britain, but few would acknowledge that outcome: war, and with any luck, independence.

There was little hope of reconciliation by 1774, the year of the First Continental Congress. The young delegate from Virginia, Thomas Jefferson, wrote an essay for his colleagues from Virginia to share among the rest of the delegates. The idea was for these arguments to be used as starting points for the Congress to refine as they debated. Jefferson however took ill and was unable to attend and gave the essay to his colleague

Monticello—Residence of Thomas Jefferson. The Miriam and Ira D. Wallach Division of Art, Prints and Photographs: New York Public Library Digital Collections.

Peyton Randolph, who would become the president of the First Continental Congress. Randolph made the decision to publish the essay as a pamphlet.

Jefferson's Virginia colleagues to the first Continental Congress such as George Wythe, Edmund Pendleton, and Peyton Randolph, saw Jefferson's essay as radical. They recognized the genius of the argumentation that Jefferson employed and set about, without his permission, to publish the essay in both America and England. According to historian Merrill Peterson, Jefferson's colleagues "Published … as the *Summary View* in Williamsburg, at once reprinted in Philadelphia in England, Jefferson's hastily penned instructions [which] opened a new chapter in the polemics of the Revolution."[1] Jefferson's tone would mark a break with the previous decades' writing and signaled the beginning of the open warfare segment of America's conflict with Britain.

The title assigned to the essay was *A Summary View of the Rights of British America*. Jefferson, as noted, wrote his essay for the benefit of his fellow members of Congress. Jefferson intended his essay strictly as an internal document, that is he did not intend it to be published for public consumption. Fellow Virginian Peyton Randolph, who was entrusted by Jefferson with the essay, sensed the significance of the arguments and decided to publish it for distribution beyond the Congress. Although Jefferson felt slighted, he did not endeavor to retract the essence of his essay once it was made known through publication.

A
SUMMARY VIEW
OF THE
RIGHTS
OF
BRITISH AMERICA.
SET FORTH IN SOME
RESOLUTIONS
INTENDED FOR THE
INSPECTION
OF THE PRESENT
DELEGATES
OF THE
PEOPLE OF VIRGINIA.
NOW IN
CONVENTION.

By a NATIVE, and MEMBER of the
HOUSE of BURGESSES.
by Thomas Jefferson.

WILLIAMSBURG:
Printed by CLEMENTINA RIND.

Title page of Thomas Jefferson's *Summary View of the Rights of British America.* Facsimile of original pamphlet.

The Essay Itself

Jefferson began his essay with a quote from one of his favorite ancient Roman writers. The well-known ancient author Cicero enjoyed a standing with the classically educated Founders above most other classical writers. Granted, there was a lot of his material which survived from the classical period which helped to ensure his enduring fame. For Jefferson though, Cicero held a unique position. As a writer and someone who respected the Latin language, Jefferson found Cicero's compositions to be particularly engaging. To a certain degree, Jefferson idolized Cicero along with several other Roman writers. In general, the Founders saw the ancient Romans of the Republican period (510 BCE to 27 BCE) to have been virtuous citizens in relation to the government. This was something they sought to emulate. "The connection between the classics and virtue was deeply ingrained and implicitly understood" by the Founders.[2]

The quote that Jefferson chose to begin his essay was directed specifically at King George III, not Parliament. The quote reads, "it is the indispensable duty of the supreme magistrate to consider himself as acting for the whole community, and obliged to support its dignity, and assign to the people, with justice, their various rights, as he would be faithful to the great trust reposed in him."[3] Without question, Jefferson identified who he saw as the main problematic figure in the dispute with Great Britain—the king. This dedication marked a break of sorts with other essayists who tended to place the blame for America's troubles with Parliament rather than with King George III. Jefferson would go on to place a significant blame on the shoulders of George III. Jefferson's influence on placing the blame more on the king rather than Parliament would echo down through the centuries to our own time. Why Jefferson felt the need to concentrate on George III can be attributed to his intense dislike of monarchy, and individual monarchs. While Parliament was elected it was the institution of monarchy and those who occupied the throne who came in for attack through Jefferson's writings. It is well known that Jefferson, in the Declaration of Independence, set out a litany of transgressions squarely placed at the feet of the monarch of Great Britain that were taken almost verbatim from his essay.

In the preface to Jefferson's essay, written by his colleagues in Congress, it was specifically noted that Jefferson was expressing "the sentiments of one of their body, whose personal attendance was prevented by an accidental illness."[4] The editors continued in the preface, "In it the sources of our present unhappy differences are traced with such faithful accuracy, and the opinions entertained by every free American expressed with such a manly firmness, that it must be pleasing to the present, and may be useful to future ages."[5] The editors were clearly writing not just for the moment, but were well aware that future generations, should the contest with Great Britain end in favor of the American colonies, would no doubt be looking at the writings of those during the years preceding warfare, to find the source of their inspiration. "Without the knowledge of the author, we have ventured to communicate his sentiments to the public; who have certainly the right to know what the best and wisest of their members have thought on a subject in which they are so deeply interested."[6] The preface, added thus by Jefferson's colleagues, clearly stated the reasons for moving the essay forward for the benefit of the public and for the benefit of future generations.

Jefferson began his essay by pointing out to the members of the Continental Congress that they should create a "humble and dutiful address [to] be presented to his majesty, begging leave to lay before him, as chief magistrate of the British empire, the united complaints of his majesty's subjects in America...."[7] Here was Jefferson looking specifically at the chief magistrate, someone that the quote from Cicero specifically identified; included in the blame are the concerns for the current state of affairs between Britain and America specifically within the purview of, as Cicero put it, the chief magistrate. Continuing, Jefferson wrote:

> To represent to his majesty that these his states have often individually made humble application to his imperial throne to obtain, through its intervention, some redress of their injured rights, to none of which was ever even an answer, condescended....[8]

By 1774 when Jefferson wrote his essay, he could look back on nearly a decade of American political writing implicating either Parliament or the king. Many of these pamphlets that were produced were known by George III and certainly by members of Parliament. Yet, it was Parliament who responded, not a monarch. It was Parliament who invited agents of the American colonies such as Benjamin Franklin and Jared Ingersoll, to set before them in 1766 to answer questions about the Stamp Act. The king during most of the decade of the 1760s, was merely an observer. Not disinterested, the king followed events closely but felt it beneath his status to intervene.

Jefferson was convinced that George III would listen to a new petition from the First Continental Congress because, "his majesty will think we have reason to expect when he reflects that he is no more than the chief officer of the people, appointed by the laws, and circumscribed with definite powers, to assist in working the great machinery of government...."[9] This was classic Jefferson testing his maturing political philosophy two years before he was to write very similar language into the Declaration of Independence. The idea that government was a great machine, directed for the benefit of the people, was classic Enlightenment thinking. That in this definition, his majesty was the chief officer of the people appointed by the laws. In other words, when it came time to create the chief magistrate of the United States, which would be our president, it was very clear not just Jefferson (who did not have a hand in drafting the Constitution as he was in Paris as American ambassador to France), but the vast majority of the Founders, recognized that the chief magistrate, or in our case president, was nothing more than a creation of the law. And within that same thinking, the law was nothing more than the creation of the people. Therefore, on page one of his essay, Jefferson made a startling connection between the power of the people to govern themselves, and the power of the government that they create, and the law, to be as one for their benefit.

After his opening commentary, Jefferson delved into the idea or concept which was common at the time, that the colonists, when they emigrated from a particular country—in this case Great Britain—carried with them not just the laws but the rights that they possessed before they emigrated. As Jefferson wrote, "our ancestors, before their emigration to America, were the free inhabitants of the British dominions and Europe, and possessed a right which nature has given to all men, of departing from the country in which chance, not choice, has placed them, of going in quest of new habitations, and of their establishing new societies, under such laws and regulations as to them shall seem most likely to promote public happiness."[10] Jefferson took the idea one step further. Emigrants not only possessed those rights which they had before they emigrated, but that indeed they had the right to create new law for their new society as they saw fit. Jefferson left immigrants with the best of both worlds.

The Saxons, already covered in some detail previously, were of great interest to Jefferson. Jefferson would be fascinated by the Anglo-Saxons until the end of his life. In fact, in a letter to a Boston bookseller written about a year before he died, he specifically was looking for unique titles on Anglo-Saxon history and the Anglo-Saxon language. These books he was looking for were to create a library at the new University of Virginia. Jefferson saw contemporary Britons as the direct descendants of the Anglo-Saxons and as such the colonists, as Britons, were also direct descendants of the Anglo-Saxons. For Jefferson the idea was to look to the most distant Britons and bring the story forward to his own time as a way to point out that in fact the direct line of not just ancestral relationships existed but a straight line of descent in patterns of law and social creation.

Indeed, Jefferson considered the new law the Saxons created in their new home in Britain to be a "system of laws which has so long been the glory and protection of that country."[11] In the very next sentence Jefferson made a rather farfetched comment—the first of many to come. He stated that once the Saxons left their ancestral German homes, that their German

"There are three particular works which I must pray you to procure for the university." Thomas Jefferson to a Boston bookseller looking for volumes for the new University of Virginia. Note the Anglo-Saxon title. Morristown NHP. Park archival collection.

countrymen never sought to impose law as restrictions on them once they reached England. Naturally, it is not fully known why the Saxons left their German home; whether they purposefully went out to establish colonies is somewhat in doubt. The fact that Jefferson put the sentence directly following the sentence concerning the system of laws is an indication of how slippery some of Jefferson's arguments could be. The Saxons could have left their ancestral homes because of overcrowding, it could have been the societal pressures created by the Roman wars on their territory. There could have been tribal warfare, and naturally, there could have been specific colonizing efforts made by certain tribes within Germany. However, this is highly unlikely. Jefferson again clarified this slippery argumentation by writing, "And it is thought that no circumstance has occurred to distinguish materially the British from the Saxon emigration."[12] Although separated by over a thousand years, the German migrations of the sixth century were identical to the English migrations in the seventeenth century. This again, was classic Jefferson. The fact that Jefferson was one of the country's most gifted writers, one of the country's most gifted thinkers, did not mean that he, when convenient, would not polish or elaborate his argumentation to make his point.

Jefferson attempted to write off the more than a century and a half of investment from Britain into the colonies by arguing that the colonists, since 1607, had been completely self-directed. Again, this is quite a stretch of the historical record and it shows how Jefferson, to make his point, would be more than willing to stretch credulity. It is true however that as the colonies became more secure and prosperous, particularly by the 1730s and 1740s, the British began to see their holdings in North America in a slightly different light. Jefferson acknowledged that had not Britain fought the French and Indian War that the colonies would more than likely have become French colonies. However, Jefferson felt that the colonies, by aligning themselves with Britain during the French and Indian War, never believed that they would somehow lose their sovereignty to Great Britain in the aftermath of the war. This was a point of intense debate among the Founders and among members of Parliament and even with the king himself. For the British, who never saw the colonies as having a separate identity or separate sovereignty, how could they suddenly become subservient to Great Britain when that was the case all along?

By 1774 when Jefferson wrote his essay the main arguments that the colonists were making had matured. Starting in 1765 through to 1774, the multiple threads of thought, the multiple angles of thought, had started to coalesce around a few basic principles. Jefferson more than any other Founder was to articulate these well-crafted and well-defined perspectives. Jefferson argued that had the colonies known the position that Great Britain would take after the French and Indian War they would have instead fought for the French rather than the British. That seems farfetched, yet Jefferson was no doubt voicing a concern that was not his alone.

What did appear to be unique to Jefferson's thinking was the alignment of American ideals and the Anglo-Saxon period of English history. Early in his essay, Jefferson sought to show, or to prove, that the colonists of the early seventeenth century were free from the imposition of rules and guidance from England, specifically from the monarch. One point which Jefferson accurately portrayed was that the early colonists would quickly change their colonies or their structure of governments from a stock company type of arrangement to a Crown colony, meaning a colony that was directed and ultimately responsible to the Crown or the monarch. This was a process that accrued through the seventeenth century. Jefferson was also correct that this type of arrangement had never existed before in British or

Chapter 11. Final Arguments for America

English government. The simple reason for that was the colonies did not exist to the extent that they had in North America until the seventeenth century. So, yes, it was true as Jefferson stated that this undertaking or approach of creating Crown colonies had never occurred in England; but Jefferson did not go on to acknowledge that there was absolutely no reason for these to occur before the seventeenth century.

Once Crown colonies were established in Jefferson's telling of the history, he said that trade with the colonies "was next the object of unjust encroachment."[13] This was a complicated statement. What exactly did he mean? Jefferson argued the colonies had never passed laws prohibiting trade beyond the British realm. It was Britain who passed such legislation, which therefore rendered it ineffective from a colonial perspective in Jefferson's mind. Jefferson's position was a familiar one within colonial leadership circles.

Here Jefferson waded into the Civil War in England between Charles I and Cromwell and his followers. Charles I had created conditions for the colonies whereby they would trade exclusively with England. Under the commonwealth headed by Oliver Cromwell, a treaty, signed in 1651, specifically stated that the colony of Virginia would have free trade with all people and nations. Jefferson would use this article of the Treaty of 1651 to emphasize his point that free trade was the foundation of the mercantile relationship between England and her colonies, or at least the colony of Virginia which Jefferson specifically was alluding to. Jefferson went on to write that under Charles II, the trade restrictions of Charles I were reinstated on Virginia and the colonies. Jefferson used the concept of trade as an argument to show just how extensive the control was which the English Parliament enjoyed over the colonies.

From the issue of trade Jefferson moved to manufacturing. It was well known at the time that Britain had very restrictive laws on any number of manufacturing schemes that presented themselves to the colonists. As an example, Jefferson cited a law, or an act passed during the reign of George II. By this law, "an American subject is forbidden to make a hat for himself of the fur which he has taken perhaps on his own soil; an instance of despotism to which no parallel can be produced in the most arbitrary ages of British history."[14] The purpose of the law that Jefferson referred to was that a trapper with beaver pelts had to send the pelts to England to be manufactured into a hat which was then shipped back to America and sold to an American. This would help ensure jobs in Britain, but it did little for American manufacturing. It goes without saying that Americans ignored many of these laws but nonetheless they were promulgated and on the books. After a few more examples of laws that were injurious to the colonists while being very generous to Englishmen, Jefferson wrote, "from which one of these conclusions must necessarily follow, either that justice is not the same in America as in Britain, or else that the British parliament pay less regard to it here than there."[15] And finally, Jefferson came to the crux of his argument: "The true ground on which we declare these acts a void is, that the British parliament has no right to exercise authority over us."[16] About a third of the way through his essay Jefferson wrote the sentence that he was building towards. Parliament, England, by extension the monarch, had no authority over the colonies. This was an extraordinary claim to make given the history of the relations, however good or bad, between England and the colonies since 1607. Nonetheless, by 1774, when Jefferson wrote these words it was clear to everyone that the only outcome would be American independence if it could be achieved.

Jefferson, at about the one-third point in his essay, completed his first argument. He wrote, "Single acts of tyranny may be ascribed to the accidental opinion of the day; but a series of oppressions, begun at a distinguished period, and pursued unalterably through every change of ministers, too plainly prove a deliberate and systematic a plan of reducing us to slavery."[17] The use of the word slavery by Jefferson has been pointed out as being hypocritical since the day he wrote it. It goes without saying that a slave owner, as Jefferson was, somehow in his mind equated the condition of slaves as equal to that of American colonists under British rule. This was without question absurd. Jefferson was clearly concerned about the so-called natural relationship between Great Britain and the American colonies. Regardless of whether Great Britain was following the law, Jefferson's main concern was whether the law itself was legal. Jefferson was much more concerned with whether the law or the laws that were passed should even have been passed. In other words, what rights, by what authority, did Great Britain exercise rule over the colonies? For Jefferson, no right existed. Taking his thinking to its extreme we would have anarchy.

By 1774 Jefferson was able to look back on all the so-called highlights of the colonial period leading up to the Revolution. Events such as the suspension of the New York legislature, the closing of the port of Boston, the Boston Tea Party, the Boston Massacre. The Boston Massacre of March 1770 was precisely what Sam Adams wanted and needed to form his radical plot. However, the upsurge Adams hoped for passed. It was not until Prime Minister North sent East India Company tea to America and threatened American merchants that events spiraled out of control towards war.

All these events Jefferson emphasized in his effort to show the tyranny of Great Britain over the colonies. Another area where Jefferson saw the tyranny of Great Britain over the American colonists was in the realm of law. Much as he would argue two years later in the Declaration of Independence, Jefferson in his essay on the summary rights of America drilled down on the idea of sending an accused person to England to stand trial; and if acquitted to somehow find their way back home. Likewise, Jefferson saw the requirement of a witness to journey at their own expense to England to give testimony in certain cases to be outlandish. This clearly would have been one area where the colonists and the British probably would have been able to compromise in any other atmosphere rather than the one that existed in the 1770s before open warfare began. Jefferson used these arguments with great dexterity, and they proved to be one of his strongest points.

Nearly two-thirds the way through his essay, after having discussed the ill fortune of those caught up in the British legal system having to find their way to England and back, Jefferson offered a paragraph summation of his thinking thus far presented:

> That these are the acts of power, assumed by a body of men, foreign to our constitutions, and unacknowledged by our laws, against which we do, on behalf of the inhabitants of British America, enter this our solemn and determined protest; and we do earnestly entreat his majesty, as yet the only mediatory power between the several states of the British empire, to recommend to his parliament of Great Britain the total revocation of these acts, which, however nugatory they be, may yet prove the cause of further discontents and jealousies among us.[18]

Jefferson now in his essay focused his enmity on King George III specifically. George had been relatively free from personal attacks up to this point, but Jefferson was hedging that by indicting both Parliament and the monarch one or the other approach would prove effective. He wrote, "It is now, therefore, the great office of his majesty, to resume the exercise of his negative power, and to prevent the passage of laws by any one legislature of the empire, which might bear injuriously on the rights and interests of another."[19] King George was made out to be an unnerved monarch, someone surprised and unsettled by the turn of events in America. A monarch who saw himself as unfit or somehow deficient for the role he found himself in. As successor to two previous Hanoverian kings, in Jefferson's mind, George was not up to the task which confronted him. Jefferson saw George as someone too easily misled by Parliament, someone who would not advocate for the interests of his colonies, and someone who was overwhelmed by the agility of his members of Parliament.

As mentioned, Jefferson's *Summary View* was a preview of his arguments of the Declaration of Independence. It is well known that in Jefferson's own handwritten draft of the Declaration he included a charge against George III of enhancing the slave trade and indeed of encouraging slavery in the colonies, which Jefferson saw as against natural law; in his essay he called it an "infamous practice."[20] While it can be argued whether Jefferson wrote this for purely political purposes or whether he genuinely felt that slavery was against the so-called laws of nature is a topic for another day. However, Jefferson went on record in his essay and took a position against the importation of slaves and indeed the entire practice of slavery in North America. In the Declaration of Independence when Jefferson tried to use this very same language, it was struck out by his colleagues on the committee which helped him fine-tune his draft. Therefore, it seems clear that this was more than just a political score on George III. Elements in American society were specifically concerned enough to remove Jefferson's language against slavery from the draft Declaration of Independence. It would seem therefore that slavery was a thread which connected the Declaration of Independence and the Constitution. Of course, the original Constitution, before the thirteenth amendment, specifically spoke about slavery (although it was couched in boutique language such as referring to the enslaved as "three-fifths of a person"). So, it seems undeniable that both founding documents were in part predicated on the practice of slavery.

Near the end of the essay Jefferson took up the idea of land ownership. Once again looking back to the Saxons and their concept of land ownership and comparing that concept of the individual land ownership with the feudal system that the Norman conquerors imposed on the Saxons. In other words, after the Norman conquest in 1066 William the Conqueror gathered all lands theoretically under the crown to be disbursed through his nobles. The Saxons, who were conquered by the Normans, held land not in a theoretical sense but in a practical sense in terms of their being the only one sole owner of a piece of property. Jefferson drew the analogy that "America was not conquered by William the Norman, nor its lands surrendered to him, or any of his successors."[21] Furthermore, Jefferson went on to argue that even though colonies submitted to charters drafted by the Crown to become Crown colonies, these charters were created through subterfuge. The emigrants Jefferson claimed were laborers, not lawyers, so how would they know the differences in the intricacies of English common law land ownership? Jefferson was correct in the sense that the early settlers were not lawyers. There were few if any who had a working knowledge of the legal process. Jefferson wrote, "[t]he fictitious principle that all lands belong originally to the king, they were early persuaded to believe the real; and accordingly, took grants of their own lands from the crown."[22]

In the last several paragraphs of the *Summary View*, Jefferson renewed his prosecution of George III. In language that was once again foreshadowing the Declaration of Independence Jefferson took up the issue of sending troops to North America. Jefferson disputed whether the king had the right to send armed forces to the colonies. Jefferson wrote, "But his majesty has no right to land a single armed man on our shores, and those whom he sends here are liable to our laws made for the suppression and

Chapter 11. Final Arguments for America

punishment of riots, routs, and unlawful assemblies; or are hostile bodies, invading us in defiance of law."[23] Jefferson was careful to draw a distinction between George III and his grandfather George II. Jefferson pointed out that George II, when he sent the Hanoverian troops to North America during the French and Indian War, secured Parliamentary consent to do so. Jefferson felt that this measure was done to prevent Englishmen from worrying whether George II could somehow bring Hanoverian troops onto English soil. Jefferson took pains to draw this distinction between the two George's, Jefferson wrote:

> He [George II] therefore applied to parliament, who passed an act for that purpose, limiting the number to be brought in and the time they were to continue. In like manner is his majesty restrained in every part of the empire.[24]

According to Jefferson's argument therefore, George III sought a different approach towards sending Hanoverian troops to North America and thus violated English law.

Jefferson continued the attack, when he wrote, "To render these proceedings still more criminal against our laws, instead of subjecting the military to the civil powers his majesty has expressly made the civil subordinate to the military."[25] Herein lay the concept which would be enshrined in the Constitution nearly fifteen years later. That is, the subjection of military power to civilian control. This concept would also become the defining feature during the revolutionary period where General Washington consistently kept himself a subordinate to the Continental Congress.

In the last paragraph of his essay, Jefferson eloquently noted, again in language which would find its way into the Declaration, that the colonists were expressing their rights, "as derived from the laws of nature, and not as the gift of their chief magistrate...."[26] Jefferson here was arguing that freedom of speech was not something that was granted by the leader or chief magistrate but rather existed for all people simply by the fact of being a person. Freedom of speech was an ideal that came before any human government and therefore was the common property of every person. Jefferson implored George III to listen to the entreaties of his people writing, "Open your breast, sire, to liberal and expanded thought. Let not the name of George the third be a blot in the page of history."[27] Here Jefferson attempted to appeal to George III's well-known desire to see himself as an enlightened monarch or someone who saw the world and his position in it, as a monarch, differently from some of the more despotic or traditional rulers of Europe.

Jefferson's brilliance and writing skills, abilities which would quickly bring him to the attention of his colleagues, were fully engaged in the ending sentence where Jefferson rose to great heights of literary composition:

> The whole art of government consists in the art of being honest. Only aim to do your duty, and mankind will give you credit where you fail. No longer persevere sacrificing the rights of one part of the empire to the inordinate desires of another; but deal out to all equal and impartial right.[28]

Jefferson ended his essay clearly as a threat to George III, the threat that the empire, or at least the colonies being part of the empire, would not maintain their position unless he took into consideration the concerns of his American colonists. Jefferson wrote, "We are willing, on our part, to sacrifice everything which reason can ask to the restoration of that tranquility for which all must wish."[29]

By 1774, when Jefferson wrote this essay, there was probably little doubt whether George III would listen to the advice and counsel of his American colonists. This essay clearly appealed to those Founders such as Patrick Henry or Samuel Adams who were already in their minds in revolt against Great Britain. Jefferson did his best to strike a balance between the Founders and public sentiment both for and against separation from Great Britain. Jefferson obviously saw the writing on the wall and yet was unwilling to say it until two years later when he was appointed to create the first draft of the Declaration of Independence, at which time he clearly looked back to his recently composed essay on the *Summary View of the Rights of British America*.

It has been pointed out before that Great Britain had, and still has, an unwritten constitution. Without question this has created problems over the centuries. Probably the defining problem occurred during the 1760s and 1770s during the era we recognize as the American founding. Historian R.B. Bernstein points out that Jefferson's *Summary View* essay was long on constitutional arguments. Many of those arguments Jefferson used with embellishment for impact in his essay. However, Jefferson was well versed in constitutional arguments and an unwritten constitution was open to more interpretation than most. Bernstein wrote, "an unwritten constitution creates even more opportunities to disagree about its meaning, as Jefferson's pamphlet showed."[30] Jefferson used his skills as a constitutional lawyer and his writing skills to create doubt, that is what a lawyer does, create doubt and poke holes in their adversaries' case. The job of a lawyer in part is to create reasonable doubt in the minds of those who are sitting in judgment. Jefferson's essay showed him arguing both for and against the British arguments; essentially poking holes where he could for dramatic effect. Clearly this was his attempt to appear as a reasonable debater; the last thing Jefferson wanted was to be labeled biased. Even with war all but certain, Jefferson strove to attempt impartiality. Jefferson's essay served its purpose by creating a strong argument for maintaining the economic boycott that was

Chapter 11. Final Arguments for America

created during the first Continental Congress and for encouraging and providing moral support for those who foresaw the inevitable war.

Historian Merrill D. Peterson created a much larger canvas upon which to place Jefferson's essay on the rights of British America. Peterson saw the early 1770s as a period of directionless opposition to Great Britain. Peterson acknowledged that the so-called hotheads, such as Patrick Henry and Dabney Carr, were still agitating for what amounted to independence. It would be Jefferson, through his essay, who gathered the various strands of thought and put them into a coherent narrative. In Peterson's telling of the story the Americans had become complacent with the relatively calm status existing between Great Britain and America. Events like the Boston "Massacre," where John Adams defended the British soldiers, only complicated America's perspective on where to draw the line in opposition to Great Britain. The Boston Tea Party was another major turning point in the first couple of years of the 1770s. The result of the destruction of the tea, the closing of the port of Boston and the passage of the Tea Act, put many of America's most radical leaders on a path towards independence—if they were not already there. Jefferson especially found the response of Great Britain to be wholly inappropriate in the Boston tea violence. He felt the punishment administered by Britain to be all out of proportion with the crime. What began as a regional, specific response by Britain escalated throughout the colonies—something Britain did not anticipate. And indeed, it was Jefferson who would organize a day of fasting and humiliation, events inspired by the Glorious Revolution, as a response to the course of acts. It was also in response to these actions that the Virginia House of Burgesses, "took the longest step yet recorded toward independence."[31] Peterson continued, "The incipient revolutionary body declared that an attack on one colony should be considered an attack on all."[32] The result of the response of Britain toward Boston prompted the colonies to begin planning for a major colony-wide gathering. It was in late summer after the day of fasting and humiliation that the colonies began electing their delegates to the first Continental Congress which was tasked to meet in Philadelphia in September of 1774.

It is important to draw the distinctions between what was occurring in 1774 and what had occurred the previous eight years in the dispute between Great Britain and the American colonies. Jefferson would acknowledge that his essay, a *Summary View*, was far bolder than most Americans were ready or willing to admit. In 1774 the American colonies were still responding and reacting to Great Britain through a paradigm that was developed by John Dickinson. It can be recalled that Dickinson, in his *Letters from a Farmer in Pennsylvania*, homed in on the idea of an external vs. internal legislation impacting taxation that Britain, through its Parliament, could exercise on the American colonies. For Dickinson, Parliament had a role relative to the colonies. With Jefferson's essay, he denied all authority of the Parliament over the colonies.

In his 1774 essay, Jefferson had been channeling the Virginian Richard Bland, who had written his own essay delving into the rights of the British colonies in 1766. Although Bland was inconclusive in his writing, Jefferson took the argument that led forward and took it to its logical conclusion, namely, independence. However, Jefferson along with several other high-minded thinkers of the period such as John Adams, "set forth the new theory of imperial connection in which the colonies were equal self-governing states owing allegiance to the king."[33] This was one reason why Jefferson, along with others, spent so much energy directly implicating King George III in somehow abdicating his ability to provide government over the colonies and somehow devolving this authority over to Parliament.

Merrill Peterson pointed out, as has been stated, that in the opening of Jefferson's *Summary View*, wherein he argued that Americans were immigrants, and had the right under natural law to establish their own legal framework as they saw fit. This was pure hyperbole on Jefferson's part. Peterson wrote, "This alleged natural right had no standing in English law, as Jefferson knew. Blackstone stated the rule: an English subject could not by any act of his own throw off his natural born allegiance."[34] Jefferson was taking liberties in his attempt to frame English law in the best light for the American colonists. The reason Jefferson felt he could get away with this was because he was quite frankly brilliant, and he knew that. He knew his ability to make an argument to cast some doubt or confusion as to British law would serve the American cause well—and it did.

The famous Jefferson biographer Dumas Malone wrote of the *Summary View*, "as a contemporary indictment of British policy it bordered on recklessness, but it was distinctive in its emphasis on philosophical fundamentals and its prophetic quality."[35] Malone also wrote that the essay was "more noteworthy for boldness and fervor than for historical precision or literary grace."[36] Ironically, Jefferson is given credit in the *Summary View* for hitting upon the idea of what became in modern times the British Commonwealth of Nations. He advocated something like a commonwealth of nations instead of the colonial system existing in 1774. This was certainly nothing new with Jefferson but coming as it did so close to actual warfare with Great Britain it has come to make Jefferson seem even more prophetic than he was. At the first Continental Congress delegates adopted some of Jefferson's language when they "claimed for the provincial assemblies the exclusive power of legislation in all matters of taxation and internal policy, subject only to the negative of the King, but they cheerfully consented to the operation of parliamentary acts that were limited to the regulation of external commerce."[37] Here the Continental Congress sought to fuse the thinking of both John

Dickinson and Thomas Jefferson (limited Parliament versus no Parliament interference in American affairs) into an idea. Malone would further write, "by attempting to ascend to the source of authority in a time of crisis he [Jefferson] laid himself open to the charge of being an impractical theorist."[38]

Concerning Jefferson's assertions that the American colonists from their first arrival in 1607 had supported themselves completely without British assistance and that the British only became interested in North America once the settlers had created something valuable, that the British could benefit from, Dumas Malone wrote, "He greatly overstated the case for the individual settlers, who could not have survived without British protection prior to the time he himself became grown. But he was not writing history; he was trying to play a part in making it by passionately pleading what seemed to him a sacred cause."[39] Malone was being rather generous with Jefferson. It is hard to fathom what Jefferson really thought his essay would accomplish, other than independence. He may even have harbored a private hope that it would be published. For Malone, the answer as to what Jefferson was really thinking was, "His chief aim was to overthrow parliamentary authority which had been unwise in practice and was wrong in principle, and at the same time to safeguard self-government."[40]

James Wilson

A substantial claim could certainly be made that James Wilson was the most interesting and unique member of the early Supreme Court. As one of only six men to sign both the Declaration of Independence and the Constitution, Wilson was clearly a Founding Father if ever there was one.[41] His education and intellectual attainments marked him early in life to be a leader, a mentor of not just men, but mankind. Yet, with all of that in the credit column of his life's ledger book, how is it that he came to die penniless in an obscure tavern in North Carolina while on the run from bill collectors when he was fifty-six?[42]

James Wilson was born on September 14, 1742, in Fifeshire, Scotland. Early in life Wilson exhibited an innate intellectual bearing which was well incubated during the heady days of the Scottish Enlightenment. His studies prepared him for his migration to the American colonies in 1765, after graduating from Saint Andrews University. He settled in Philadelphia and began to study law. Fortunately for Wilson, he was accepted to study with John Dickinson, a highly learned and capable attorney who himself became a Founder. After successfully practicing law for several years, Wilson was eager to lend his voice to the growing crisis between the colonies and Britain. In 1774, the same year as Thomas Jefferson's pamphlet the *Summary*

View, Wilson published his own pamphlet called *Considerations on the Nature and Extent of the Legislative Authority of the British Parliament*. Wilson was elected to the Second Continental Congress and continued to prosper in his legal practice. In the early 1780s he began to become involved with land speculation, and in less than twenty years he would be dead, buried in a pauper's grave.

In the vast North American continent, land speculation was not uncommon—in fact quite a few Founders engaged in the practice. Certainly, men of means were engaged, and over-extended, in the contest to create wealth and to determine western settlement and expansion. Men from all economic strata engaged if they could; those at the top, like George Washington, to those unnamed of lesser financial standing, all entered the frenzied market. It produced some immense fortunes, but more likely it created financial hardship and burden. For James Wilson, sadly, the latter occurred.

It was also during these eleven years between 1776 and 1787 that Wilson became heavily involved with banking and land speculation that would ultimately lead to his downfall. He was a director of the Bank of North America when banks were not viewed favorably at all. In fact, Wilson was occasionally the target of vandals and mob violence by those who saw banks as the bastions of the moneyed elite.

Even when he was appointed to the Supreme Court in 1789, there were signs of trouble in his shaky financial portfolio. As early as 1782, Wilson was bargaining over the price of furniture he was selling to satisfy a debt. In a letter of February 9, 1782, Wilson wrote "On reconsidering, more maturely, the [language?] of my last letter to you, I am apprehensive that your reassessing the appraised value of the furniture, as it will not discharge the whole of your demand, may [?] some legal difficulties in the [?] which it may be necessary to take for reassessing the remediation of the debt."[43] Wilson was concerned that the appraised value of the furniture was not high enough to eliminate the debt owed to his creditors and therefore was looking to have the appraisal reconsidered.

Eleven years later, Wilson, now a Supreme Court Justice, entered an agreement with William Bingham on July 17, 1793. Wilson borrowed £5,013 to be repaid, with interest, by February 1, 1794. This brief seven-month loan was to be repaid at £5,506, meaning the original loan carried an approximate ten percent interest rate.[44] Wilson's practice of staying one step ahead of one creditor by engaging another creditor lasted nearly fifteen years and presented a sorry commentary on the life of someone so brilliant. This was someone forced to sell his household furnishings to cover the debts incurred in land speculation and other investments in the highly turbulent financial world of post–Revolutionary America.

Chapter 11. Final Arguments for America

It seems almost incongruous that such a uniquely brilliant legal mind would descend into financial ruin. Of course, not all the blame for his collapse can be placed at Wilson's feet. The unimaginably chaotic financial world of post–Revolutionary America was nearly indecipherable, and some elements of Wilson's collapse were certainly out of his control. However, in the late 1770s and for the next decade, Wilson was simply one of the greatest theoretical legal thinkers in the United States.

During the Second Continental Congress, Wilson was a reliable voice for an independent United States before and after the Declaration of Independence. His arguments invariably centered around legal reasoning; generally, formulated along the lines of Britain having abrogated their legal duties to the colonies. Wilson was perhaps the best prepared to follow this line of thought. For Wilson, the law was paramount, without law, there would be no liberty, without liberty, no law. The two concepts or perspectives were fused, and to Wilson they formed the essence of the American colonial revolt.

More significantly, it was Wilson's conception of natural law versus human law. To Wilson, natural law constituted some impenetrable law that existed outside the realm of human law; for Wilson, and ultimately America, human law and liberty were what was at stake in the struggle with Britain. While George Washington is given more than his fair share for the military victory over Britain, Wilson is all but forgotten for his victory over the concepts of the Declaration of Independence, which he did sign. In other words, Wilson, due to his intense involvement in the American political process between 1776 and 1787 (the years of the Declaration and the Constitution) became the victor in the struggle to find the foundation of American liberty: human law. Those eleven years saw *Nature's God* in the Declaration become *We the People* in the Constitution. "It was Wilson who wrote the intellectual threads of his generation into a theory of popularly based government combined to the rule of law."[45]

Wilson strove throughout his life to bring together the various elements of an emerging American consciousness. "Wilson attempted to blend the ideas of liberty and the rule of law with the new idea of popular sovereignty."[46] As one of only six men to sign both the Declaration of Independence and the Constitution, he had as much to do with the intellectual underpinnings of the American founding as any man. Wilson not only signed both of America's founding documents, he was instrumental in drafting both. Records indicate he was a seminal figure during the debates in 1776 and in 1787. Wilson's agile mind allowed him to address "…the law in broad, often bold strokes that encompassed philosophy, psychology, and political theory."[47] Much of his writing outside of the law was reflected by his research about the law as well. In the new nation, virtue was of paramount importance for being a citizen. Wilson, through his writings, was most closely associated with those who saw citizenship as a "...close relationship among public virtue, moral commitment to the public interest, and respect for the will of the people based on their intrinsic good."[48]

Wilson's Essay

James Wilson is a Founding Father that few could name. If for no other reason, his essay, *Considerations on the Nature and Extent of the Legislative Authority of the British Parliament*, deserves to be reviewed. Fortunately, Wilson was a significant member of the Founding generation whose essay, written in 1768, the decade under consideration by this book, was not published until 1774, the same year as Jefferson's. Whether Jefferson was aware of Wilson's essay is not known but given that Wilson wrote his essay six years before it was published, he, and not Jefferson, should receive credit for the argument that Parliament had no control over the colonies in either internal or external affairs. What makes this proposition so unique for Wilson is that he was a law student of John Dickinson. Dickinson, the most famous writer of the 1760s, had developed the argument that Parliament could control external, but not internal, affairs. Between Dickinson and Wilson lies a classic case of a teacher making one argument and the pupil making the exact opposite.

Wilson began his essay by jumping immediately into the matter at hand. He asked, "No question can be more important to Great Britain, and to the colonies, then this—does the legislative authority of the British parliament extend over them?"[49] This seems like such an elementary question, yet it is a question that engaged the greatest minds, in both Britain and America, between 1765 and 1774. Everyone from John Dickinson and Thomas Jefferson to James Wilson thought they had the answer. Wilson argued that the colonies were asking no more than what was due to them as Englishmen, like Jefferson. This was a familiar refrain that nearly every polemicist on the topic relied on. Wilson also cast the cause of the colonies as the cause of the British constitution. This was another familiar argument which the American writers made frequently. Wilson made a reference to William Blackstone and his *Commentaries on the Laws of England* within the first several paragraphs and it would be largely upon Blackstone that Wilson based his essay. Blackstone's *Commentaries* were literally fresh off the press in 1768 when Wilson composed his essay. Wilson likely acquired a copy of Blackstone (four volumes in all) and read it in a relatively short period of time. He quoted Blackstone—and criticized him—for reflecting the views of the British nobility who Wilson felt argued that political power must reside fully within one component of the political system and be disbursed downward to the lowest levels. The lowest levels were to work to make sure that the policy which initiated at the top and ran to the bottom ran equally smooth from the bottom to the top. This was a concept that was quickly becoming anathema to the American Founders who gradually came to see power running in just the opposite direction, that is from the bottom to the top.

Wilson looked immediately to the source or topic under consideration. He phrased it in a formal question, "Let me now be permitted to ask, will it ensure an increase in the happiness of the American colonies, that the parliament of Great Britain should possess a supreme, irresistible, uncontrolled authority over them? Is such an authority consistent with their liberty?"[50] Wilson did not even consider that the colonies were a part of Great Britain. He saw them as already separate political entities whose connection to Great Britain could be of no benefit to them. To answer these questions Wilson set out to examine the liberties that the British people enjoyed; likewise, he wanted to compare whether the American colonists enjoyed the same liberties as Englishmen. Should the liberties enjoyed by Englishmen be found to not correspond with those enjoyed by the colonists then the American colonists would have no further connection with the British government. Or, as Wilson phrased it, "the undeniable consequence will be, that the colonists are not under the same obligations to entrust their liberties into the hands of the same legislature...."[51]

For Wilson, the most powerful political tool the British voters had was the vote. Without the vote, Englishmen lacked the ability to remove those legislators who were not living up to their potential, who were threatening or endangering English liberties; without the vote the ability to remove politicians, English liberties would not exist. This worked well if everyone who could vote did. Wilson acknowledged that there are vast segments of society which were unable to vote. Still, those who could vote should vote. Voting is the greatest weapon that a free citizen has. This is where Wilson confronted the idea of virtual representation, something that the English ministers argued the American colonists had. The idea of virtual representation meant that although there was not a representative that one may have voted for meant that there was nonetheless a virtual representative with your best interests in mind. Wilson expanded this concept of virtual representation while not having voting privileges. Wilson, as with every other Founder, saw the idea of virtual representation as disingenuous. However, we need to bear in mind that the Founders had no conception either of voting that could equate to our notions presently.

For Wilson, "The first maxims of jurisprudence are ever kept in view—that all power is derived from the people—that their happiness is the end of government."[52] New parliaments, those with new members recently elected allow the king to understand "the immediate sense of the nation."[53] This encapsulated the power of voting in Wilson's view. Frequent turnover of officials in theory represented the will of the people. Frequent elections therefore ensured that the king had the best representatives regarding the feelings of those who elected members of Parliament. By this argument, frequent elections were best. Infrequent elections were damaging; without a frequent, scheduled, relied upon turnover in Parliament it would be difficult for the king or the monarch to understand the climate in which they were trying to govern. In theory this was superb and naturally required citizens to vote.

Of the three major writers we looked at in this book, Dickinson, Jefferson, and Wilson, without doubt Wilson is the most gifted scholar. Jefferson is by far the most rhetorical of the three and in a certain measure humorous; while Dickinson, after making his argument concisely, needlessly dragged his *Letters from a Farmer in Pennsylvania* to a less than convincing conclusion. Wilson, who read law under Dickinson, was every bit as well-versed in legal understanding as Dickinson and Jefferson, but it was Wilson who used his learning to the greatest extent. This perhaps made Wilson's essay not as accessible to the average colonist who may not have had the benefit of a legal education as Wilson did. Blackstone's *Commentaries on the Laws of England* had just been published in 1768 and he quickly became the authority on law, or English common law. Wilson, like Dickinson and Jefferson, used the imagery of slavery to indicate the condition and the status of the American colonists under British Parliamentary rule. Naturally, to us today this is the height of insensitivity and frankly at the time there were those who pointed out that the American colonists were in no way, shape, or form to be compared to the status of the enslaved African in America. Yet the imagery of the colonists as being slaves under the English system persisted. Wilson went so far in his essay to argue that the clergy in England had worked multiple times throughout English history to influence voting members of society, and by extension those who could not vote who lived with the consequences of votes cast by others. Wilson made a not so subtle jab at the power of an established religion which naturally would be rejected in the United States. He wrote that the clergy at times became, "Enemies alike to their king and to their country, their sole and unvaried aim was to reduce both to the most abject status of mission and slavery."[54]

Wilson began his attack on the issue of taxation by quoting the English scholar Lord Bracton: "One of the most ancient maxims of the English law is, that no freeman can be taxed at pleasure."[55] Wilson would go on to make probably the most sustained arguments over the issue of taxation and the issue of representation in Parliament. Wilson drew examples from Bracton, from Bacon, from Coke, and from Blackstone. Freemen here was used in connection with the idea of being politically free by having the vote. This was a concept that went back to Magna Carta and something the British or English took as a birthright. Wilson saw this aspect of the English constitution in dramatic and patriotic terms:

> Such is the admirable temperament of the British constitution! Such the glorious fabric of Britain's liberty, the pride of her citizens, the envy of her neighbors, planned by her legislators, erected by her patriots, maintained the entire by numerous generations past! May it be maintained entire by numerous generations to come![56]

On this basis, Wilson argued why should Englishmen hold the American colonists in contempt? Are not the American colonists asking for what is theirs as true born Englishmen?

Wilson embarked on a soliloquy midway through his essay on whether members of Parliament could adequately represent American colonists. Wilson wrote:

> [A]re the representatives of the commons of Great Britain the representatives of the Americans? Are they elected by the Americans? Are they such as the Americans, if they had the power of election, would probably elect? Do they know the interest of the Americans? Does their own interest prompt them to pursue the interest of the Americans? If they do not pursue it, had the Americans Power to punish them? Can the Americans remove unfaithful members at every new election? Can members, whom the Americans do not elect; with whom the Americans are not connected in interest; whom the Americans cannot remove; over whom the Americans have no influence—can such members be styled, with any propriety, the magistrates of the Americans?[57]

This argument, somewhat out of context as this was approached earlier in the essay, was a topic Wilson, or virtually any Founder, would not let their readers lose sight of. Wilson went so far as to quote debates in the House of Commons where he stated the members of Parliament themselves had the power to legislate for the government comes solely from the electors; "We had no legislative authority but what we derived from them."[58] Overall, Wilson provided by far the most extensive and well-documented argument for whether the British Parliament could speak for the American colonists. John Dickinson and Thomas Jefferson both took it as an almost established fact without really saying where that fact could be found or referenced. It was Wilson who would provide that reference.

Two-thirds the way through his essay Wilson endeavored to provide a point by point count of how and why English law was applicable to both people who lived in England and in the colonies. Wilson wrote, "What has been already advanced will suffice to show, that it is repugnant to the essential maxims of jurisprudence, to the ultimate end of all governments, to the genius of the British constitution, and to the liberty and happiness of the colonies, that they should be bound by the legislative authority of the parliament of Great Britain. Such a doctrine is not less repugnant to the voice of her laws. In order to evince this, I shall appeal to some authorities from the books of the law, which show expressly, or by a necessary implication, that the colonies are not bound by the acts of the British parliament; because they had no share in the British legislature."[59]

The case of *Blankard vs. Galdy*, adjudicated in 1693, was the most compelling legal case which Wilson was to rely on. Although it was a complicated case (the case contradicted itself) it did hold, "that all laws in force in England were in force in the country newly inhabited by English subjects."[60] Again, while this case had many plots and subplots not necessarily applicable to the American colonists of the 1760s, nonetheless a broader reading of the decision certainly bolstered Wilson's argument. More than any writer of his generation James Wilson summed up what would be the cause of nearly two decades of verbal debate and the wholesale reversal in the entire concept of government as it was known in the eighteenth century. The power of the case that began in Jamaica, one of the British colonies in the 1690s, would signal the end of the British empire as it stood in 1768. It was determined in the *Blankard* case of 1693, "That the acts of parliament or statutes of England were not in force in Jamaica. This decision is explicit in favor of America; for whatever was resolved concerning Jamaica is equally applicable to every American colony."[61] Indeed, several years later the same chief justice who ruled in the Jamaica case would also rule similarly in a case which involved the colony of Virginia. The 1693 Jamaica case showed just how complicated the concept of English colonial law was. English law was in force, and English law was not in force. Clearly a dichotomy existed that should have been settled through Parliament.

William Blackstone too wrote on the issue of whether English law followed explorers and settlers when they occupied the new land. Blackstone wrote:

> For it is held, that if an uninhabited country be discovered and planted by English subjects, all the English laws are immediately there in force. For as the law is the birthright of every subject, so wherever they go they carry their laws with them. But in conquered or ceded countries, that have already laws of their own, the king may indeed alter and change those laws; but till he does change them, the ancient laws of the country remain....[62]

Blackstone further wrote in his highly influential *Commentaries on the Laws of England*:

> Our American plantations are principally of this latter sort, being obtained in the last century either by right of conquest and driving out the natives (with what natural justice I shall not at present inquire) or by treaties. And therefore, the common law of England, as such, has no allowance or authority there; they

being no part of the mother country, but distinct (though dependent) dominions. They are subject however to the control of the parliament; though ... not bound by any acts of parliament, unless particularly named.[63]

This observation by Blackstone is as confusing as it is not confusing. They are subject to the control Parliament, while not being bound by Parliament unless particularly named. That no doubt produced a particularly knotty issue for debate.

In a footnote Wilson discussed William Blackstone when he wrote, "It is plain that Blackstone understood the opinion of the judge's—that the colonies are bound by acts of the British parliament if named in them—to be founded on the principle of conquest. It will not be improper to insert his commentary upon the resolutions respecting America."[64] British legal opinion concerning whether the colonies were in fact subject to parliamentary rule was not something that was agreed upon. Scholars have varying opinions with various points within those opinions. Whether citing Blackstone, Chief Justice Holt, Edward Coke, or Sir Matthew Hale, among others, these are genuine debates which should have happened—rather than having been allowed to descend into warfare. Many of these issues could and should have been determined legislatively.

James Wilson responded in his essay to William Blackstone's argument concerning dependency of colonies on Great Britain. Wilson wrote:

> The original and true ground of the superiority of Great Britain over the American colonies is not shown in any book of the law, unless, as I have already observed, it be derived from the right of conquest. But I have proved, and I hope satisfactorily, that this is all together inapplicable to the colonists. The original of the superiority of Great Britain over the colonies is, then, unaccounted for; and when we consider the ingenuity and pains which have lately been employed at home on this subject, we may justly conclude, that the only reason why it is not accounted for, is, that it cannot be accounted for.[65]

Similarly, Wilson also referenced *Calvin*'s case, argued in 1607–1608, which determined that persons born within territory held by the king enjoy the benefits of English law.[66]

Wilson also relied on the writings of Francis Bacon (someone John Dickinson greatly admired) to further his argument concerning where the loyalty of the colonists should lie. According to Bacon, Wilson wrote, "my Lord Bacon had no conception that the parliament would or ought to interpose, either in the settlement or the government of the colonies. The only relation, in which he says the colonists must still continue, is that of subjects: the only dependency, which they ought to acknowledge, is a dependency on the crown."[67] This was an argument that the colonists would make over and over between 1765 and the outbreak of hostilities in 1775. However, as we have seen, Jefferson took great pains in his essay to attack

George III to great extent. (In fact, even today it is George III, and not Parliament, who carries the weight of America's greatest bogeyman.)

Wilson wrapped up his essay by stating, "Now we have explained the dependence of the Americans. They are the subjects of the king of Great Britain. They owe him allegiance. They have a right to the benefits which arise from preserving that allegiance inviolate."[68] Wilson's last paragraph struck a high note:

> The connection and harmony between Great Britain and us, which it is her interest and ours mutually to cultivate, and on which her prosperity, as well as ours, so materially depends, will be better preserved by the operation of the legal prerogatives of the crown, then by the exertion of an unlimited authority by parliament.[69]

Of the three major American essayists who have been reviewed in this book, John Dickinson, Thomas Jefferson, and James Wilson, all three exhibited unique writing quality and style. Their arguments do overlap in certain points which results in a familiar refrain that is common to any student of American history. The phrase taxation without representation is as common as if it had been written by Shakespeare. Yet it was not written by Shakespeare, and this represented a serious flashpoint in relations between the American colonies and Great Britain. What Dickinson, Jefferson, and Wilson brought to the table was an encyclopedic knowledge of English common law. Dickinson had a great fund of English history to draw on as well. Jefferson made the attempt at history and historical connection, but ultimately got sidelined by his own rhetoric. Jefferson's literary genius clearly got the better of his skills as a legal researcher. That is where Wilson came into the picture. His reliance on legal precedent rather than history was something neither Dickinson nor Jefferson relied on to the extent that Wilson did. It is clearly no contest which of the three essayists ranks the highest in the popular American imagination of the twenty-first century. Jefferson has one of the most beautiful monuments in Washington, D.C. His home is a magnet for visitors from around the world. John Dickinson has a college named for him although it is nowhere near is well known as Jefferson's University of Virginia. Dickinson's home in Dover, Delaware, is also a historic site but only receives a sliver of the visitors which Monticello receives. Dickinson even wrote the "Liberty Song," a song set to the music of English composer William Boyce, which is still popular and performed today, yet most people have no idea that Dickinson wrote the words. James Wilson is totally forgotten partly because of his disgrace at having been forced into debt due to his excessive land speculation. Yet to read the three side by side today in the twenty-first century, Wilson's is the one that reads closest to a language that we would recognize. This would seem to make Wilson the obvious candidate for being the one most remembered. Yet that is not the case.

It is a popular comment that anyone wanting to understand the Constitution, or the American system of government should read the *Federalist* papers, or the Constitution. It could be just as easily said concerning the Revolution that if someone wanted to understand that event, they should read Wilson's essay. Dickinson, Jefferson, and many other essayists, created compelling works. But the one that without question rises above them all and should be a standard starting point for anyone wanting to understand the Revolution should be the essay by the Scotsman James Wilson.

Conclusions

In many ways the dispute between America and Britain is truly Old World versus New World. Britain was trying to maintain ancient concepts of colony governance while America was trying at first to modify it, but ultimately ended up completely abolishing it. The experiences which Americans lived every day simply did not translate into British or European politics or ways of life. For good or bad, virtually every aspect of the old country became Americanized sooner rather than later upon arrival by immigrants. It simply became too difficult for Britain to keep up with the changes and challenges. No one among the colonists seriously thought Britain was going to modify or amend its policies without a fight. Although the prospect of revolt was frightening to most, independence was more enticing than the fright of revolt.

It seems abundantly clear, despite seemingly endless protestations to the contrary, that the colonial leaders of the 1760s wanted independence. Whatever that independence looked like they may not have fully articulated. Perhaps they had in mind some type of commonwealth status such as exists today. It will never be known because it was never written about at the time. And Britain was still grappling with trying to comprehend the new geo-political order brought about by the victory in the French and Indian War.

The colonial leaders, nearly all of whom were American aristocracy or gentry, led the colonies in a way that even out-classed England. In the 1760s and 1770s, American leaders sought to protect their status, not just economically, but politically as well. The non-voting members of society, poor whites, women, the enslaved, were deemed of little consequence at the time. The documents the Founders created have been wonderfully elastic in that they have since come to include those excluded at the Founding. What made it all work in part was, for the time, endless resources, and opportunities for those non-aristocratic Americans to have a chance at what came to be encouragingly called the American Dream.

Appendix 1. Crevecoeur—What Is an American?

Crevecoeur's monumental question, "What is an American?" no doubt may have struck some at the time as absurd. From the basic geographical perspective an American was someone who lived in America. But just below the surface of this innocent reply is a complex, multi-layered definition approximating an answer.

An American was whatever they wanted to be; that was part of the lure of the colonies (and later states). There was no one answer to which Crevecoeur or anyone during the time he wrote could have answered. America was still raw, new, unfounded, unsettled. America was in constant motion, forever in a state of becoming. The decades between the 1760s and the turn of nineteenth century saw America attempt to define itself and provide an answer to Crevecoeur.

Naturally this is a European perspective to the answer; Native Americans and those marginalized had no reasonable answer much less even caring about the original question. Yet the answer to Crevecoeur had a meaning and has a meaning even today. It is worthwhile to understand Crevecoeur's own perspective.

Here, in selections from Letter III, Crevecoeur answers what an American is:

Crevecoeur

I wish I could be acquainted with the feelings and thoughts which must agitate the heart and present themselves to the mind of an enlightened Englishman, when he first lands on this continent.[1] He must greatly rejoice that he lived at a time to see this fair country discovered and settled; he must necessarily feel a share of national pride, when he views the chain of settlements which embellishes these extended shores. When he says to himself, this is the work of my countrymen, who, when convulsed by factions, afflicted by a variety of miseries, and wants, restless and impatient, took refuge here. They brought along with them their national genius, to which they principally owe what liberty they enjoy, and what substance they possess. Here he sees the industry of his native country displayed in a new manner, and traces in their works the embryos of all the arts, sciences, and ingenuity which nourish in Europe. Here he beholds fair cities, substantial villages, extensive fields, an immense country filled with decent houses, good roads, orchards, meadows, and bridges, where a hundred years ago all was wild, woody, and uncultivated! What a train of pleasing ideas this fair spectacle must suggest; it is a prospect which must inspire a good citizen with the most heartfelt pleasure. The difficulty consists in the manner of viewing so extensive a scene. He is arrived on a new continent; a modern society offers itself to his contemplation, different from what he had hitherto seen. It is not composed, as in Europe, of great lords who possess everything, and of a herd of people who have nothing. Here are no aristocratical families, no courts, no kings, no bishops, no ecclesiastical dominion, no invisible power giving to a few a very visible one; no great manufacturers employing thousands, no great refinements of luxury. The rich and the poor are not so far removed from each other as they are in Europe. Some few towns excepted, we are all tillers of the earth, from Nova Scotia to West Florida. We are a people of cultivators, scattered over an immense territory, communicating with each other by means of good roads and navigable rivers, united by the silken bands of mild government, all respecting the laws, without dreading their power, because they are equitable. We are all animated with the spirit of an industry which is unfettered and unrestrained, because each person works for himself. If he travels through our rural districts he views not the hostile castle, and the haughty mansion, contrasted with the clay-built hut and miserable cabin, where cattle and men help to keep each other warm, and dwell in meanness, smoke, and indigence. A pleasing uniformity of decent competence appears throughout our habitations. The meanest of our log-houses is a dry and comfortable habitation. Lawyer or merchant are the fairest titles our towns afford; that of a farmer is the only appellation of the rural inhabitants of our country. It must take some time ere he can reconcile himself to our dictionary, which is but short in words of dignity, and names of honor. There, on a Sunday, he sees a congregation of respectable farmers and their wives, all clad in neat homespun, well mounted, or riding in their own humble wagons. There is not among them an esquire, saving the unlettered magistrate. There he sees a parson as simple as his flock, a farmer who does not riot on the labor of others. We have no princes, for whom we toil, starve, and bleed: we are the most perfect society now existing in the world. Here man is free as he ought to be; nor is this pleasing equality so transitory as many others are. Many ages will not see the shores of our great lakes replenished with inland nations, nor the unknown bounds of North America entirely peopled. Who can tell how far it extends? Who can tell the millions of men whom it will feed and contain? For no European foot has as yet travelled half the extent of this mighty continent!

In this great American asylum, the poor of Europe have by some means met together, and in consequence of various causes; to what purpose should they ask one another what countrymen they are? Alas, two thirds of them had no country. Can a wretch who wanders about, who works and starves, whose life is a continual scene of sore affliction or pinching penury; can that man call England or any other kingdom his country? A country that had no bread for him, whose fields procured him no harvest, who met with nothing but the frowns of the rich, the severity of the laws, with jails and punishments; who owned not a single foot of the extensive surface of this planet? No! Urged by a variety of motives, here they came. Everything has tended to regenerate them; new laws, a new mode of living, a new social system; here they are become men: in Europe they were as so many useless plants, wanting vegetative mold, and refreshing showers; they withered, and were mowed down by want, hunger, and war; but now by the power of transplantation, like all other plants they have taken root and flourished! Formerly they were not numbered in any civil lists of their country, except in those of the poor; here they rank as citizens. By what invisible power has this surprising metamorphosis been performed? By that of the laws and that of their industry. The laws, the indulgent laws, protect them as they arrive, stamping on them the symbol of adoption; they receive ample rewards for their labors; these accumulated rewards procure them lands; those lands confer on them the title of freemen, and to that title every benefit is affixed which men can possibly require. This is the great operation daily performed by our laws. From whence proceed these laws? From our government. Whence the government? It is derived from the original genius and strong desire of the people ratified and confirmed by the crown. This is the great chain which links us all, this is the picture which every province exhibits, Nova Scotia excepted. There the crown has done all; either there were no people who had genius, or it was not much attended to: the consequence is, that the province is very thinly inhabited indeed; the power of the crown in conjunction with the mosquitos has prevented men from settling there. Yet some parts of it flourished once, and it contained a mild harmless set of people. But for the fault of a few leaders, the whole were banished [the driving of the French from Nova Scotia during the French and Indian War]. The greatest political error the crown ever committed in America, was to cut off men from a country which wanted nothing but men!

    What attachment can a poor European emigrant have for a country where he had nothing? The knowledge of the language, the love of a few kindred as poor as himself, were the only cords that tied him: his country is now that which gives him land, bread, protection, and consequence: ... What then is the American, this new man? He is either a European, or the descendant of an European, hence that strange mixture of blood, which you will find in no other country. I could point out to you a family whose grandfather was an Englishman, whose wife was Dutch, whose son married a French woman, and whose present four sons have now four wives of different nations. He is an American, who, leaving behind him all his ancient prejudices and manners, receives new ones from the new mode of life he has embraced, the new government he obeys, and the new rank he holds. He becomes an American by being received in the broad lap of our great Alma Mater. Here individuals of all nations are melted into a new race of men, whose labors and posterity will one day cause great changes in the world. Americans are the western pilgrims, who are carrying along with them that great mass of arts, sciences, vigor, and industry which began long since in the east; they will finish the great circle. The Americans were once scattered all over Europe; here they are incorporated into one of the finest systems of population which has ever appeared, and which will hereafter become distinct by the power of the different climates they inhabit. The American ought therefore to love this country much better than that wherein either he or his forefathers were born. Here the rewards of his industry follow with equal steps the progress of his labor; his labor is founded on the basis of nature, SELF-INTEREST: can it want a stronger allurement? Wives and children, who before in vain demanded of him a morsel of bread, now, fat and frolicsome, gladly help their father to clear those fields whence exuberant crops are to arise to feed and to clothe them all; without any part being claimed, either by a despotic prince, a rich abbot, or a mighty lord. Here religion demands but little of him; a small voluntary salary to the minister, and gratitude to God; can he refuse these? The American is a new man, who acts upon new principles; he must therefore entertain new ideas, and form new opinions. From involuntary idleness, servile dependence, penury, and useless labor, he has passed to toils of a very different nature, rewarded by ample subsistence—This is an American.

Appendix 2.
The Language of the Stamp Act

Of all the episodes surrounding the American Founding few looms as large in the American imagination as the Stamp Act. A seemingly innocuous tax—one that had been around in England since the seventeenth century—it ballooned out of all proportion and ultimately doomed British control of North America.

Great Britain: Parliament—The Stamp Act, March 22, 1765

An act for granting and applying certain stamp duties, and other duties, in the British colonies and plantations in America, towards further defraying the expenses of defending, protecting, and securing, the same; and for amending such parts of the several acts of parliament relating to the trade and revenues of the said colonies and plantations, as direct the manner of determining and recovering the penalties and forfeitures therein mentioned.[1]

WHEREAS by an act made in the last session of parliament, several duties were granted, continued, and appropriated, towards defraying the expenses of defending, protecting, and securing, the British colonies and plantations in America: and whereas it is just and necessary, that provision be made for raising a further revenue within your Majesty's dominions in America, towards defraying the said expenses: we, your Majesty's most dutiful and loyal subjects, the commons of Great Britain in parliament assembled, have therefore resolved to give and grant unto your Majesty the several rates and duties herein after mentioned; and do most humbly beseech your Majesty that it may be enacted, and be it enacted by the King's most excellent majesty, by and with the advice and consent of the lords spiritual and temporal, and commons, in this present parliament assembled, and by the authority of the same, That from and after the first day of November, one thousand seven hundred and sixty five, there shall be raised, levied, collected, and paid unto his Majesty, his heirs, and successors, throughout the colonies and plantations in America which now are, or hereafter may be, under the dominion of his Majesty, his heirs and successors.

For every skin or piece of vellum or parchment, or sheet or piece of paper, on which shall be ingrossed, written or printed, any declaration, plea, replication, rejoinder, demurrer, or other pleading, or any copy thereof, in any court of law within the British colonies and plantations in America, a stamp duty of three pence.

For every skin or piece of vellum or parchment, or sheet or piece of paper, on which shall be ingrossed, written or printed, any special bail and appearance upon such bail in any such court, a stamp duty of two shillings.

For every skin or piece of vellum or parchment, or sheet or piece of paper, on which shall be ingrossed, written, or printed, any petition, bill, answer, claim, plea, replication, rejoinder, demurrer, or other pleading in any court of chancery or equity within the said colonies and plantations, a stamp duty of one shilling and six pence.

For every skin or piece of vellum or parchment, or sheet or piece of paper, on which shall be ingrossed, written, or printed, any copy of any petition, bill, answer, claim, plea, replication, rejoinder, demurrer, or other pleading in any such court, a stamp duty of three pence.

For every skin or piece of vellum or parchment, or sheet or piece of paper, on which shall be ingrossed, written, or printed, any monition, libel, answer, allegation, inventory, or renunciation in ecclesiastical matters in any court of probate, court of the ordinary, or other court exercising ecclesiastical jurisdiction within the said colonies and plantations, a stamp duty of one shilling.

For every skin or piece of vellum or parchment, or sheet or piece of paper, on which shall be ingrossed, written, or printed, any copy of any will (other than the probate thereof) monition, libel, answer, allegation, inventory, or renunciation in ecclesiastical matters in any such court, a stamp duty of six pence.

Appendix 3.
Language from the Repeal of the Stamp Act

The Stamp Act generated the first sustained effort by Americans to collectively oppose British policy. Repeal of the Stamp Act marked the end of a two-year struggle to organize thoughts and reactions into a coherent rejection of British foreign policy. It was perhaps the Americans' only unique victory against the British—the Revolution required the assistance of the French, Spanish, and Dutch to ultimately defeat Britain militarily.

Great Britain: Parliament—An Act Repealing the Stamp Act; March 18, 1766

Whereas an Act was passed in the last session of Parliament entitled, an Act for granting and applying certain stamp duties, and other duties in the British colonies and plantations in America towards further defraying the expenses of defending, protecting, and securing the same; and for amending such parts of the several Acts of Parliament relating to the trade and revenues of the said colonies and plantations as direct the manner of determining and recovering the penalties and forfeitures therein mentioned; and whereas the continuance of the said Act would be attended with many inconveniencies, and may be productive of consequences greatly detrimental to the commercial interests of these kingdoms; may it therefore please your most excellent majesty that it may be enacted; and be it enacted by the King's most excellent majesty, by and with the advice and consent of the Lords Spiritual and Temporal, and Commons, in this present Parliament assembled, and by the authority of the same, that from and after the first day of May, one thousand seven hundred and sixty-six, the above-mentioned Act, and the several matters and things therein contained, shall be, and is and are hereby repealed and made void to all intents and purposes whatsoever.[1]

Appendix 4.
The Language
of the Declaratory Act

The euphoria over the repeal of the Stamp Act was quickly dashed by news of the Declaratory Act. Colonists, who struggled to make a legal argument against the Stamp Act often reverted to the opinion that Parliament had no right to tax the colonies. This viewpoint was immediately rejected by the British through the Declaratory Act.

Great Britain: Parliament—The Declaratory Act; March 18, 1766

An act for the better securing the dependency of his majesty's dominions in America upon the crown and parliament of Great Britain.

Whereas several of the houses of representatives in his Majesty's colonies and plantations in America, have of late against law, claimed to themselves, or to the general assemblies of the same, the sole and exclusive right of imposing duties and taxes upon his majesty's subjects in the said colonies and plantations; and have in pursuance of such claim, passed certain votes, resolutions, and orders derogatory to the legislative authority of parliament, and inconsistent with the dependency of the said colonies and plantations upon the crown of Great Britain: may it therefore please your most excellent Majesty, that it may be declared; and be it declared by the King's most excellent majesty, by and with the advice and consent of the lords spiritual and temporal, and commons, in this present parliament assembled, and by the authority of the same, that the said colonies and plantations in America have been, are, and of right ought to be, subordinate unto, and dependent upon the imperial crown and parliament of Great Britain; and that the King's majesty, by and with the advice and consent of the lords spiritual and temporal, and commons of Great Britain, in parliament assembled, had before, and of right ought to have, full power and authority to make laws and statutes of sufficient force and validity to bind the colonies and people of America, subjects of the crown of Great Britain, in all cases whatsoever....[1]

II. And be it further declared and enacted by the authority aforesaid, that all resolutions, votes, orders, and proceedings, in any of the said colonies or plantations, whereby the power and authority of the parliament of Great Britain, to make laws and statutes as aforesaid, is denied, or drawn into question, are, and are hereby declared to be, utterly null and void to all in purposes whatsoever.

Appendix 5.
Massachusetts Circular Letter to the Colonial Legislatures: February 11, 1768

The Massachusetts legislature, during a relative lull in legislative matters, took it upon themselves to reach out to other colonies in the hopes of maintaining the pressure on Britain against taxation and Parliamentary interference against colonial governments.

A synopsis of the feelings entertained by the Massachusetts legislature and shared throughout colonial North America:

> The House of Representatives of this province have taken into their serious consideration the great difficulties that must accrue to themselves and their constituents by the operation of several Acts of Parliament, imposing duties, and taxes on the American colonies.[1]
>
> As it is a subject in which every colony is deeply interested, they have no reason to doubt but your house is deeply impressed with its importance, and that such constitutional measures will be come into as are proper. It seems to be necessary that all possible care should be taken that the representatives of the several assemblies, upon so delicate a point, should harmonize with each other. The House, therefore, hope that this letter will be candidly considered in no other light than as expressing a disposition freely to communicate their mind to a sister colony, upon a common concern, in the same manner as they would be glad to receive the sentiments of your or any other house of assembly on the continent.
>
> The House have humbly represented to the ministry their own sentiments, that his Majesty's high court of Parliament is the supreme legislative power over the whole empire; that in all free states the constitution is fixed, and as the supreme legislative derives its power and authority from the constitution, it cannot overleap the bounds of it without destroying its own foundation; that the constitution ascertains and limits both sovereignty and allegiance, and, therefore, his Majesty's American subjects, who acknowledge themselves bound by the ties of allegiance, have an equitable claim to the full enjoyment of the fundamental rules of the British constitution; that it is an essential, unalterable right in nature, engrafted into the British constitution, as a fundamental law, and ever held sacred and irrevocable by the subjects within the realm, that what a man has honestly acquired is absolutely his own, which he may freely give, but cannot be taken from him without his consent; that the American subjects may, therefore, exclusive of any

consideration of charter rights, with a decent firmness, adapted to the character of free men and subjects, assert this natural and constitutional right.

It is, moreover, their humble opinion, which they express with the greatest deference to the wisdom of the Parliament, that the Acts made there, imposing duties on the people of this province, with the sole and express purpose of raising a revenue, are infringements of their natural and constitutional rights; because, as they are not represented in the British Parliament, his Majesty's commons in Britain, by those Acts, grant their property without their consent.

This House further are of opinion that their constituents, considering their local circumstances, cannot, by any possibility, be represented in the Parliament; and that it will forever be impracticable, that they should be equally represented there, and consequently, not at all; being separated by an ocean of a thousand leagues. That his Majesty's royal predecessors, for this reason, were graciously pleased to form a subordinate legislature here, that their subjects might enjoy the unalienable right of a representation; also, that considering the utter impracticability of their ever being fully and equally represented in Parliament, and the great expense that must unavoidably attend even a partial representation there, this House thinks that a taxation of their constituents, even without their consent, grievous as it is, would be preferable to any representation that could be admitted for them there.

Upon these principles, and also considering that were the right in Parliament ever so clear, yet, for obvious reasons, it would be beyond the rules of equity that their constituents should be taxed on the manufactures of Great Britain here, in addition to the duties they pay for them in England, and other advantages arising to Great Britain, from the Acts of trade, this House have preferred a humble, dutiful, and loyal petition, to our most gracious sovereign, and made such representations to his Majesty's ministers, as they apprehended would tend to obtain redress. They have also submitted to consideration, whether any people can be said to enjoy any degree of freedom if the Crown, in addition to its undoubted authority of constituting a governor, should appoint him such a stipend as it may judge proper, without the consent of the people, and at their expense; and whether, while the judges of the land, and other civil officers, hold not their commissions during good behaviour, their having salaries appointed for them by the Crown, independent of the people, hath not a tendency to subvert the principles of equity, and endanger the happiness and security of the subject.

In addition to these measures, the House have written a letter to their agent which he is directed to lay before the ministry; wherein they take notice of the hardships of the Act for preventing mutiny and desertion, which requires the governor and council to provide enumerated articles for the king's marching troops, and the people to pay the expenses; and also, the commission of the gentlemen appointed commissioners of the customs, to reside in America, which authorizes them to make as many appointments as they think fit, and to pay the appointees what sum they please, for whose malconduct they are not accountable; from whence it may happen that officers of the Crown may be multiplied to such a degree as to become dangerous to the liberty of the people, by virtue of a commission, which does not appear to this House to derive any such advantages to trade as many have supposed.

These are the sentiments and proceedings of this House; and as they have too much reason to believe that the enemies of the colonies have represented them to his Majesty's ministers, and to the Parliament, as factious, disloyal, and having a disposition to make themselves independent of the mother country, they have taken occasion, in the most humble terms, to assure his Majesty, and his ministers, that, with regard to the people of this province, and, as they doubt not, of all the colonies, the charge is unjust. The House is fully satisfied that your assembly is too generous and liberal in sentiment to believe that this letter proceeds from an ambition of taking the lead, or dictating to the other assemblies. They freely submit their opinions to the judgment of others; and shall take it kind in your house to point out to them anything further that may be thought necessary.

This House cannot conclude, without expressing their firm confidence in the king, our common head and father, that the united and dutiful supplications of his distressed American subjects will meet with his royal and favorable acceptance.

Appendix 6.
James Wilson: From *Considerations on the Nature and Extent of the Legislative Authority of the British Parliament*

Forgotten today, James Wilson was in the major ranks of Founding Fathers. His writings influenced many of his colleagues with their deeply researched and lucidly argued points. Below are excerpts from his pamphlet published in 1774 on the authority of the British Parliament.

What has been already advanced will suffice to show, that it is repugnant to the essential maxims of jurisprudence, to the ultimate end of all governments, to the genius of the British constitution, and to the liberty and happiness of the colonies, that they should be bound by the legislative authority of the parliament of Great Britain.[1] Such a doctrine is not less repugnant to the voice of her laws. In order to evince this, I shall appeal to some authorities from the books of the law, which show expressly, or by a necessary implication, that the colonies are not bound by the acts of the British parliament; because they have no share in the British legislature.

The first case I shall mention was adjudged in the second year of Richard the third [1485]. It was a solemn determination of all the judges of England, met in the exchequer chamber, to consider whether the people in Ireland were bound by an act of parliament made in England. They resolved, "that they were not, as to such things as were done in Ireland; but that what they did out of Ireland must be conformable to the laws of England, because they were the subjects of England. 'Ireland' said they, 'has a parliament, who make laws; and our statutes do not bind them; *because they do not send knights to parliament:* but their persons are the subjects of the king, in the same manner as the inhabitants of Calais, Gascoigne, and Guienne.'"

This is the first case which we find in the books upon this subject; and it deserves to be examined with the most minute attention.

    1. It appears, that the matter under consideration was deemed, at that time, to be of the greatest importance: for ordinary causes are never adjourned into the exchequer chamber; only such are adjourned there as are of uncommon

weight, or of uncommon difficulty. "Into the exchequer chamber," says my Lord Coke, "all cases of difficulty in the king's bench, or common pleas, &c. are, and of ancient time have been, adjourned, and there debated, argued, and resolved, by all the judges of England and barons of the exchequer." This court proceeds with the greatest deliberation, and upon the most mature reflection. The case is first argued on both sides by learned counsel, and then openly on several days, by all the judges. Resolutions made with so much caution, and founded on so much legal knowledge, may be relied on as the surest evidences of what is law.

2. It is to be observed, that the extent of the legislative authority of parliament is the very *point* of the adjudication. The decision was not incidental or indigested: it was not a sudden opinion, unsupported by reason and argument: it was an express and deliberate resolution of that very doubt, which they assembled to resolve.

3. It is very observable, that the reason, which those reverend sages of the law gave, why the people in Ireland were not bound by an act of parliament made in England, was the same with that, on which the Americans have founded their opposition to the late statutes made concerning them. The Irish did not send members to parliament; and, therefore, they were not bound by its acts. From hence it undeniably appears, that parliamentary authority is derived *solely* from representation—that those, who are bound by acts of parliament, are bound for this only reason, because they are represented in it. If it were not the *only* reason, parliamentary authority might subsist independent of it. But as parliamentary authority fails wherever this reason does not operate, parliamentary authority can be founded on no other principle. The law never ceases, but when the reason of it ceases also.

4. It deserves to be remarked, that no exception is made of any statutes, which bind those who are not represented by the makers of them. The resolution of the judges extends to *every* statute: they say, without limitation—"our statutes do not bind them." And indeed the resolution ought to extend to every statute; because the reason, on which it is founded, extends to every one. If a person is bound only because he is represented, it must certainly follow that wherever he is not represented he is not bound. No sound argument can be offered, why one statute should be obligatory in such circumstances, and not another. If we cannot be deprived of our property by those, whom we do not commission for that purpose; can we without any such commission, be deprived, by them, of our lives? Have those a right to imprison and gibbet us, who have not a right to tax us?

5. From this authority it follows, that it is by no means a rule, that the authority of parliament extends to all the subjects of the crown. The inhabitants of Ireland were the subjects of the king as of his crown of England; but it is expressly resolved, in the most solemn manner, that the inhabitants of Ireland are not bound by the statutes of England. Allegiance to the king and obedience to the parliament are founded on very different principles. The former is founded on protection: the latter, on representation. An inattention to this difference has produced, I apprehend, much uncertainty and confusion in our ideas concerning the connexion, which ought to subsist between Great Britain and the American colonies.

Appendix 6

6. The last observation which I shall make on this case is, that if the inhabitants of Ireland are not bound by acts of parliament made in England, *a fortiori,* the inhabitants of the American colonies are not bound by them. There are marks of the subordination of Ireland to Great Britain, which cannot be traced in the colonies. A writ of errour lies from the king's bench in Ireland, to the king's bench, and consequently to the house of lords, in England; by which means the former kingdom is subject to the control of the courts of justice of the latter kingdom. But a writ of errour does not lie in the king's bench, nor before the house of lords, in England, from the colonies of America. The proceedings in their courts of justice can be reviewed and controlled only on an appeal to the king in council.

Appendix 7.
Albany Plan of Union 1754

It is proposed that humble application be made for an act of Parliament of Great Britain, by virtue of which one general government may be formed in America, including all the said colonies, within and under which government each colony may retain its present constitution, except in the particulars wherein a change may be directed by the said act, as hereafter follows.[1]

    1. That the said general government be administered by a President-General, to be appointed and supported by the crown; and a Grand Council, to be chosen by the representatives of the people of the several Colonies met in their respective assemblies.

That within [several] months after the passing such act, the House of Representatives that happen to be sitting within that time, or that shall especially for that purpose convened, may and shall choose members for the Grand Council, in the following proportion, that is to say,

Massachusetts Bay 7
New Hampshire 2
Connecticut 5
Rhode Island 2
New York 4
New Jersey 3
Pennsylvania 6
Maryland 4
Virginia 7
North Carolina 4
South Carolina 4

———
48

    2. Who shall meet for the first time at the city of Philadelphia, being called by the President-General as soon as conveniently may be after his appointment.

    3. That there shall be a new election of the members of the Grand Council every three years; and, on the death or resignation of any member, his

place should be supplied by a new choice at the next sitting of the Assembly of the Colony he represented.

4. That after the first three years, when the proportion of money arising out of each Colony to the general treasury can be known, the number of members to be chosen for each Colony shall, from time to time, in all ensuing elections, be regulated by that proportion, yet so as that the number to be chosen by any one Province be not more than seven, nor less than two.

5. That the Grand Council shall meet once in every year, and oftener if occasion require, at such time and place as they shall adjourn to at the last preceding meeting, or as they shall be called to meet at by the President-General on any emergency; he having first obtained in writing the consent of seven of the members to such call, and sent duly and timely notice to the whole.

6. That the Grand Council have power to choose their speaker; and shall neither be dissolved, prorogued, nor continued sitting longer than six weeks at one time, without their own consent or the special command of the crown.

7. That the members of the Grand Council shall be allowed for their service ten shillings sterling per diem, during their session and journey to and from the place of meeting; twenty miles to be reckoned a day's journey.

8. That the assent of the President-General be requisite to all acts of the Grand Council, and that it be his office and duty to cause them to be carried into execution.

9. That the President-General, with the advice of the Grand Council, hold or direct all Indian treaties, in which the general interest of the Colonies may be concerned; and make peace or declare war with Indian nations.

10. That they make such laws as they judge necessary for regulating all Indian trade.

11. That they make all purchases from Indians, for the crown, of lands not now within the bounds of particular Colonies, or that shall not be within their bounds when some of them are reduced to more convenient dimensions.

12. That they make new settlements on such purchases, by granting lands in the King's name, reserving a quitrent to the crown for the use of the general treasury.

13. That they make laws for regulating and governing such new settlements, till the crown shall think fit to form them into particular governments.

14. That they raise and pay soldiers and build forts for the defense of any of the Colonies, and equip vessels of force to guard the coasts and protect the trade on the ocean, lakes, or great rivers; but they shall not impress men in any Colony, without the consent of the Legislature.

15. That for these purposes they have power to make laws, and lay and levy such general duties, imposts, or taxes, as to them shall appear most equal and just (considering the ability and other circumstances of the inhabitants in the several Colonies), and such as may be collected with the least inconvenience to the people; rather discouraging luxury, than loading industry with unnecessary burdens.

16. That they may appoint a General Treasurer and Particular Treasurer in each government when necessary; and, from time to time, may order the

sums in the treasuries of each government into the general treasury; or draw on them for special payments, as they find most convenient.

17. Yet no money to issue but by joint orders of the President-General and Grand Council; except where sums have been appropriated to particular purposes, and the President-General is previously empowered by an act to draw such sums.

18. That the general accounts shall be yearly settled and reported to the several Assemblies.

19. That a quorum of the Grand Council, empowered to act with the President-General, do consist of twenty-five members; among whom there shall be one or more from a majority of the Colonies.

20. That the laws made by them for the purposes aforesaid shall not be repugnant, but, as near as may be, agreeable to the laws of England, and shall be transmitted to the King in Council for approbation, as soon as may be after their passing; and if not disapproved within three years after presentation, to remain in force.

21. That, in case of the death of the President-General, the Speaker of the Grand Council for the time being shall succeed, and be vested with the same powers and authorities, to continue till the King's pleasure be known.

22. That all military commission officers, whether for land or sea service, to act under this general constitution, shall be nominated by the President-General; but the approbation of the Grand Council is to be obtained, before they receive their commissions. And all civil officers are to be nominated by the Grand Council, and to receive the President-General's approbation before they officiate.

23. But, in case of vacancy by death or removal of any officer, civil or military, under this constitution, the Governor of the Province in which such vacancy happens may appoint, till the pleasure of the President-General and Grand Council can be known.

24. That the particular military as well as civil establishments in each Colony remain in their present state, the general constitution notwithstanding; and that on sudden emergencies any Colony may defend itself, and lay the accounts of expense thence arising before the President-General and General Council, who may allow and order payment of the same, as far as they judge such accounts just and reasonable.

Appendix 8.
William Blackstone:
Excerpt from the Introduction to *Commentaries on the Laws of England*

Adapted from William Blackstone's introduction to his monumental *Commentaries on the Laws of England*. The result was the entry point for modern Anglo-American law and a classic English speech. Blackstone would guide generations of lawyers through the maze of law via his immensely popular study of English law. In this excerpt, he calls for the addition of a liberal arts education to complement legal training.

> For I think it is past dispute that those gentlemen, who resort to the inns of court with a view to pursue the profession, will find it expedient (whenever it is practicable) to lay the previous foundations of this, as well as every other science, in one of our learned universities.[1] We may appeal to the experience of every sensible lawyer, whether anything can be more hazardous or discouraging than the usual entrance on the study of the law. A raw and unexperienced youth, in the most dangerous season of life, is transplanted on a sudden into the midst of allurements to pleasure, without any restraint or check but what his own prudence can suggest; with no public direction in what course to pursue his enquiries; no private assistance to remove the distresses and difficulties, which will always embarrass a beginner. In this situation he is expected to sequester himself from the world, and by a tedious lonely process to extract the theory of law from a mass of undigested learning; or else by an assiduous attendance on the courts to pick up theory and practice together, sufficient to qualify him for the ordinary run of business. How little therefore is it to be wondered at, that we hear of so frequent miscarriages; that so many gentlemen of bright imaginations grow weary of so unpromising a search, and addict themselves wholly to amusements, or other less innocent pursuits; and that so many persons of moderate capacity confuse themselves at first setting out, and continue ever dark and puzzled during the remainder of their lives!
>
> The evident want of some assistance in the rudiments of legal knowledge, has given birth to a practice, which, if ever it had grown to be general, must have proved of extremely pernicious consequence: I mean the custom, by some so very warmly recommended, to drop all liberal education, as of no use to lawyers; and to place them, in its

stead, at the desk of some skillful attorney; in order to initiate them early in all the depths of practice, and render them more dexterous in the mechanical part of business. A few instances of particular persons (men of excellent learning, and unblemished integrity) who, in spite of this method of education, have shone in the foremost ranks of the bar, have afforded some kind of sanction to this illiberal path to the profession, and biased many parents, of shortsighted judgment, in its favor: not considering, that there are some geniuses, formed to overcome all disadvantages, and that from such particular instances no general rules can be formed; nor observing, that those very persons have frequently recommended by the most forcible of all examples, the disposal of their own off-spring, a very different foundation of legal studies, a regular academic education. Perhaps too, in return, I could now direct their eyes to our principal feats of justice, and suggest a few hints, in favor of university learning, but in these all who hear me, I know, have already prevented me.

Making therefore due allowance for one or two shining exceptions, experience may teach us to foretell that a lawyer thus educated to the bar, in subservience to attorneys and solicitors, will find he has begun at the wrong end. If practice be the whole he is taught, practice must also be the whole he will ever know: if he be uninstructed in the elements and first principles upon which the rule of practice is founded, the least variation from established precedents will totally distract and bewilder him … he must never aspire to form, and seldom expect to comprehend, any arguments drawn a priori, from the spirit of the laws and the natural foundations of justice.

Nor is this all; for (as few persons of birth, or fortune, or even of scholastic education, will submit to the drudgery of servitude and the manual labor of copying the trash of an office) should this infatuation prevail to any considerable degree, we must rarely expect to see a gentleman of distinction or learning at the bar. And what the consequence may be, to have the interpretation and enforcement of the laws (which include the entire disposal of our properties, liberties, and lives) fall wholly into the hands of obscure or illiterate men, is matter of very public concern.

The inconveniences here pointed out can never be effectually prevented, but by making academic education a previous step to the profession of the common law, and at the same time making the rudiments of the law a part of academic education. For sciences are of a sociable disposition, and flourish best in the neighborhood of each other; nor is there any branch of learning, but may be helped and improved by assistances drawn from other arts. If therefore the student in our laws hath formed both his sentiments and style, by perusal and imitation of the purest classical writers, among whom the historians and orators will best deserve his regard; if he can reason with precision, and separate argument from fallacy, by the clear simple rules of pure unsophisticated logic; if he can fix his attention, and steadily pursue truth through any [of] the most intricate deduction, by the use of mathematical demonstrations; if he has enlarged his conceptions of nature and art, by a view of the several branches of genuine; experimental, philosophy; if he has contemplated those maxims reduced to a practical system in the laws of imperial Rome; if he has done this or any part of it, (though all may be easily done under as able instructors as ever graced any feats of learning) a student thus qualified may enter upon the study of the law with incredible advantage and reputation. And if, at the conclusion, or during the acquisition of these accomplishments, he will afford himself here a year or two's farther leisure, to lay the foundation of his future labors in a solid scientific method, without thirsting too early to attend that practice which it is impossible he should rightly comprehend, he will afterwards proceed with the greatest ease, and will unfold the most intricate points with an intuitive rapidity and clearness.

I shall not insist upon such motives as might be drawn from principles of economy, and are applicable to particulars only: I reason upon more general topics. And therefore to the qualities of the head, which I have just enumerated, I cannot but add those of the heart; affectionate loyalty to the king, a zeal for liberty and the constitution, a sense of real honor, and well-grounded principles of religion; as necessary to form a truly valuable English lawyer, a Hyde, a Hale, or a Talbot. And, whatever the ignorance of some, or unkindness of others, may have heretofore untruly suggested, experience will warrant us to affirm, that these endowments of loyalty and public spirit, of honor and religion, are nowhere to be found in more high perfection than in the two universities of this kingdom [Oxford and Cambridge].

Chapter Notes

Preface

1. Jack P. Greene, and Craig B. Yirush, eds., *Exploring the Bounds of Liberty; Political Writings of Colonial British America From the Glorious Revolution to the American Revolution* Volume 1 (Carmel: Liberty Fund Inc., 2018), xii.
2. David L. Jacobson, "John Dickinson's Fight Against Royal Government, 1764," *The William and Mary Quarterly* 19, no. 1 (Jan., 1962), 85.
3. Winston S. Churchill, *The Age of Revolution* (New York: Dodd, Mead, and Company, 1980), 113.

Chapter 1

1. Georgian Papers Online; GEO/ADD/32/1074.
2. David Hawke, *The Colonial Experience* (New York: Macmillan Publishing Company, 1990), 399.
3. Charles A. Beard, Mary R. Beard, *The Rise of American Civilization, Volume 1, The Agricultural Era* (New York: The Macmillan Company, 1927), 126.
4. Alan Taylor, *Colonial America: A Very Short Introduction* (Oxford: Oxford University Press, 2013), 93.
5. Hawke, *The Colonial Experience*, 402.
6. Jack P. Greene, and Craig B. Yirush, ed., *Exploring the Bounds of Liberty; Political Writings of Colonial British America From the Glorious Revolution to the American Revolution* Volume 1 (Carmel: Liberty Fund Inc., 2018), xiv.
7. Hawke, *The Colonial Experience*, 404.

Chapter 2

1. John V. Jezierski, "Parliament or People: James Wilson and Blackstone on the Nature and Location of Sovereignty," *Journal of History of Ideas* Vol. 32, No. 1 (Jan.—Mar., 1971), 97.
2. Alan Taylor, *Colonial America: A Very Short Introduction* (Oxford: Oxford University Press, 2013), 90.
3. Charles A. Beard, Mary R. Beard, *The Rise of American Civilization, Volume 1, The Agricultural Era* (New York: The Macmillan Company, 1927), 37.
4. *Ibid.*, 112.
5. *Ibid.*
6. *Ibid.*, 43.
7. *Ibid.*, 119.
8. Taylor, *Colonial America: A Very Short Introduction*, 56.
9. *Ibid.*, 65.
10. Beard, *The Rise of American Civilization, Volume 1, The Agricultural Era*, 52.
11. *Ibid.*, 112.
12. *Ibid.*, 118.
13. Taylor, *Colonial America: A Very Short Introduction*, 90.
14. Beard, *The Rise of American Civilization, Volume 1, The Agricultural Era*, 30.
15. *Ibid.*, 129.
16. David Hawke, *The Colonial Experience* (New York: Macmillan Publishing Company, 1990), 501.
17. David Levin, ed. *Francis Parkman: France and England in North America, Volume II* (New York: Literary Classics of the United States, 1983), 1073.
18. Charles M. Andrews, *Colonial Folkways, A Chronicle of American Life in the Reign of the Georges* (New Haven: Yale University Press, 1920), 213.

19. *Ibid.*, 210–211.
20. *Ibid.*, 213.
21. *Ibid.*
22. *Ibid.*, 215.
23. Hawke, *The Colonial Experience*, 372.
24. Taylor, *Colonial America: A Very Short Introduction*, 102.
25. *Ibid.*, 7.
26. Hawke, *The Colonial Experience*, 477.
27. Beard, *The Rise of American Civilization, Volume 1, The Agricultural Era*, 32.
28. Lawrence Henry Gipson, *The Coming of the Revolution, 1763–1775* (New York: Harper & Row Publishers, 1954), 7.
29. Taylor, *Colonial America: A Very Short Introduction*, 74.
30. Hawke, *The Colonial Experience*, 475.
31. Taylor, *Colonial America: A Very Short Introduction*, 69.
32. *Ibid.*, 71.
33. The Dred Scott case decision was delivered by the United States Supreme Court on March 6, 1857. In a 7–2 ruling, Chief Justice Roger Taney, writing for the majority, ruled that Dred Scott, an enslaved African, who had resided in a Free State and territory was not thereby entitled to his freedom. Not being enough, Taney went on to expand on the case by writing that African Americans were not and could never be citizens of the United States. This is universally seen as one of the, if not the most, infamous cases ever decided by the Court. Had Taney simply ruled on the narrow parameters of whether an enslaved person residing in a free state could sue for their freedom the case may have been forgotten to history. However, Taney's animus to "once and for all" place African Americans in a second class of citizenship has forever made the case an infamous watchword for racism.
34. There is debate over whether the Africans who arrived in Jamestown on the ship in 1620 were actual slaves or indentured servants. However, it is known that enslaved Africans first arrived in the New World with Europeans in 1619. For all intents and purposes, enslaved Africans were ensconced in the colonies by the 1620s.
35. Beard, *The Rise of American Civilization, Volume 1, The Agricultural Era*, 173.
36. *Ibid.*, 174.
37. Albert E. Stone, ed., *Letters from an American Farmer and Sketches of Eighteenth-Century America* (New York: Viking Penguin, 1981), 10.
38. Daniel J. Boorstin, *The Lost World of Thomas Jefferson* (Chicago: University of Chicago Press, 1981), 3.
39. Stone, ed., *Letters from an American Farmer and Sketches of Eighteenth-Century America*, 8.
40. *Ibid.*, 82.
41. *Ibid.*, 70.
42. *Ibid.*, 69.
43. James P. Myers, Jr., "Crevecoeur: Concealing and Revealing the Secret Self." *Early American Literature* 49, no. 2 (2014), 357–401.
44. Stone, ed., *Letters from an American Farmer and Sketches of Eighteenth-Century America*, 35.
45. *Ibid.*, 37.
46. *Ibid.*, 66.
47. *Ibid.*, 67.
48. *Ibid.*
49. *Ibid.*, 70.
50. Taylor, *Colonial America: A Very Short Introduction*, 88.

Chapter 3

1. David Hawke, *The Colonial Experience* (New York: Macmillan Publishing Company, 1990), 396.
2. Probably the most famous is that by Henry Wadsworth Longfellow, the poem *Evangeline*.
3. Jane E. Calvert, ed., *The Complete Writings and Selected Correspondence of John Dickinson, Volume 1, 1751–1758* (Newark: University of Delaware Press, 2020), 134.
4. Will Durant, *The Age of Louis XIV* (Norwalk: The Easton Press, 1992), 706.
5. David Levin, ed. *Francis Parkman: France and England in North America, Volume II* (New York: Literary Classics of the United States, 1983), 938.
6. Patrice Louis-Rene Higonnet, "The Origins of the Seven Years' War," *The Journal of Modern History* 40, no. 1 (Mar., 1968), 68.
7. *Ibid.*, 69.
8. Calvert, ed., *The Complete Writings and Selected Correspondence of John Dickinson, Volume 1, 1751–1758*, 123.
9. *Ibid.*, 125.

10. *Ibid.*, 134.
11. Arthur R. Ropes, "The Causes of the Seven Years' War," *Transactions of the Royal Historical Society* 4 (1889), 148.
12. Winston S. Churchill, *The Age of Revolution* (Norwalk: The Easton Press, 1992), vii.
13. *Ibid.*
14. Adapted from Alan Taylor, *Colonial America: A Very Short Introduction* (Oxford: Oxford University Press, 2013), 108.
15. Durant, *The Age of Louis XIV*, 714.
16. An interesting side note to the War of Austrian Succession occurred in 1743 at Dettingen when French and British forces met. It was the last time a British king (George II) not only commanded in the field but fought hand-to-hand in the action after he lost his horse—the battle was a draw and George II unscathed.
17. Levin, ed. *Francis Parkman: France and England in North America, Volume II*, 744–745.
18. George M. Wrong, *The Conquest of New France, A Chronicle of the Colonial Wars* (New Haven: Yale University Press, 1920), 93.
19. Levin, ed. *Francis Parkman: France and England in North America, Volume II*, 745.
20. Wrong, *The Conquest of New France, A Chronicle of the Colonial Wars*, 94.
21. Higonnet, "The Origins of the Seven Years' War," 67.
22. Stephen Brumwell, *George Washington; Gentleman Warrior* (New York: Quercus, 2012), 29.
23. John Rhodehamel, ed. *George Washington: Writings* (New York: Literary Classics of the United States, 1997), 17.
24. *Ibid.*, 26.
25. *Ibid.*, 28.
26. As quoted in Parkman (Sparks' pupil), Levin, ed. *Francis Parkman: France and England in North America, Volume II*, 947.
27. *Ibid.*, 1075.
28. *Ibid.*, 1071.
29. Rhodehamel, ed. *George Washington: Writings*, 34–35.

Chapter 4

1. Winston S. Churchill, *The Age of Revolution* (Norwalk: The Easton Press, 1992), 137.
2. *Ibid.*
3. Peter D.G. Thomas, *George III—King and Politicians, 1760-1770* (Manchester: Manchester University Press, 2002), 281.
4. George M. Wrong, *The Conquest of New France, A Chronicle of the Colonial Wars* (New Haven: Yale University Press, 1920), 215.
5. Morristown National Historical Park, Lloyd W. Smith archival collection, MORR 12118.
6. Morristown National Historical Park, Lloyd W. Smith archival collection, MORR 12118.
7. Morristown National Historical Park, Lloyd W. Smith archival collection, MORR 12118.
8. Thomas, *George III—King and Politicians, 1760-1770*, 28–29.
9. Churchill, *The Age of Revolution*, 139.
10. Morristown National Historical Park, Lloyd W. Smith archival collection, MORR 11014.
11. Morristown National Historical Park, Lloyd W. Smith archival collection, MORR 11014.
12. David Levin, ed. *Francis Parkman: France and England in North America, Volume II* (New York: Literary Classics of the United States, 1983), 1477.
13. *Ibid.*, 1475.
14. Gordon S. Wood, ed., *The American Revolution—Writings from the Pamphlet Debate Volume I, 1764-1772* (New York: Literary Classics of the United States), xv.
15. *Ibid.*, xx.
16. Levin, ed. *Francis Parkman: France and England in North America, Volume II*, 1477.
17. Will Durant, *Rousseau and Revolution* (Norwalk: The Easton Press, 1992), 62.
18. Wood, ed., *The American Revolution—Writings from the Pamphlet Debate Volume I, 1764-1772*, 4.
19. Thomas, *George III—King and Politicians, 1760-1770*, 35.
20. Wood, ed., *The American Revolution—Writings from the Pamphlet Debate Volume I, 1764-1772*, 7.
21. Francis Bacon, *The Essays or Counsels Civil and Moral* (Norwalk, The Easton Press, 1980), 61.
22. Wood, ed., *The American Revolution—Writings from the Pamphlet Debate Volume I, 1764-1772*, 9.

23. Churchill, *The Age of Revolution*, 151.
24. An interesting note is the famous image of the snake cut in pieces representing the colonies dates from the efforts to gather support for a plan of union in 1754. The image is often mistaken as having been created for the Revolution.
25. Benjamin Franklin, *The Autobiography of Benjamin Franklin* Reprint (Danbury: Grolier Enterprises Corp., 1980), 124.
26. Ibid.
27. Jack P. Greene, and Craig B. Yirush, eds., *Exploring the Bounds of Liberty; Political Writings of Colonial British America From the Glorious Revolution to the American Revolution* Volume 2 (Carmel: Liberty Fund Inc., 2018), 1375.
28. Alison Gilbert Olson, "The British Government and Colonial Union, 1754," *The William and Mary Quarterly* 17 no. 1 (Jan., 1960), 23.
29. French philosopher Voltaire was one who did not see the struggle in North America as one of great significance. In his highly influential book *Candide*, published in 1759, just as Pitt was beginning his massive influx of money and supplies, Voltaire has one of the characters in the book comment on the war. Nearing the coast of England, Cunegonde asks Martin what sort of people the English are, "You know England; are the people there as mad as they are in France?" To this Martin replies, "'Tis another sort of madness, you know these two nations are at war for a few acres of snow in Canada, and that they are spending more on this fine war than all Canada is worth. It is beyond my poor capacity to tell you whether there are more madmen in one country than in the other...." Voltaire, *Candide* (Norwalk: The Easton Press, 1977), 97.
30. Colin G. Calloway, *The Scratch of a Pen, 1763 and the Transformation of North America* (Oxford: Oxford University Press, 2006), 41.
31. Ibid., 24.
32. Walter Isaacson, *Benjamin Franklin, An American Life* (New York: Simon and Schuster, 2003), 158.
33. Greene and Yirush, eds., *Exploring the Bounds of Liberty; Political Writings of Colonial British America*, 1373.
34. Ibid., 1374.
35. Ibid., 1378.
36. Ibid., 1380.
37. Ibid., 1383.
38. Olson, "The British Government and Colonial Union, 1754," 22.
39. Greene and Yirush, eds., *Exploring the Bounds of Liberty; Political Writings of Colonial British America*, 1376–1377.
40. Frederic Austin Ogg, *The Old Northwest—A Chronicle of the Ohio Valley and Beyond* (New Haven: Yale University Press, 1920), 7.
41. Ibid.
42. Calloway, *The Scratch of a Pen, 1763 and the Transformation of North America*, 66.
43. Ogg, *The Old Northwest—A Chronicle of the Ohio Valley and Beyond*, 10.
44. Ibid., 11.
45. Ibid., 15.
46. Calloway, *The Scratch of a Pen, 1763 and the Transformation of North America*, 74.
47. David Hawke, *The Colonial Experience* (New York: Macmillan Publishing Company, 1990), 396.
48. Alan Taylor, *Colonial America: A Very Short Introduction* (Oxford: Oxford University Press, 2013), 103.
49. Crevecoeur as quoted in *Ibid*.
50. Ibid., 104.

Chapter 5

1. As quoted in Carl Becker, *The Eve of the Revolution, A Chronicle of the Breach with England* (New Haven: Yale University Press, 1920), 10–11.
2. Winston S. Churchill, *The Age of Revolution* (Norwalk: The Easton Press, 1992), 154.
3. John Brooke, *King George III; A Biography of America's Last Monarch* (New York: McGraw-Hill Book Company, 1972), ix.
4. Ibid., 162.
5. Ibid., 56–57.
6. Ibid., 7.
7. The Royal Archives have made the works of the Hanovarian monarchs available online via scanned manuscripts starting in 2018.
8. Brooke, *King George III; A Biography of America's Last Monarch*, xv.
9. Ibid., 44.
10. Bonamy Dobree, ed., *The Letters of King George III* (London: Cassell & Company Ltd., 1968), 3.
11. Jeremy Black, *George III: America's*

Last King (New Have: Yale University Press, 2008), 21.
12. Georgian Papers Online; GEO/ADD/32/1072.
13. Georgian Papers Online; GEO/ADD/32/1072.
14. Georgian Papers Online; GEO/ADD/32/1072.
15. Georgian Papers Online; GEO/ADD/32/1072.
16. Brooke, *King George III; A Biography of America's Last Monarch*, 44.
17. *Ibid.*, 76.
18. *Ibid.*, 77.
19. *Ibid.*, 7.
20. Georgian Papers Online; GEO/ADD/32/1072.
21. Georgian Papers Online; GEO/ADD/32/1116.
22. Georgian Papers Online; GEO/ADD/32/1073.
23. Black, *George III: America's Last King*, 10.
24. *Ibid.*, 12.
25. Morristown National Historical Park, Lloyd W. Smith archival collection, MORR 11014.
26. Black, *George III: America's Last King*, 68.
27. *Ibid.*, 58.
28. *Ibid.*, 81.
29. Stephen Smith, *Taxation: A Very Short Introduction* (Oxford: Oxford University Press, 2015), 8.
30. Quoted in *Ibid.*, 3.
31. Georgian Papers Online; GEO/ADD/32/1100.
32. Georgian Papers Online; GEO/ADD/32/1099.
33. Georgian Papers Online; GEO/ADD/32/1099.
34. Georgian Papers Online; GEO/ADD/32/1099.
35. Georgian Papers Online; GEO/ADD/32/1101.
36. Georgian Papers Online; GEO/ADD/32/1101.
37. Georgian Papers Online; GEO/ADD/32/1106.
38. Bonamy Dobree, ed., *The Letters of King George III* (London: Cassell & Company Ltd., 1968), 41.
39. *Ibid.*, 42.
40. Becker, *The Eve of the Revolution*, 35.
41. As quoted in *Ibid.*, 42.
42. *Ibid.*

43. *Ibid.*, 62.
44. *Ibid.*, 64.
45. Dobree, ed., *The Letters of King George III*, 37.
46. *Ibid.*, 73.
47. *Ibid.*, 34.
48. Peter D.G. Thomas, *George III—King and Politicians, 1760-1770* (Manchester: Manchester University Press, 2002), 35.
49. Becker, *The Eve of the Revolution, A Chronicle of the Breach with England*, 50.
50. Thomas, *George III—King and Politicians, 1760-1770*, 189.
51. *Ibid.*
52. *Ibid.*, 200.

Chapter 6

1. Claire Priest, "The Stamp Act and the Political Origins of American Legal and Economic Institutions," *Faculty Scholarship Series*. Paper 4934, 885.
2. *Ibid.*, 888.
3. Charles A. Beard, Mary R. Beard, *The Rise of American Civilization, Volume 1, The Agricultural Era* (New York: The Macmillan Company, 1927), 187.
4. Morristown National Historical Park, Lloyd W. Smith archival collection, MORR 9859.
5. Priest, "The Stamp Act and the Political Origins of American Legal and Economic Institutions," 891.
6. Ralph Frasca, "Benjamin Franklin's Printing Network and the Stamp Act," *Pennsylvania History: A Journal of Mid-Atlantic Studies* 71, no. 4 (Autumn, 2004), 403.
7. *Ibid.*, 414.
8. *Ibid.*, 403-404.
9. As quoted in *Ibid.*, 405.
10. *Ibid.*, 406.
11. *Ibid.*, 408.
12. David Levin, ed. *Francis Parkman: France and England in North America, Volume II* (New York: Literary Classics of the United States, 1983), 938.
13. As quoted in Lawrence Henry Gipson, *The Coming of the Revolution, 1763-1775* (New York: Harper & Row Publishers, 1954), 76.
14. *Ibid.*, 69.
15. *Ibid.*, 73.
16. Edmund S. Morgan, "The Postponement of the Stamp Act," *The William and Mary Quarterly* 7, no. 3 (Jul., 1950), 366.

17. David Lindsay Keir, *The Constitutional History of Modern Britain since 1485* (New York: W.W. Norton Company, 1969), 358.
18. *Ibid.*, 358.
19. *Ibid.*, 357.
20. Edmund S. Morgan, "Colonial Ideas of Parliamentary Power 1764–1766," *The William and Mary Quarterly* 5, no. 3 (Jul., 1948), 320.
21. *Ibid.*, 325.
22. *Ibid.*, 366.
23. Peter D.G. Thomas, *George III—King and Politicians, 1760–1770* (Manchester: Manchester University Press, 2002), 130.
24. Carl Becker, *The Eve of the Revolution, A Chronicle of the Breach with England* (New Haven: Yale University Press, 1920), 73.
25. Gipson, *The Coming of the Revolution, 1763–1775*, 88.
26. The Virginia Resolves were largely the work of Patrick Henry. Numbering five, these resolutions were introduced to the House of Burgesses on May 29, 1765. The fifth resolution, nearly calling for independence, was rejected by the Burgesses.
27. Becker, *The Eve of the Revolution, A Chronicle of the Breach with England*, 81.
28. David L. Jacobson, *John Dickinson and The Revolution in Pennsylvania 1764–1776* (Berkeley: University of California Press, 1965), 33.
29. John V. Jezierski, "Parliament or People: James Wilson and Blackstone on the Nature and Location of Sovereignty," *Journal of History of Ideas* Vol. 32, No. 1 (Jan.–Mar., 1971), 103.
30. Morgan, "The Postponement of the Stamp Act," 370.

Chapter 7

1. Gordon S. Wood, *The American Revolution—Writings from the Pamphlet Debate Volume I, 1764-1772* (New York: Literary Classics of the United States), 42.
2. *Ibid.*, 45.
3. *Ibid.*, 50, in footnote.
4. *Ibid.*, 51.
5. *Ibid.*, 66.
6. *Ibid.*
7. *Ibid.*, 69–70.
8. *Ibid.*, 75.
9. *Ibid.*, 91.
10. *Ibid.*, 167.
11. *Ibid.*, 179.
12. *Ibid.*, 203.
13. *Ibid.*, 240.
14. *Ibid.*, 126.
15. *Ibid.*, 129.
16. *Ibid.*
17. *Ibid.*, 135.
18. Walter Isaacson, *Benjamin Franklin, An American Life* (New York: Simon and Schuster, 2003), 222.
19. Edmund S. Morgan, "The Postponement of the Stamp Act," *The William and Mary Quarterly* 7, no. 3 (Jul., 1950), 370.
20. Wood, *The American Revolution—Writings from the Pamphlet Debate Volume I, 1764–1772*, 336.
21. *Ibid.*, 340.
22. *Ibid.*
23. Edmund S. Morgan, "Colonial Ideas of Parliamentary Power 1764–1766," *The William and Mary Quarterly* 5, no. 3 (Jul., 1948), 324.
24. David L. Jacobson, "John Dickinson's Fight Against Royal Government, 1764," *The William and Mary Quarterly* 19, no. 1 (Jan., 1962), 73.
25. *Ibid.*, 78.
26. *Ibid.*, 70.
27. *Ibid.*
28. Paul Leicester Ford, *The Writings of John Dickinson, Vol. 1 Political Writings 1764–1774*, Reprint (Philadelphia: The Historical Society of Pennsylvania, 1895), 151.
29. *Ibid.*, 152.
30. *Ibid.*, 154.
31. Wood, *The American Revolution—Writings from the Pamphlet Debate Volume I, 1764–1772*, 341.
32. *Ibid.*, 352.
33. *Ibid.*, 354.
34. *Ibid.* It is hard not to envision multiple sets of rolling eyes at this statement.
35. *Ibid.*
36. Claire Priest, "The Stamp Act and the Political Origins of American Legal and Economic Institutions," *Faculty Scholarship Series.* Paper 4934, 876.
37. *Ibid.*
38. *Ibid.*, 893.
39. *Ibid.*, 876.
40. *Ibid.*, 895.
41. *Ibid.*, 900.
42. *Ibid.*, 881.
43. Charles A. Beard, Mary R. Beard, *The Rise of American Civilization, Volume 1,*

The Agricultural Era (New York: The Macmillan Company, 1927), 184.

44. Priest, "The Stamp Act and the Political Origins of American Legal and Economic Institutions," 881.

45. Arthur M. Schlesinger, "The Colonial Newspapers and the Stamp Act," *The New England Quarterly* 8, no. 1 (Mar., 1935), 63.

46. *Ibid.*, 64.
47. *Ibid.*, 66–67.
48. *Ibid.*, 67.
49. *Ibid.*, 72.
50. *Ibid.*, 72–73.
51. *Ibid.*, 73.
52. *Ibid.*, 79.
53. *Ibid.*, 80.
54. *Ibid.*, 81.

55. John Brooke, *King George III; A Biography of America's Last Monarch* (New York: McGraw-Hill Book Company, 1972), 129.

56. *Ibid.*
57. As quoted in *Ibid.*

58. Peter D.G. Thomas, *George III—King and Politicians, 1760–1770* (Manchester: Manchester University Press, 2002), 133.

59. Jeremy Black, *George III: America's Last King* (New Haven, Yale University Press, 2008), 84.

60. Charles J. Stille, *The Life and Times of John Dickinson, 1732–1808* (Philadelphia: The Historical Society of Pennsylvania, 1891), 28.

61. *Ibid.*, 29.

Chapter 8

1. Jack P. Greene, and Craig B. Yirush, eds., *Exploring the Bounds of Liberty; Political Writings of Colonial British America From the Glorious Revolution to the American Revolution* Volume 1 (Carmel: Liberty Fund Inc., 2018), xiii.

2. Trevor Colbourn, *The Lamp of Experience, Whig History and the Intellectual Origins of the American Revolution* (Indianapolis: The Liberty Fund, 1998), 132.

3. H. Trevor Colbourn, "John Dickinson: Historical Revolutionary," *The Pennsylvania Magazine of History and Biography* 83, no. 3 (Jul., 1959), 273.

4. Jane E. Calvert, ed., *The Complete Writings and Selected Correspondence of John Dickinson, Volume 1, 1751–1758* (Newark: University of Delaware Press, 2020), 2.

5. *Ibid.*, 10.

6. *Ibid.*, 27.
7. *Ibid.*, 10.
8. *Ibid.*, 48.
9. *Ibid.*, 16.
10. *Ibid.*, 76.
11. *Ibid.*, 62.
12. *Ibid.*

13. William Murchison, *The Cost of Liberty, The Life of John Dickinson* (Wilmington: ISI Books, 2013), 10.

14. Eric Stockdale, and Randy J. Holland, *Middle Temple Lawyers and the American Revolution* (Eagan: Thomson West, 2007), 61.

15. Calvert, ed., *The Complete Writings and Selected Correspondence of John Dickinson, Volume 1, 1751–1758*, 19.

16. *Ibid.*, 134.
17. *Ibid.*, 60.
18. *Ibid.*, 55.
19. *Ibid.*, 73.

20. Will Durant, and Ariel Durant, *The Age of Reason Begins* (Norwalk: The Easton Press, 1992), 170.

21. Calvert, ed., *The Complete Writings and Selected Correspondence of John Dickinson, Volume 1, 1751–1758*, 55.

22. *Ibid.*
23. *Ibid.*, 19.
24. *Ibid.*
25. *Ibid.*, 81.
26. *Ibid.*, 137.

27. Jane E. Calvert, ed., *The Complete Writings and Selected Correspondence of John Dickinson, Volume 2, Set Two of Notes for Paxton v. Vandyke, [1759]* (Newark: University of Delaware Press, 2020), Page number unavailable.

28. Stockdale, and Holland, *Middle Temple Lawyers and the American Revolution*, 63.

29. Calvert, ed., *The Complete Writings and Selected Correspondence of John Dickinson, Volume 1, 1751–1758*, 30.

30. *Ibid.*, 30.
31. *Ibid.*
32. *Ibid.*, 60.
33. *Ibid.*
34. *Ibid.*
35. *Ibid.*, 134.

36. Charles J. Stille, *The Life and Times of John Dickinson, 1732–1808* (Philadelphia: The Historical Society of Pennsylvania, 1891), 45.

37. *Ibid.*, 67–68.

38. The acts passed by Parliament throughout the 1760s were: 1764—the Sugar

Act, and the Currency Act. 1765—the Quartering Act, and the Stamp Act. 1766—the Declaratory Act. 1767—Townshend Acts.

39. Kenneth Campbell, "Legal Rights", *The Stanford Encyclopedia of Philosophy* (Winter 2017 Edition), 1.

40. Gregory S. Ahern, "Experience Must Be Our Only Guide: John Dickinson and the Spirit of American Republicanism" (PhD diss., The Catholic University of America, 1996), 106.

41. *Ibid.*, 107.

42. Milton E. Flower, *John Dickinson, Conservative Revolutionary* (Charlottesville: The University Press of Virginia, 1983), 65.

43. Stille, *The Life and Times of John Dickinson, 1732–1808*, 83.

44. David L. Jacobson, *John Dickinson and The Revolution in Pennsylvania 1764–1776* (Berkeley: University of California Press, 1965), 27.

45. Stille, *The Life and Times of John Dickinson, 1732–1808*, 80–81.

46. *Ibid.*, 85.

47. *Ibid.*, 87.

48. Flower, *John Dickinson, Conservative Revolutionary*, 65.

49. Flower, *John Dickinson, Conservative Revolutionary*, 65.

50. Ahern, "Experience Must Be Our Only Guide," 105.

51. Gordon S. Wood, ed., *The American Revolution—Writings from the Pamphlet Debate Volume I, 1764–1772* (New York: Literary Classics of the United States), 410.

52. *Ibid.*, 409.

53. *Ibid.*

54. *Ibid.*, 489.

55. John V. Jezierski, "Parliament or People: James Wilson and Blackstone on the Nature and Location of Sovereignty," *Journal of History of Ideas* Vol. 32, No. 1 (Jan.–Mar., 1971), 95.

56. Gregory S. Ahern, "Experience Must Be Our Only Guide," 107.

57. *Ibid.*, 114.

58. *Ibid.*, 120.

59. Wood, ed., *The American Revolution—Writings from the Pamphlet Debate Volume I, 1764–1772*, 410.

60. *Ibid.*, 411.

61. *Ibid.*

62. *Ibid.*

63. *Ibid.*, 411–412.

64. *Ibid.*, 413.

65. *Ibid.*

66. *Ibid.*, 413–414.

67. *Ibid.*, 414.

68. *Ibid.*

69. *Ibid.*, 414–415.

70. *Ibid.*, 421.

71. *Ibid.*

72. *Ibid.*, 422.

73. *Ibid.*

74. *Ibid.*, 423.

75. *Ibid.*, 426.

76. *Ibid.*, 427.

77. *Ibid.*, 429.

78. *Ibid.*, 432.

79. *Ibid.*

80. *Ibid.*, 441.

81. *Ibid.*, 444.

82. *Ibid.*

83. *Ibid.*, 449.

84. *Ibid.*, 451.

85. *Ibid.*, 453.

86. *Ibid.*, 463.

87. *Ibid.*, 473.

88. *Ibid.*, 475.

89. *Ibid.*, 475–476.

90. Carl Becker, *The Eve of the Revolution, A Chronicle of the Breach with England* (New Haven: Yale University Press, 1920), 133–134.

91. Ahern, "Experience Must Be Our Only Guide," 104.

92. Flower, *John Dickinson, Conservative Revolutionary*, 69.

Chapter 9

1. Stephen Smith, *Taxation: A Very Short Introduction* (Oxford: Oxford University Press, 2015), 6.

2. Baron De Montesquieu, *The Spirit of Laws,* Reprint (Birmingham: The Legal Classics Library, 1984), 266.

3. Stanley N. Katz, ed., William Blackstone, *Commentaries on the Laws of England Volume 1* Reprint (Chicago: The University of Chicago Press, 1979), 163.

4. John V. Jezierski, "Parliament or People: James Wilson and Blackstone on the Nature and Location of Sovereignty," *Journal of History of Ideas* Vol. 32, No. 1 (Jan.–Mar., 1971), 96.

5. Katz, ed., William Blackstone, *Commentaries on the Laws of England Volume 1*, 271.

6. *Ibid.*

7. *Ibid.*, 320.

8. *Ibid.*, 271.

9. *Ibid.*, 296.
10. *Ibid.*
11. *Ibid.*
12. *Ibid.*, 296–297.
13. *Ibid.*, 297.
14. *Ibid.*
15. *Ibid.*, 312.
16. Isaac Kramnick, ed., *The Portable Edmund Burke* (New York: Penguin Books, 1999), 242.
17. *Ibid.*, 244.
18. *Ibid.*, 246.
19. *Ibid.*, 247.
20. *Ibid.*
21. *Ibid.*, 248.
22. Anne Pallister, *Magna Carta, The Heritage of Liberty* (Norwalk: The Easton Press, 1994), 43.
23. *Ibid.*, 55.
24. *Ibid.*, 56.
25. *Ibid.*, 57.
26. Kramnick, ed., *The Portable Edmund Burke*, 233.
27. Alan Ramsay, *Reflections Moral and Political on Great Britain and Her Colonies* Facsimile (Norwalk: The Easton Press, ND), 2 (preface).
28. Ramsay, *Reflections Moral and Political* Facsimile, 2 (preface).
29. *Ibid.*, 3 (preface).
30. *Ibid.*, 2.
31. *Ibid.*
32. *Ibid.*, 3.
33. *Ibid.*, 10–11.
34. *Ibid.*, 19.
35. *Ibid.*
36. *Ibid.*
37. *Ibid.*, 20.
38. *Ibid.*
39. *Ibid.*
40. *Ibid.*
41. *Ibid.*, 26.
42. *Ibid.*
43. *Ibid.*, 26–27.
44. *Ibid.*, 27.
45. *Ibid.*, 28.
46. *Ibid.*, 29.
47. *Ibid.*, 32.
48. *Ibid.*
49. *Ibid.*
50. *Ibid.*, 33.
51. *Ibid.*, 34.
52. *Ibid.*, 36.
53. *Ibid.*, 37.
54. *Ibid.*
55. *Ibid.*, 41.
56. *Ibid.*
57. *Ibid.*, 44.
58. *Ibid.*
59. *Ibid.*
60. *Ibid.*
61. *Ibid.*, 45.
62. *Ibid.*
63. *Ibid.*, 48.
64. *Ibid.*
65. *Ibid.*, 52.
66. *Ibid.*
67. *Ibid.*, 3
68. *Ibid.*
69. *Ibid.*, 6.
70. *Ibid.*, 27–28.
71. *Ibid.*, 50.
72. *Ibid.*
73. *Ibid.*, 51.
74. *Ibid.*, 54–55.
75. *Ibid.*, 63.
76. *Ibid.*, 64.

Chapter 10

1. John Phillip Reid, *Jurisprudence of Liberty*, in Ellis Sandoz, ed., *The Roots of Liberty; Magna Carta, Ancient Constitution, and the Anglo-American Tradition of Rule of Law* (Indianapolis: The Liberty Fund, 1993), 189.
2. David Hawke, *The Colonial Experience* (New York: Macmillan Publishing Company, 1990), 272–273.
3. *Ibid.*, 272.
4. Winston S. Churchill, *The New World* (New York: Dodd, Mead and Company, 1980), 308.
5. Charles M. Andrews, *The Fathers of New England, A Chronicle of the Puritan Commonwealths* (New Haven: Yale University Press, 1920), 175.
6. *Ibid.*, 176.
7. *Ibid.*
8. *Ibid.*, 185.
9. *Ibid.*
10. *Ibid.*, 186.
11. Theodore B. Lewis, "A Revolutionary Tradition, 1689–1774: There was a Revolution Here as Well as in England" *The New England Quarterly* 46, No. 3 (Sep., 1973), 433.
12. Churchill, *The New World*, 316.
13. Hawke, *The Colonial Experience*, 265–266.
14. Lewis, "A Revolutionary Tradition, 1689–1774," 433.
15. *Ibid.*, 434.
16. *Ibid.*, 438.

17. Hawke, *The Colonial Experience*, 273.
18. Lewis, "A Revolutionary Tradition, 1689-1774," 425.
19. Andrews, *The Fathers of New England*, 190.
20. *Ibid.*, 192.
21. Hawke, *The Colonial Experience*, 272.
22. *Ibid.*, 265.
23. Reid, *Jurisprudence of Liberty*, 191.
24. *Ibid.*, 192.
25. As quoted in *Ibid.*, 203.
26. *Ibid.*, 204.
27. *Ibid.*, 205.
28. *Ibid.*, 210.
29. *Ibid.*, 212.
30. *Ibid.*, 216.
31. S.A. Handford, ed., *Tacitus: The Agricola and The Germania* (London: Penguin Books, 1970), 24.
32. *Ibid.*, 25.
33. *Ibid.*, 27.
34. *Ibid.*, 28.
35. H. Trevor Colbourn, "John Dickinson: Historical Revolutionary," *The Pennsylvania Magazine of History and Biography* 83, no. 3 (Jul., 1959), 280.
36. *Ibid*.
37. Reid, *Jurisprudence of Liberty*, 240.
38. Henry Adams, et al., *Essays in Anglo-Saxon Law* (Clark: The Lawbook Exchange, Ltd., 2017), 1.
39. Frederick Pollock, "Anglo-Saxon Law," *The English Historical Review* Vol. 8, No. 30 (Apr., 1893), 239-240.
40. *Ibid.*, 239.
41. Matthew Hale, *The History and Analysis of the Common Law of England* Reprint. (Brimingham: The Legal Classics Library, 1987), 58.
42. Pollock, "Anglo-Saxon Law," 243.
43. Hale, *The History and Analysis of the Common Law of England* Reprint, 58.
44. *Ibid.*, 64.
45. Kevin Crossley-Holland, ed., *The Anglo-Saxon World, An Anthology* (Oxford: Oxford University Press, 2009), 26.
46. John Baker, *An Introduction to English Legal History* (Oxford: Oxford University Press, 2019), 4.
47. *Ibid*.

Chapter 11

1. Merrill D. Peterson, *Thomas Jefferson and the New Nation* (Norwalk: The Easton Press, 1987), 71.
2. Carl Richard, *The Founders and the Classics* (Cambridge: Harvard University Press, 1996), 37.
3. Thomas Jefferson, *A Summary View of the Rights of British America* Reprint (Norwalk: The Easton Press, nd), verso of title page.
4. *Ibid.*, 2.
5. *Ibid*.
6. *Ibid*.
7. *Ibid.*, 5.
8. *Ibid*.
9. *Ibid*.
10. *Ibid.*, 6.
11. *Ibid*.
12. *Ibid*.
13. *Ibid.*, 8.
14. *Ibid.*, 10.
15. *Ibid*.
16. *Ibid.*, 11.
17. *Ibid*.
18. *Ibid.*, 16.
19. *Ibid*.
20. *Ibid.*, 17.
21. *Ibid.*, 20.
22. *Ibid.*, 20-21.
23. *Ibid.*, 21.
24. *Ibid.*, 22.
25. *Ibid*.
26. *Ibid*.
27. *Ibid*.
28. *Ibid.*, 22-23.
29. *Ibid.*, 23.
30. R. B. Bernstein, *Thomas Jefferson* (London: The Folio Society, 2008), 23.
31. Peterson, *Thomas Jefferson and the New Nation*, 70.
32. *Ibid*.
33. *Ibid.*, 73.
34. *Ibid*.
35. Dumas Malone, *Jefferson the Virginian* (Boston: Little, Brown and Company, 1948), 182.
36. *Ibid*.
37. *Ibid.*, 184.
38. *Ibid*.
39. *Ibid.*, 185.
40. *Ibid.*, 186.
41. The six men were: George Clymer (Pennsylvania), Benjamin Franklin (Pennsylvania), Robert Morris (Pennsylvania), George Read (Delaware), Roger Sherman (Connecticut), and James Wilson (Pennsylvania).
42. In 1906 James Wilson was reinterred in Christ Churchyard, Philadelphia.

43. Morristown National Historical Park. Lloyd W. Smith archival collection MORR 1248.
44. Morristown National Historical Park. Lloyd W. Smith archival collection MORR 1258.
45. Kermit L. Hall, Mark David Hall, eds., *Collected Works of James Wilson*, Volume 1 (Indianapolis: Liberty Fund, 2007), xi. The Declaration of Independence and the Constitution are two vastly different documents. Each had a specific purpose behind its creation. One area, however, were there is similarity is in their unique grounding, or attempts to frame their respective purposes in a higher being as in the Declaration, and just the opposite with the Constitution. The Declaration grounds itself in Nature's God—not a god of an organized religion, but more a pantheistic version of a god free from anthropomorphic designs. The Constitution grounds itself in the people, it is a man-made law designed for people—by and for people. People of course in 1787 meant white, male, property owning non-aristocrats. The meaning of people to the Founders was taken from the Latin *populares*, meaning non-aristocracy, which the new United States certainly was. There were and are no nobility in the country. Therefore, people did not mean people in the twenty-first century inclusive meaning, it meant not-noble white males who could vote.
46. Hall, Hall, eds., *Works of James Wilson*, xiv.
47. *Ibid*.
48. *Ibid.*, xv.
49. *Ibid.*, 3.
50. *Ibid.*, 5.
51. *Ibid.*, 6.
52. *Ibid.*, 9.
53. *Ibid*.
54. *Ibid.*, 12.
55. *Ibid.*, 13.
56. *Ibid.*, 14.
57. *Ibid.*, 15.
58. *Ibid.*, 15, footnote.
59. *Ibid.*, 18.
60. *Ibid.*, 21, footnote.
61. *Ibid.*, 22.
62. William Blackstone, *Commentaries on the Laws of England, Of the Rights of Persons* Reprint (Chicago: The University of Chicago Press, 1979), 104–105.
63. *Ibid.*, 105.
64. Hall, Hall, eds., *Works of James Wilson*. 23, footnote.
65. *Ibid*. 25.
66. *Ibid.*, 26, footnote.
67. *Ibid.*, 28.
68. *Ibid.*, 29–30.
69. *Ibid.*, 30.

Appendix 1

1. Albert E. Stone, *Letters from an American Farmer and Sketches of Eighteenth-Century America* (New York: Viking Penguin, 1981), 66–70.

Appendix 2

1. Avalon Law, accessed 1–20–2020. https://avalon.law.yale.edu/18th_century/stamp_act_1765.asp

Appendix 3

1. Avalon Law, accessed 1–20–2020. https://avalon.law.yale.edu/18th_century/repeal_stamp_act_1766.asp

Appendix 4

1. Avalon Law, accessed 1–20–2020. https://avalon.law.yale.edu/18th_century/declaratory_act_1766.asp

Appendix 5

1. Avalon Law, accessed 1–20–2020. https://avalon.law.yale.edu/18th_century/mass_circ_let_1768.asp

Appendix 6

1. Kermit L. Hall, Mark David Hall, eds., *Collected Works of James Wilson*, Volume 1 (Indianapolis: Liberty Fund, 2007), 19–21.

Appendix 7

1. Avalon Law, accessed 1–20–2020. https://avalon.law.yale.edu/18th_century/albany.asp

Appendix 8

1. Avalon Law, accessed 1–20–2020. https://avalon.law.yale.edu/18th_century/blackstone_intro.asp#1

Bibliography

Articles

Ahern, Gregory S. "Experience Must Be Our Only Guide: John Dickinson and the Spirit of American Republicanism." PhD diss., The Catholic University of America, 1996.
Anderson, Fred. "Review of The Impact of the Seven Years' War on Massachusetts Provincial Soldiers." *Reviews in American History* 13, no. 4 (Dec., 1985), 512–517.
Bullion, John L. "Review of A Great and Necessary Measure: George Grenville and the Genesis of the Stamp Act, 1763–1765." *The Virginia Magazine of History and Biography* 92, no 1 (Jan., 1984), 103–104.
Calvert, Jane E. "Myth-Making and Myth-Breaking in the Historiography on John Dickinson." *Journal of the Early Republic* Vol. 34, No. 3 (Fall 2014), 467–480.
Campbell, Kenneth, "Legal Rights." *The Stanford Encyclopedia of Philosophy* (Winter 2017 Edition).
Chaffin, Robert J. "The Townshend Acts of 1767." *The William and Mary Quarterly* 27, no. 1 (Jan. 1970), 90–121.
Charters, Erica. "The Caring Fiscal-Military State During the Seven Years War, 1756–1763." *The Historical Journal* 52, no. 4 (December 2009), 921–941.
Colbourn, H. Trevor. "John Dickinson: Historical Revolutionary." *The Pennsylvania Magazine of History and Biography* 83, no. 3 (Jul., 1959), 271–292.
_____. "Thomas Jefferson's use of the Past." *The William and Mary Quarterly* Vol. 15, No. 1 (Jan., 1958), 56–70.
Dowd, Gregory Evans. "The French King Wakes up in Detroit: 'Pontiac's War'" in Rumor and History." *Ethnohistory* Vol. 37, No. 3 (Summer, 1990), 254–278.
Ellis, Joseph. "Habits of Mind and an American Enlightenment." *American Quarterly* Vol. 28, No. 2, Special Issue: An American Enlightenment (Summer, 1976), 150–164.
Engelman, F.L. "Cadwallader Colden and the New York Stamp Act Riots." *The William and Mary Quarterly* 10, no. 4 (Oct., 1953), 560–578.
Frasca, Ralph. "Benjamin Franklin's Printing Network and the Stamp Act." *Pennsylvania History: A Journal of Mid-Atlantic Studies* 71, no. 4 (Autumn, 2004), 403–419.
Freiberg, Malcolm. "An Unknown Stamp Act Letter." *Proceedings of the Massachusetts Historical Society* Third Series, 78 (1966), 138–142.
Gipson, Lawrence Henry. "Review of The Albany Congress and Plan of Union." *The William and Mary Quarterly* Vol. 13, No. 3 (Jul., 1956), 419–424.
Grant, Charles S. "Pontiac's Rebellion and the British Troop Moves of 1763." *The Mississippi Valley Historical Review* Vol. 40, No. 1 (Jun., 1953), 75–88.
Grant, William L. "Canada Versus Guadeloupe, An Episode of the Seven Years' War." *The American Historical Review* 17, no. 4 (Jul., 1912), 735–743.
Green, Jack P., and Henry McCulloh. "A Dress of Horror: Henry McCulloh Objections to the Stamp Act." *Huntington Library Quarterly* 26, no. 3 (May, 1963), 253–262.
Higonnet, Patrice Louis-Rene. "The Origins of the Seven Years' War." *The Journal of Modern History* 40, no. 1 (Mar., 1968), 57–90.

Iannini, Christopher. "The Itinerant Man: Crevecoeur's Caribbean, Raynal's Revolution, and the Fate of Atlantic Cosmopolitanism." *The William and Mary Quarterly* Third Series, 61, no. 2 (Apr. 2004), 201–234.
Jacobson, David L. "John Dickinson's Fight Against Royal Government, 1764." *The William and Mary Quarterly* 19, no. 1 (Jan., 1962), 64–85.
Jehlen, Myra. "J. Hector St. John Crevecoeur: A Monarcho-Anarchist in Revolutionary America." *American Quarterly* 31, no. 2 (Summer, 1979), 204–222.
Jezierski, John V. "Parliament or People: James Wilson and Blackstone on the Nature and Location of Sovereignty." *Journal of History of Ideas* Vol. 32, No. 1 (Jan.–Mar., 1971), 95–106.
Langford, Paul. "Review of George III by John Brooke." *The English Historical Review* 89, no. 350 (Jan., 1974), 196–197.
Lawson, Karol Ann Peard. "Charles Wilson Peale's "John Dickinson": An American Landscape as Political Allegory." *Proceedings of the American Philosophical Society* Vol. 136, No. 4 (Dec., 1992), 455–486.
Lemay, J. A. Leo. "John Mercer and the Stamp Act in Virginia, 1764–1765." *The Virginia Magazine of History and Biography* 91, no. 1 (Jan., 1983), 3–38.
Lewis, Theodore B. "A Revolutionary Tradition, 1689–1774: There was a Revolution Here as Well as in England." *The New England Quarterly* 46, no. 3 (Sep., 1973), 424–438.
MacLeod, D. Peter. "Microbes and Muskets: Smallpox and the Participation of the Amerindian Allies of New France in the Seven Years' War." *Ethnohistory* 39, no. 1 (Winter, 1992), 42–64.
Main, Jackson Turner. "Lawrence Henry Gipson: Historian." *Pennsylvania History: A Journal of Mid-Atlantic Studies* 36, no. 1 (January, 1969), 22–48.
Miller, E. J. "The Virginia Legislature and the Stamp Act." *The William and Mary Quarterly* 21, no. 4 (Apr., 1913), 233–248.
Morgan, Edmund S. "Colonial Ideas of Parliamentary Power 1764–1766." *The William and Mary Quarterly* 5, no. 3 (Jul., 1948), 311–341.
_____. "The Postponement of the Stamp Act." *The William and Mary Quarterly* 7, no. 3 (Jul., 1950), 353–392.
_____. "Thomas Hutchinson and the Stamp Act." *The New England Quarterly* 21, no. 4 (Dec., 1948), 459–492.
Myers, James P., Jr. "Crevecoeur: Concealing and Revealing the Secret Self." *Early American Literature* 49, no. 2 (2014), 357–401.
Nelson, William. "Review of The Writings of John Dickinson." *The American Historical Review* 2, no. 2 (Jan., 1897), 362–363.
Olson, Alison Gilbert. "The British Government and Colonial Union, 1754." *The William and Mary Quarterly* 17, no. 1 (Jan., 1960), 22–34.
Pollock, Frederick. "Anglo-Saxon Law." *The English Historical Review* Vol. 8, No. 30 (Apr., 1893), 239–271.
Priest, Claire. "The Stamp Act and the Political Origins of American Legal and Economic Institutions." *Faculty Scholarship Series.* Paper 4934.
Richards, Carl J. "A Dialogue with the Ancients: Thomas Jefferson and Classical Philosophy and History." *Journal of the Early Republic* Vol. 9, No. 4 (Winter, 1989), 431–455.
Ropes, Arthur R. "The Causes of the Seven Years' War." *Transactions of the Royal Historical Society* 4 (1889), 143–170.
Schlesinger, Arthur M. "The Colonial Newspapers and the Stamp Act." *The New England Quarterly* 8, no. 1 (Mar., 1935), 63–83.
Spindel, Donna J. "The Stamp Act Crisis in the British West Indies." *Journal of American Studies* 11, no. 2 (Aug., 1977), 203–221.
Steel, Ian. "Governors or Generals? A Note on Martial Law and the Revolution of 1689 in English America." *The William and Mary Quarterly* Vol. 46, No. 2 (Apr., 1989), 304–314.
_____. "Origins of Boston's Revolutionary Declaration of 18 April 1689." *The New England Quarterly* Vol. 62, No. 1 (Mar., 1989), 75–81.
Stockton, Constant Noble. "Hume—Historian of the English Constitution." *Eighteenth-Century Studies* Vol. 4, No. 3 (Spring, 1971), 277–293.
Wilson, Douglas L. "Jefferson v. Hume." *The William and Mary Quarterly* Vol. 46, No. 1 (Jan., 1989), 49–70.

Wright, Louis B. "William Byrd's Defense of Sir Edmund Andros." *The William and Mary Quarterly* Vol. 2, No. 1 (Jan., 1945), 47–62.

Books

Adams, Henry, et al., *Essays in Anglo-Saxon Law*. Clark: The Lawbook Exchange, Ltd., 2017.
Andrews, Charles M. *Colonial Folkways, A Chronicle of American Life in the Reign of the Georges*. New Haven: Yale University Press, 1920.
_____. *The Fathers of New England, A Chronicle of the Puritan Commonwealths*. New Haven: Yale University Press, 1920.
Bacon, Francis. *The Essays or Counsels Civil and Moral*. Norwalk: The Easton Press, 1980.
Baker, John. *An Introduction to English Legal History*. Oxford: Oxford University Press, 2019.
Beard, Charles A., and Mary R. *The Rise of American Civilization, Volume 1, The Agricultural Era*. New York: The Macmillan Company, 1927.
Becker, Carl. *The Eve of the Revolution, A Chronicle of the Breach with England*. New Haven: Yale University Press, 1920.
Bernstein, R.B. *Thomas Jefferson*. London: The Folio Society, 2008.
Black, Jeremy. *George III; America's Last King*. New Haven: Yale University Press, 2008.
Blackstone, William. *Commentaries on the Laws of England, Of the Rights of Persons*. Reprint. Chicago: The University of Chicago Press, 1979.
Boorstin, Daniel J. *The Lost World of Thomas Jefferson*. Chicago: University of Chicago Press, 1981.
Bowen, Catherine Drinker. *Francis Bacon, The Temper of a Man*. Boston: Little, Brown and Company, 1963.
Brooke, John. *King George III; A Biography of America's Last Monarch*. New York: McGraw-Hill, 1972.
Brumwell, Stephen. *George Washington, Gentleman Warrior*. New York: Quercus, 2012.
Butterfield, Herbert. *George III and the Historians*. New York: The Macmillan Company, 1959.
Calloway, Colin G. *The Indian World of George Washington*. Oxford: Oxford University Press, 2018.
_____. *The Scratch of a Pen, 1763 and the Transformation of North America*. Oxford: Oxford University Press, 2006.
Calvert, Jane E., ed. *The Complete Writings and Selected Correspondence of John Dickinson, Volume 1, 1751–1758*. Newark: University of Delaware Press, 2020.
_____, ed. *The Complete Writings and Selected Correspondence of John Dickinson, Volume 2*. Newark: University of Delaware Press, 2020.
_____. *Quaker Constitutionalism and the Political Thought of John Dickinson*. Cambridge: Cambridge University Press, 2009.
Churchill, Winston S. *The Age of Revolution*. New York: Dodd, Mead, and Company, 1980.
_____. *The Age of Revolution*. Norwalk: The Easton Press, 1992.
_____. *The New World*. New York: Dodd, Mead and Company, 1980.
Colbourn, Trevor. *The Lamp of Experience, Whig History and the Intellectual Origins of the American Revolution*. Indianapolis: The Liberty Fund, 1998.
Crossley-Holland, Kevin, ed., *The Anglo-Saxon World, An Anthology*. Oxford: Oxford University Press, 2009.
Dobree, Bonamy, ed. *The Letters of King George III*. London: Cassell & Company Ltd., 1968.
Durant, Will. *The Age of Louis XIV*. Norwalk: The Easton Press, 1992.
_____, and Ariel Durant. *The Age of Reason Begins*. Norwalk: The Easton Press, 1992.
_____. *Rousseau and Revolution*. Norwalk: The Easton Press, 1992.
Fears, J. Rufus, ed. *Selected Writings of Lord Acton, Volume 1, Essays in the History of Liberty*. Indianapolis: Liberty Fund, 1985.
Flower, Milton E. *John Dickinson, Conservative Revolutionary*. Charlottesville: The University Press of Virginia, 1983.
Ford, Paul Leicester. *The Writings of John Dickinson, Vol. 1 Political Writings 1764–1774* Reprint. Philadelphia: The Historical Society of Pennsylvania, 1895.

Franklin, Benjamin. *The Autobiography of Benjamin Franklin* Reprint. Danbury: Grolier Enterprises Corp., 1980.
Gipson, Lawrence Henry. *The Coming of the Revolution, 1763–1775.* New York: Harper & Row Publishers, 1954.
Greene, Jack P., and Yirush, Craig B., eds. *Exploring the Bounds of Liberty; Political Writings of Colonial British America From the Glorious Revolution to the American Revolution.* Carmel: Liberty Fund Inc., 2018.
Hale, Matthew. *The History and Analysis of the Common Law of England.* Reprint. Brimingham: The Legal Classics Library, 1987.
Hall, Kermit L., and Mark David Hall, eds. *Collected Works of James Wilson.* Volume 1. Indianapolis: Liberty Fund, 2007
Handford, S.A., ed. *Tacitus: The Agricola and The Germania.* London: Penguin Books, 1970.
Hawke, David. *The Colonial Experience.* New York: Macmillan Publishing Company, 1990.
Hicks, Frederick C. *Men and Books Famous in the Law.* Reprint. Clark: The Lawbook Exchange, Ltd., 2008.
Isaacson, Walter. *Benjamin Franklin, An American Life.* New York: Simon & Schuster, 2003.
Jacobson, David L. *John Dickinson and The Revolution in Pennsylvania, 1764–1776.* Berkeley: University of California Press, 1965.
Jefferson, Thomas. *A Summary View of the Rights of British America.* Reprint. Norwalk: Easton Press, nd.
Katz, Stanley N., ed., William Blackstone, *Commentaries on the Laws of England Volume 1.* Chicago: The University of Chicago Press, 1979.
Keir, David Lindsay. *The Constitutional History of Modern Britain since 1485.* New York: W.W. Norton Company, 1969.
Kramnick, Isaac, ed., *The Portable Edmund Burke.* New York: Penguin Books, 1999.
Levin, David, ed. *Francis Parkman: France and England in North America, Volume II.* New York: Literary Classics of the United States, 1983.
Loughlin, Martin. *The British Constitution, A Very Short Introduction.* Oxford: Oxford University Press, 2013.
Malone, Dumas. *Jefferson the Virginian.* Boston: Little, Brown and Company, 1948.
Montesquieu, Baron De. *The Spirit of Law.*, Reprint. Birmingham: The Legal Classics Library, 1984.
Murchison, William. *The Cost of Liberty, The Life of John Dickinson.* Wilmington, DE: ISI Books, 2013.
Namier, Lewis. *England in the Age of the American Revolution.* London: Macmillan and Company, 1961.
_____. *The Structure of Politics at the Accession of George III.* London: Macmillan and Company, 1978.
Ogg, Frederic Austin. *The Old Northwest—A Chronicle of the Ohio Valley and Beyond.* New Haven: Yale University Press, 1920.
Oliver, Lisi. *The Beginnings of English Law.* Toronto: University of Toronto Press, 2002.
Pallister, Anne. *Magna Carta, The Heritage of Liberty.* Norwalk: The Easton Press, 1994.
Peterson, Merrill D. *Thomas Jefferson and the New Nation.* Norwalk: The Easton Press, 1987.
Radice, Betty, ed. *The Agricola and the Germania.* London: Penguin Books, 1970.
Ramsay, Alan. *Reflections Moral and Political on Great Britain and Her Colonies.* Facsimile. Norwalk: The Easton Press, ND.
Rhodehamel, John, ed. *George Washington: Writings.* New York: Literary Classics of the United States, 1997.
Richard, Carl. *The Founders and the Classics.* Cambridge: Harvard University Press, 1996.
Sandoz, Ellis, ed. *The Roots of Liberty; Magna Carta, Ancient Constitution, and the Anglo-American Tradition of Rule of Law.* Indianapolis: The Liberty Fund, 1993.
Smith, Stephen. *Taxation: A Very Short Introduction.* Oxford: Oxford University Press, 2015.
Stille, Charles J. *The Life and Times of John Dickinson, 1732–1808.* Philadelphia: The Historical Society of Pennsylvania, 1891.
Stockdale, Eric, and Randy J. Holland. *Middle Temple Lawyers and the American Revolution.* Eagan: Thomson West, 2007.

Stone, Albert E. *Letters from an American Farmer and Sketches of Eighteenth-Century America*. New York: Viking Penguin, 1981.
Taylor, Alan. *Colonial America: A Very Short Introduction*. Oxford: Oxford University Press, 2013.
Thomas, Peter D.G. *George III—King and Politicians, 1760–1770*. Manchester: Manchester University Press, 2002.
Voltaire. *Candide*. Norwalk: The Easton Press, 1977.
Wood, Gordon S. *The American Revolution—Writings from the Pamphlet Debate Volume I, 1764–1772*. New York: Literary Classics of the United States, 2015.
Wormser, Rene. *The Story of Law and the Men Who Made it—From the Earliest Times to the Present*. New York: Simon & Schuster, 1962.
Wrong, George M. *The Conquest of New France, A Chronicle of the Colonial Wars*. New Haven: Yale University Press, 1920.
Zane, John Maxcy. *The Story of Law*. Indianapolis: Liberty Fund, 1998.

Websites

Avalon Law at Yale: https://avalon.law.yale.edu/
Georgian Papers Online: http://gpp.rct.uk., January, 2019. GEO/ADD/32/1–2485.
New York Public Library: The Miriam and Ira D. Wallach Division of Art, Prints and Photographs: Print Collection, The New York Public Library. New York Public Library Digital Collections. Accessed July 23, 2020.
http://digitalcollections.nypl.org/items
Stanford Encyclopedia of Philosophy: https://plato.stanford.edu/archives/win2017/entries/legal-rights/
Yale Law School Legal Scholarship Repository: http://digitalcommons.law.yale.edu/fss_papers/4934

Index

Adams, Samuel 200
Albany Plan of Union 57–62, 230
Andros, Edmund 173–177
Anglo-Saxons 179–185, 192–193

Bacon, Francis 56, 130–133, 211
Blackstone, William 102, 154–156, 206, 210–211, 233
Braddock, Edward 40, 46–47
Burke, Edmund 157–161

Charles II (British monarch) 3, 12, 14
Charles II (Spanish monarch) 36–37
Churchill, John 37–39
Common Law 104, 123, 127, 133–134, 180, 182–184
Cook, Edward 130–133, 211
Crevecoeur, Michel Guillaume Jean de (*What Is an American*) 25–30, 215

Declaratory Act 86, 122–123, 137–138, 142–143
de Menneville, Michel-Ange Du Quesue (Marquis de Duquesne) 33, 40–41
de Secondat, Charles-Louis (Baron Montesquieu) 153–154
Dickinson, John 90, 100–102, 112; *Farmers Letters* 124–152, 179
Dinwiddie, Robert 33, 40, 43

Enlightenment (intellectual movement) 23, 25, 71, 133, 154, 164, 191

Farmers Letters 124–152, 179
Fort Necessity 33; role of George Washington 45–47
Franklin, Benjamin 8, 23–26, 57–59; before House of Commons 109–118; debate with David Ramsay 161–172
French and Indian War 31–55

George III (British monarch) 69–79, 122, 161, 190, 197–200, 212
Grenville, George (British prime minister) 81, 85, 94, 109, 249

Hanbury, John 127–129

Henry, Patrick 98; Virginia Resolves 98–99, 100, 116, 200
Hopkins, Stephen 59, 61, 108–109
Hutchinson, Thomas 97–98

Inns of Court 7, 126–127, 129–130, 146

James II (British monarch) 3, 36–37, 175–178
Jefferson, Thomas (*A Summary View*) 187–203

liberty (as a concept) 64, 71, 73, 92–93, 136, 138, 143, 162
Louis XIV (French monarch) 36–37, 39

Native Americans (loyalties split between French and British) 31, 41–42, 56–59
Natural Law 104–105, 123, 139, 160, 197, 202, 205
newspapers (role in 1760s America) 45, 89, 90, 118–121, 138, 243

Otis, James 103–105

Pitt, William 32–33, 48–49, 52, 54, 56
Pontiac (Native America leader) 62, 64–66, 83
Proclamation Act 81

Ramsay, Alan 161–172
Stamp Act 73, 84–85
Stamp Act Congress 96, 100, 112, 136, 142
Stuart, John (Earl of Bute) 73–75
A Summary View 187–203

Townshend Duties 86–87, 142–145

Virginia Resolves 98–99, 100, 116, 200

Wars of Austria and Spanish Succession 35–42
What Is an American 25–30, 215
Whately, Thomas 93, 106–108
William and Mary (Joint British monarchs) 160, 175, 177
Wilson, James 129; as essayist 203–213

255

www.ingramcontent.com/pod-product-compliance
Lightning Source LLC
Chambersburg PA
CBHW032035300426
44117CB00009B/1073